The Word That Causes Death's Defeat

ANNA AKHMATOVA

The Word That Causes Death's Defeat

Poems of Memory

Translated, with an introductory biography,

critical essays, and commentary, by

Nancy K. Anderson

Yale University Press   New Haven & London

Published with assistance from the foundation established in memory of
Philip Hamilton McMillan of the Class of 1894, Yale College.

Designed by James J. Johnson and set in Nofret Roman type by
Keystone Typesetting, Inc.
Printed in the United States of America.

Library of Congress Cataloging-in-Publication Data

Akhmatova, Anna Andreevna, 1889–1966.
 [Poems. English. Selections]
 The word that causes death's defeat : poems of memory / Anna Akhmatova ;
translated, with an introductory biography, critical essays, and commentary,
by Nancy K. Anderson.–1st ed.
  p. cm.
 Includes bibliographical references and index.
ISBN 0-300-10377-8 (alk. paper)
 1. Akhmatova, Anna Andreevna, 1889–1966–Translations into English. 2.
Akhmatova, Anna Andreevna, 1889–1966. I. Anderson, Nancy K., 1956– II. Title.
 PG3476.A217 2004
 891.71'42–dc22
 2004006295

A catalogue record for this book is available from the British Library.

10 9 8 7 6 5 4 3 2 1

Contents

§ § §

Contents

Preface

Enough has been written about Akhmatova that the addition of another book on her calls for some justification. Perhaps the best way to describe what this book proposes to do is to explain how it came into being.

Some books are the realization of a preconceived plan, like a building constructed in strict conformity with the architect's blueprints. Others, including this one, are like the work of a builder who, as he sees the project begin to take form, suddenly realizes how many possibilities it offers and responds by adding feature upon feature, until the result is a vast elaboration of an initially simple concept.

In the case of this book, the original concept was to offer a new translation of *Poem Without a Hero*. While Akhmatova's first readers had consistently praised the poem for its musicality, most of the English translations of it I had seen were in free verse, which failed to give any sense of the work's sound or rhythm. The one honorable exception to this rule (at least to my knowledge) is D. M. Thomas's translation. Thomas chose to keep Akhmatova's exact meter while reducing the *Poem*'s end rhymes to assonances (sometimes quite weak ones); I chose to strengthen the stanza structure by keeping the end rhymes (or at least inexact rhymes) while using a meter compatible with, rather than the same as, Akhmatova's.

While the initial idea of translating *Poem Without a Hero* was straight-forward enough, the first addition to the plan occurred almost imme-diately. Translating the *Poem* into English, I realized, implied the wish to make it accessible to more than just the limited number of specialists in Russian literature and culture (most of whom, after all, would be able to read the work in the original). But the *Poem* is such a complex work, and so deeply rooted in the experience of Akhmatova's generation, that a nonspecialist encountering it for the first time might well be disoriented. Accordingly, I decided that guidance was needed, in the form of a critical essay and a commentary. The critical essay would discuss the main themes and images, while the commentary would be keyed to individual lines and would identify historical and literary allusions, give variant readings, point out problems of translation, and so on. I intended that every reader should read the critical essay all the way through; the commentary I regard as to some extent optional. Some readers might want to read through it simultaneously with the *Poem*; others may refer to it only when some individual line baffles them. To make it possible for a nonspecialist to read the commentary straight through, if so desired, I have tried to make it reasonably comprehensive without being overly detailed.

For readers whose ambitions to learn more about *Poem Without a Hero* had not been sated by the commentary, I included two more sections, which I relegated to the status of appendixes to indicate their optional nature. The first is a translation of the earliest known edition of *Poem*, written in 1942, some two decades before the final version. The second is a selection of entries from the personal notebooks that Akhmatova kept during the last years of her life, from 1958 to 1966, reflecting her thoughts about the *Poem* in those years. Both of these sections theoretically could themselves have been the object of further exposition and commentary, but because they were included essentially as notes to the *Poem*, any further comment on them would be glosses on glosses—a form that I found a bit too Talmudic to pursue.

This completed the first round of additions. The second round occurred when I began to think about *Poem Without a Hero* in the context of Akhmatova's creative biography. Work on the *Poem* began in 1940, a year that Akhmatova would later speak of as her poetic zenith. Thus I turned to the other works written in that fruitful year in order to determine what recurring themes (if any) could be found, what ideas and emotions were dominant in Akhmatova's artistic consciousness at that time. The year 1940 is associated with two other major works by Akhmatova in addition to *Poem Without a Hero*: *Requiem,* parts of which were written earlier but which assumed its definitive form in 1940, and *The Way of All the Earth.* It soon became clear to me that these poems were united by the theme of memory, the danger of its loss over time, and the will to preserve it.

Requiem grew out of the experience of the Stalinist terror, when many people close to Akhmatova, including her only son, were arrested. As a poem, it responds to this suffering with both a private lyric response and a public epic one. On a purely personal level, the poet–narrator strives to find a way to bear the burden of her constant awareness of her son's ordeal. She is tempted to escape, to forget her pain, whether by simply numbing herself, emotionally distancing herself from a life that is at once agonizingly real and grotesquely unreal, or by the more dramatic means of death or madness. Ultimately, however, she finds the strength to take upon herself the role of witness to suffering and death, as she invokes the image of Mary, the mother of Jesus, standing at the foot of the Cross. This personal act of witness gives rise to a public one, as the grieving mother recognizes her own pain in the face of every woman who lost a loved one to the Terror and accepts the responsibility to speak for all those who are too frightened or crushed in spirit to tell their own stories. The poet cannot save the victims; but through her conscious act of memory, through the creation of a poem that serves as a monument to them, she can prevent the second death that would occur if they were forgotten.

Whereas *Requiem* seeks to ensure that the memory of the present (as seen from the poet's vantage point in 1940) will be preserved in the future, *The Way of All the Earth* seeks to return from the world of the present to a past preserved in memory. Its central image is the holy city of Kitezh, which, according to an old Russian legend, escaped desecration at the hands of marauding infidels by miraculously vanishing from the earth. The narrator of *The Way of All the Earth* is described as a woman of Kitezh trying to find her way home to the now-lost city; on another level, she is clearly Akhmatova herself, trying to find a way back to her past, to her youth in the more innocent era before the First World War. But each past scene to which the poet–narrator returns has been frighteningly altered, as if the terrible events of the future–her present–had already cast their shadows before. In the world of the living, the world of time and change, what is and what has been cannot be disentangled; the clock cannot be turned back from the agonies of the present, there is no earthly road that leads to Kitezh. Yet beyond time, on the far side of death, Kitezh continues to exist, unchanged and unchangeable, as a memory and a summoning vision.

This same sense of the complex relationship between present and past, in which living memory can neither wholly recover nor wholly lose any past time, lies at the foundation of *Poem Without a Hero*. The poem opens on New Year's Eve of 1940 as the narrator awaits a "Guest from the Future"; instead she is visited by the ghosts of her past who are celebrating New Year's Eve in 1913, heedless of the rapidly approaching tragedies of war, revolution, and dictatorship. In this case, history itself has become a threat to memory. The distance between the Russia of 1940 and the Russia of 1913 is so great that the poet–narrator has all but forgotten the world of her younger self; and when that world unexpectedly reemerges into her consciousness, even though her recollections are factual, she experiences them in the disturbingly vivid yet fragmentary manner of a dream.

This sense of estrangement from her past, however, is only one of the enemies of memory confronted by the narrator of *Poem Without a Hero*. Viewing her prerevolutionary youth from the perspective of the Stalin era, when moral choices could literally be a matter of life and death, Akhmatova regards the artistic and bohemian circles with which she was once associated as aesthetically brilliant but lacking a moral compass. Forgetting the past would be easier, more comfortable, than facing memories that evoke guilt; but conscience nevertheless drives the poet–narrator to revisit an obscure tragedy and to see in it a portent of the destruction to come. And after overcoming her own reluctance to remember, the poet–narrator must then surmount the obstacles placed in the way of her writing by a regime that has no interest in preserving a truthful account of events, either pre- or postrevolutionary. In response, echoing motifs from *Requiem*, the poet–witness speaks of the mass arrests of the Stalin years as well as of the heavy–handed official attempts to discredit and silence her—attempts which, her Muse assures her, are destined to fail. Finally, after conquering all these enemies of memory, the poet–narrator is able to reestablish the broken links between past and present and thus to set her own sufferings and those of her generation in a meaningful context.

The three major poems associated with the year 1940, then, are the-

matically linked compositions. And given that fact, presenting them to-
gether would offer greater insight into each work than presenting any
one of them in isolation. I thus undertook new translations of *Requiem*
and *The Way of All the Earth* not in the spirit of criticizing any existing
translation but simply to complete the work I had started by translating
Poem Without a Hero. And, just as *Poem Without a Hero* had its own literary
apparatus, so *Requiem* and *The Way of All the Earth* were followed by critical
discussions. However, while the sheer number of small but cumulatively
significant points in *Poem Without a Hero* had required the creation of a
separate section of commentary to prevent them from crowding out any
overall consideration of the work, no such difficulty in integrating a
discussion of details with the whole presented itself when I addressed
the shorter, less complex *Requiem* and *The Way of All the Earth*.

At this point, the design of the work seemed settled. First would be
the new translations of the three poems. Next, the reader, who would
already have formed some thoughts on the works, would be able to
benefit from (or argue with) my understanding of them, as set forth in
three critical essays. This would be followed by the material related to a
yet deeper examination of *Poem Without a Hero*, that is, the commentary
and the two appendices.

Everything seemed in order—and then the third and final round of
expansion began. It was motivated by the realization that I could not
expect an American nonspecialist to pick up an English translation of
Akhmatova's poems and read it with the same understanding that a
Russian brings to the original. Imagine a reader from Novgorod opening
a copy of *The Adventures of Huckleberry Finn*. Such a reader would not know
the relevant facts of Twain's biography (such as his youth on the Mis-
sissippi) or be able to recognize the extent to which the book reflects
such major themes in American history as the role of the frontier and the
tragic scar of slavery. In short, the Russian reader would be lacking cru-
cial information that an American reader would possess simply by hav-
ing grown up in American society. The average educated American is in
somewhat the same position with regard to Akhmatova: a compatriot
will automatically draw upon a whole constellation of biography, his-
tory, and cultural assumptions that is much less familiar to an outsider.

Accordingly, to make the poems more accessible to nonspecialist
readers, I decided to preface them with an account of Akhmatova's life

and times covering all the relevant information a reader should possess before encountering *Requiem, The Way of All the Earth,* and *Poem Without a Hero.* Although closest in form to biography, this introduction does not quite fall under that heading, first, because its selection of facts is based upon their importance in understanding a specific set of Akhmatova's works, rather than in understanding the entire course of her life (in particular, the discussion of her prerevolutionary poetic career is compressed); and second, because it goes beyond the normal bounds of biography to address not only Akhmatova's life and works, but also the larger historical and political forces that shaped the society in which she lived and that were echoed in her writings.

Thus the completed work can be summarized as follows: new metrical translations of *Requiem, The Way of All the Earth,* and *Poem Without a Hero* preceded by an introduction offering biographical and historical background and followed by a critical discussion and exposition of the three works. Although this book is made up of numerous genres–biography, poetry in translation, criticism, commentary–they are united in a single goal: to increase the reader's ability to understand and appreciate three works by one of the twentieth century's great poets.

A Note on Style

§ § §

Because this book is meant to be accessible to the nonspecialist reader, in my transliterations of Russian names I have preferred spellings that would help an English speaker to pronounce the name correctly (or at least less incorrectly): thus Gumilyov rather than Gumilev, Yesenin rather than Esenin, and Mayakovsky rather than Maiakovskii. An exception has been made when a particular form has become so well established in English that an alternative would be disconcerting: for example, Khrushchev rather than the more phonetically correct Khrushchov.

Adult Russians typically address one another by first name and patronymic (a name derived from one's father's name): thus Akhmatova was Anna Andreyevna (daughter of Andrei) Akhmatova, while her son was Lev Nikolaevich (son of Nikolai) Gumilyov. Russians also use affectionate diminutives of first names: for example, Lev might be known as Lyova to his close friends and Lyovushka to his doting mother or grandmother. To avoid confusing readers not familiar with such forms, I have kept the use of patronymics and diminutives to a minimum.

Prior to 1918, Russians used the Julian calendar, which lagged twelve days behind the Gregorian (Western) calendar in the nineteenth century and thirteen days in the twentieth. Thus the day on which Akhmatova was born was considered by a Russian to be June 11, 1889, while a westerner regarded it as June 23, 1889; and the October Revolution of 1917 took place on Western-style November 7, 1917. Dates throughout are given as they were perceived by Russians at the time—"Old Style" prior to Russia's adoption of the Gregorian calendar in 1918, "New Style" thereafter.

PART I

Biographical and Historical Background

CHAPTER 1
Youth and Early Fame, 1889–1916

§ § §

S HE WAS NOT BORN ANNA AKHMATOVA. She came into the world on June 11, 1889, as Anna Andreyevna Gorenko, the daughter of a naval officer named Andrei Antonyevich Gorenko and his wife, Inna Erazmovna. When she was seventeen, it came to her father's attention that she was so unladylike as to aspire to recognition as a poet, and he warned her not to bring shame upon his name. She replied, "I don't need your name" and promptly disowned the entire masculine side of her lineage by choosing as her literary name the maiden name of her maternal grandmother, Akhmatova.[1] It was not only a defiant act, but also a creative one. It is difficult to believe that "Anna Gorenko" would have captured the imagination in the same way as "Anna Akhmatova"–"a name that is a great sigh / Falling into a depth without name," as the other great female poet of her generation, Marina Tsvetayeva, wrote in admiration. One might say that the inspired self-naming of Anna Akhmatova was the first instance of the pattern that governed her life: the attempts of men in authority to silence her would rouse her Muse to yet more eloquently impassioned speech.

Akhmatova was born near Odessa, on the Black Sea, but when she was two years old her family moved to Tsarskoe Selo (now Pushkin), just a few miles from the capital, Saint Petersburg. Tsarskoe Selo (the tsar's

3

village) was a small but grandiose town dominated by the Catherine Palace, built by Peter the Great's daughter Elizabeth as a Russian Baroque answer to Versailles. In later years, Akhmatova was to look back upon this vanished world in a set of sketches of her girlhood. Her recollections of Tsarskoe Selo themselves suggest the style of an earlier aristocratic era, when memoirists regarded public examination of their own feelings as inappropriate and preferred to concentrate on describing the charac-teristic details of the world around them: the view from Anna's bedroom window onto a side street overgrown with nettles and burdock, the train ride for outings to nearby Pavlovsk,and the scent of strawberries for sale in the station store. This classicist ethos of clear-eyed observation and self-restraint is a characteristic trait of all her poems, from the earliest to the last.

Yet equally characteristic of Akhmatova is a thoroughly romantic strain of self-consciousness, a sense of herself as someone special, some-one fated to live a consuming drama, whether personal or historical. This tendency also appears in reminiscences of her girlhood, where it is linked with the summers her family spent on the Black Sea. By Akhma-tova's account, at the seacoast the proper young lady of Tsarskoe Selo revealed her true colors as a bold nonconformist who delighted in shocking respectable society. In an age when women decorously covered themselves while bathing by the shore, the young Anna Gorenko would run about sunburned and hatless, jump headlong into the sea and swim like a fish, wearing a thin dress with nothing on beneath. When an aunt rebuked the thirteen-year-old girl for such conduct, saying, "If I were your mama, I would cry all the time," she retorted, "It's better for both of us that you're not my mama."[2] Such bohemianism was, of course, a fitting trait for a budding poet: at age thirteen, Akhmatova claimed, she had already read Charles-Pierre Baudelaire, Paul Verlaine, and all the *poètes maudits* in the original and had written her first poem two years before.[3]

Akhmatova regarded herself as destined to be a poet, but she would have been the first to point out that one must learn to be a good poet. And during her childhood in the 1890s, Russian poetry was at a low point in its history. The average educated Russian had come to regard poetry as a frivolous aesthetic self-indulgence. The only book of poetry in the Gorenko household was a volume of Nikolai Nekrasov, a contem-porary of Tolstoy and Dostoyevsky whose poems were widely admired not for their strikingly innovative poetic language and forms, but for their socially conscious depictions of the hard life of the peasantry. Nevertheless, poetry was not completely lacking in defenders. The 1890s saw the rise of a new literary movement, which named itself Symbolism in homage to its French contemporaries, but which also drew inspiration from Edgar Allan Poe, Dostoyevsky, and the philosopher–mystic Vladimir Solovyov (who died in 1900). Symbolism was fascinated by the irrational, the extreme, the otherworldly. It saw the poet as the bearer of a hidden truth which could be expressed only indirectly, through symbols. The young poets who made up the movement undertook their chosen task with great enthusiasm, and by the turn of the twentieth century had produced a considerable amount of literary scandal and some good poems. It was in the midst of this literary ferment that the young Akhmatova found her own poetic voice. And she was brought into this artistic world by another young aspiring poet, who was also to become her husband–Nikolai Gumilyov.

Akhmatova and Gumilyov met on Christmas Eve, 1903, when the fourteen–year–old Anna and a girlfriend went out shopping for Christmas tree ornaments and ran into the seventeen–year–old Nikolai and his older brother. The girlfriend, who already knew "the Gumilyov boys," made the introductions and noticed that Anna seemed unimpressed. Gumilyov, however, apparently felt love at first sight, and the next few years of their relationship would be a dizzying set of variations on the old theme, "Much ado there was, God wot, / He would love and she would not."⁴ In the fall of 1904, Anna's older sister Inna married Sergei von Shtein. Every Thursday the young von Shteins invited friends for tea and conversation, and Gumilyov, an acquaintance of von Shtein, seized the occasion to meet Anna regularly. He also made it a point to cultivate the acquaintance of Anna's brother Andrei, two years her senior and one year Gumilyov's junior. At Easter 1905, Anna's refusal to take his courtship seriously drove Nikolai to despair. He attempted suicide, which frightened and angered Anna, and she broke off the relationship with him.

The year 1905 was a tumultuous one, both for the Gorenko family and for the country. The Russian government's expansionism in the Far East had brought it into conflict with Japan, which had its own imperialist agenda. In 1904, the Japanese declared war. The tsarist government, although caught off guard, was initially confident of European superiority to "Asiatics" and convinced that a victorious war would shore up its sagging domestic support. But Russia's Far Eastern military command was inept, and the supply lines across thousands of miles of Siberia were inadequate. In December 1904, the Russians surrendered the key fortress of Port Arthur in northern China. Instead of victory shoring up the regime, defeat was undermining it; and the number of troops stationed in Asia meant that fewer were available to put down uprisings in European Russia. On January 9, 1905, a group of unarmed Petersburg workers led by a priest undertook a march to the palace to present a petition of their grievances to the tsar. They were fired upon by mounted troops, and in the close quarters of the crowded street, casualties were heavy–ninety-two deaths, according to the official figures; several times that, according to unofficial ones. "Bloody Sunday," as the massacre came to be called, was the start of a series of labor strikes and peasant rebellions throughout the country. In May 1905, as the Russian Pacific Squadron sailed toward Vladivostok through the Strait of Tsushima, off the southern coast of Japan, it was attacked by the faster and more modern fleet of Admiral Heihachiro Togo and annihilated. The Gorenkos, as a naval family, felt the blow particularly painfully. More than fifty years later, Akhmatova would write, "January 9 and Tsushima were a shock that lasted my whole life, and since it was the first one, it was especially terrible."[5] That summer, the world of Anna's childhood fell apart: her father left her mother for his mistress, and Inna Erazmovna took the children and moved to Eupatoria, in the Crimea. The lonely Anna, as she later recalled, "pined for Tsarskoe Selo and wrote a great number of incompetent poems."[6]

In October 1905, as Tsar Nicholas II was preparing to issue the semi-constitution known as the October Manifesto, the twenty-year-old Nikolai Gumilyov published his first volume of poems, the proudly titled *Path of the Conquistadors*. He sent a copy to Andrei Gorenko, but even though many of the poems were dedicated to Anna, he did not dare to send her a copy. Contact between the two was renewed in the fall of 1906, when Anna wrote to Gumilyov, then in Paris studying literature at the Sorbonne. It is not clear what prompted her to break her long silence; perhaps she wanted to respond to Gumilyov's expressions of sympathy for the family following Inna von Shtein's death from tuberculosis in July

1906. In any event, Gumilyov promptly wrote back to the seventeen-year-old Anna with a marriage proposal. The letters that Akhmatova was writing at this time to her widowed brother-in-law Sergei, the member of her family circle in whom she most confided, show that she was deeply in love with another man who did not return her affection. Nevertheless, she accepted Gumilyov's proposal, and in February 1907 she wrote to von Shtein, "I am going to marry my childhood friend, Nikolai Stepanovich Gumilyov. He has loved me for 3 years now, and I believe that it is my fate to be his wife. Whether or not I love him, I do not know, but it seems to me that I do." In a second letter written four days later, she added, "I am poisoned for my whole life; bitter is the poison of unrequited love! Will I be able to begin to live again? Certainly not! But Gumilyov is my Fate, and I obediently submit to it. Don't condemn me, if you can. I swear to you, by all that is holy to me, that this unhappy man will be happy with me."[7]

But in June 1907, when Gumilyov returned from Paris to see Anna, she again quarreled with him and made it clear to him that she was "not innocent" (to use the quaint expression of his biographer).[8] He returned to Paris alone, and before the year was out he made two more suicide attempts. January 1908 saw the publication of his second book of poems, *Romantic Flowers*, with a dedication to Anna Andreyevna Gorenko. Back in Russia, he proposed again in April 1908 and was again refused. Searching for new experiences and inspirations, in September 1908 Gumilyov set off for Egypt, while the nineteen-year-old Akhmatova enrolled in prelaw in the Kiev Advanced Courses for Women. He returned to Crimea in the late spring of 1909, again proposed to Akhmatova, and was again refused. He asked her if she loved him, and she replied, "I don't love you, but I consider you an outstanding individual."[9]

Certainly Gumilyov was outstandingly persistent, and he finally got his way. According to Akhmatova's recollections, she decided to marry him when she read a phrase in a letter he wrote to her in fall 1909, "I've come to understand that the only things in the world that interest me are those related to you."[10] Given Gumilyov's many avowals, it is difficult to believe that one declaration more or less could have been so crucial. Perhaps his sheer insistence confirmed her previously expressed belief that he was her fate. In any event, at the end of November 1909, when Gumilyov was passing through Kiev en route to Africa, he again proposed to Akhmatova, and this time she said yes. He was so afraid she would not go through with the wedding that in February 1910, when he returned to Russia and she came to meet him at the station, he introduced her to several of his friends but did not mention that she was his fiancée. The wedding did take place, however, in Kiev on April 25, 1910, nine days after the publication of the groom's third book of poems, *Pearl.* Akhmatova's family regarded the marriage as doomed from the start and registered their disapproval by refusing to attend—an absence which offended the twenty–year–old bride but did not deter her. A week later, the young couple left for a honeymoon in Paris.

It was Akhmatova's first trip outside Russia, but, like any educated prerevolutionary Russian, she was fluent in French and had been brought up on French culture. Gumilyov, who knew the city well, proudly escorted his bride to museums, exhibitions, and cafes. Years later she recalled her strolls through the city: "The construction of the new boulevards on the living body of Paris (as described by Zola) had not yet been completely finished (Boulevard Raspail). Werner, a friend of Edison's, pointed out two tables in the Taverne de Panthéon and said: 'And those are your Social Democrats—the Bolsheviks sit here, the Mensheviks over there.'"[11]

There were other compatriots in Paris, however, who interested Akhmatova much more than political exiles, for this was the period of the first great triumphs of Sergei Diaghilev's Ballets Russes. Diaghilev represented in dance and opera the same discontent with art dominated by social consciousness that in literature had given rise to Symbolism. Realism had been the artistic keynote of the preceding generation; the new generation regarded ordinary life as drab and prized theatricality as an escape from it. Guided by this love of theatricality and Richard Wagner's doctrine of the *Gesamtkunstwerk*, or "unified work of art," Diaghilev and his collaborators achieved some of their greatest successes in the fields of opera and ballet. In 1908, Diaghilev arranged for the first complete performance of Modest Moussorgsky's *Boris Godunov* (in the Nikolai Rimsky-Korsakov arrangement) to be staged at the Paris Opéra, with Fyodor Chaliapin singing the title part. The set designs were by Alexander Benois and Alexander Golovin, both painters of note in their own right, and the costumes were the work of Ivan Bilibin, a specialist in folk art. Chaliapin instantly became the world's most famous basso, and the production won rave reviews. Success, for Diaghilev, was only an incentive to aim higher. Starting in 1909, he brought the Ballets Russes to the West for a series of tours, first in Paris and then through the capitals of Europe. For the first time the West saw the dancing of Vaslav Nijinsky, Tamara Karsavina, and Anna Pavlova, and these now-legendary dancers were brilliantly supported by the contributions of Michel Fokine as choreographer and Benois and Leon Bakst as stage designers. In 1910, the Ballets Russes staged a new work based on a Russian folktale, with music composed by an unknown twenty-six-year-old: the Paris premiere of Igor Stravinsky's *Firebird* made him an overnight celebrity. Continuing in the vein of Russian popular tradition, Stravinsky turned to the characters of the puppet theater presented at country fairs and during the festivities of Maslenitsa (the Russian pre-Lenten carnival). The result was the ballet *Petrouchka*, which had its premiere in Paris in 1911 with Nijinsky in the title role; it was to become Nijinsky's favorite part.

After a month in Paris, Akhmatova and Gumilyov returned to Petersburg. On their way back, they found themselves in the same train compartment with an acquaintance, the poet and critic Sergei Makovsky, with whom they enthusiastically shared their impressions of Diaghilev's operas and ballets. Makovsky was strongly impressed by his female companion, not merely as the "wife of the poet," but as a person in her own right: "Everything about the appearance of the Akhmatova of that time–tall, thin, quiet, very pale, with a sorrowful crease to her mouth and satiny bangs on her forehead (the fashion in Paris)–was attractive and evoked a feeling half of touched curiosity, half of pity."[12] His description suggests Akhmatova's self-evaluation some fifty years later: "In 1910, when people met the twenty-year-old wife of N. Gumilyov, pale, dark-haired, very slender and graceful, with beautiful hands and a Bourbon profile, it never crossed their minds that this person already had behind her a vast and painful experience of life, that the poems of 1910–11 were not a beginning, but a continuation."[13]

Through all the years of Gumilyov's courtship, Akhmatova had been writing poems. She later regarded most of them as unsatisfactory juvenilia, with the result that only about twenty of the poems she wrote before 1910 survive. Gumilyov, however, felt that she deserved encouragement and in 1907 printed one of her poems in a brief-lived journal, *Sirius*, that he published in Paris. After Gumilyov and Akhmatova returned from their honeymoon, he took his new wife to the Tower, the celebrated literary and philosophical salon presided over by the poet and polymath Vyacheslav Ivanov. Ivanov privately asked her if she wrote poetry, and when she recited two of her poems to him, he said ironically, "What lush Romanticism!"[14] Gumilyov also did not hesitate to criticize her poems and suggested that she take up some other form of art. She was exceptionally lithe–why didn't she consider becoming a dancer?

Akhmatova recognized the justice of her husband's criticism but did not give up her goal of becoming a poet. Instead, she used the new opportunities she had in Petersburg to improve her work. In September 1910, Gumilyov set off on a trip to Ethiopia, while Akhmatova, who remained in Petersburg, began a course of literary studies. Gumilyov had told her of his admiration for the little-known poet Innokenty Annensky, who had been headmaster of the Tsarskoe Selo lyceum when Gumilyov was a student there. Now Akhmatova was allowed to read the proofs of Annensky's collection of verse *The Cypress Chest*. Annensky, who had died in 1909, had been out of the poetic mainstream because, unlike the Symbolists, he regarded art primarily in psychological rather than mystical terms. This characteristic fitted Akhmatova's half-formed artistic aspirations and enabled her to learn from Annensky in a way she had not been able to from any other of her older contemporaries. As she studied *The Cypress Chest*, "read[ing] it as if the world had ceased to exist," she discovered her poetic identity: "Poems came at an even flow– nothing like it had ever happened before. I searched, I found, I lost. I sensed (rather dimly) that I was beginning to succeed."[15]

By November or December 1910, Akhmatova was confident enough to send four of her new poems to Valery Bryusov, one of the founding fathers of Symbolism and an early mentor of Gumilyov, and to ask for his opinion. In the artistic circles of Saint Petersburg, where everybody knew and gossiped about everybody else, the word quickly spread that the wife of the poet Gumilyov was turning out to be a gifted poet in her own right. She was asked to read her work at various gatherings and finally, on March 14, 1911, was asked to read at the Tower. When she finished, Ivanov dramatically invited her to sit at his right hand, in the place where Annensky had used to sit, and declared to the assembled company, "Here is a new poet who will reveal to us that which remained undisclosed in the recesses of Annensky's soul."[16]

The young Akhmatova succeeded so dramatically not only because of her gifts, but also because she had appeared at the right moment. The great literary flowering of nineteenth–century Russia had produced no women writers of a stature comparable to George Eliot in England or George Sand in France. By the early twentieth century, what Russians called the woman question had become pressing enough that a woman writer speaking with a distinctly feminine sensibility could finally hope for a positive reception. It was just such a woman's perspective that Akhmatova brought to Russian poetry. Most of her early poems were on the traditionally feminine topic of love, often unhappy love. But whereas in a typical nineteenth–century Russian love poem the male poet addressed his praises or pleas to a beautiful and silent woman, in Akhmatova's poems the woman's emotions and experience are central, and the man is seen only through her eyes:

> Under the dark veil my hands tensed and clutched:
> "You're white as a sheet—what's happened to you?"
> I poured grief for him and he drank it up
> Until he got drunk on that bitter brew.
>
> I'll never forget the twist of his mouth,
> How, as he left, he could hardly walk straight.
> I didn't touch the railing as I ran out,
> I ran after him as far as the gate.
>
> I gasped as I shouted: "It was a joke,
> All of it. Don't leave me, please, or I'll die!"
> He had such a calm cruel smile as he spoke:
> "It's windy out here. Go on back inside."

Akhmatova's lyrics plunge into the narrative without pausing to supply background (is the man a lover? a husband? and how exactly did the woman hurt him?), thus creating an effect of unexpected intimacy, as if the reader had accidentally overheard a personal conversation or come across a page from the diary of a stranger. The reader's sense of being an intimate observer of the narrator's life is heightened by the precise and realistic details she supplies: her dash down the stairs, in which she refuses to slow down and hold on to the banister despite the long skirts that presumably encumbered her, and her gasping for breath when she stops running. One could readily imagine this poem as a scene in a movie. Indeed, many of the young Akhmatova's readers found her lyrics

11

so grippingly real that they assumed that the first-person narrator and the author must be one and the same and that the poems were directly autobiographical documents. Such a misunderstanding annoyed Akhmatova, but it undoubtedly helped to make her a literary celebrity.

Her sudden recognition in literary circles meant little to Akhmatova, who had already seen enough of the personal intrigues that were involved to regard reputation-makers with distrust. But one person's approval was very important to her: that of Gumilyov, who returned from Africa on March 25, 1911. Years later, she would still delight in remembering her triumph: "During our first conversation he casually asked me, 'Did you write any poetry?' I, secretly rejoicing, answered, 'Yes.' He asked me to read, listened to several poems and said, 'You are a poet—you need to make a book.' "[17]

By the standards of the time, Gumilyov's willingness to accept his wife not merely as an artist, but as an artist in his own field—hence, in a sense, a competitor—is remarkable. Perhaps one reason he did not resent her independence was that his own adventurous nature, his Hemingwayesque fascination with the "primitive" and exotic, would have made it very difficult for him to find happiness with a traditional domestic-minded wife.

Another form of unconventionality in the Gumilyovs' marriage was manifested a few months later. At the beginning of May 1911 Gumilyov and Akhmatova again went to Paris; he stayed only a few days, while she remained there for two months. During that time, Akhmatova renewed her relationship with an impoverished, little-known artist whom she had met the previous year, the twenty-six-year-old Amedeo Modigliani. He and she would go for long strolls on the cobblestone streets of Paris, where horses rather than cars were still the normal means of transport, and discuss the poems of Verlaine, Baudelaire, and Stephane Mallarmé. Once Akhmatova came to his studio but found he was not there. She was carrying a large bouquet of red roses, and, seeing an open window above the studio's locked gates, she impulsively threw the roses in. Later Modigliani asked her how she had gotten in to leave the roses, and she explained what she had done. He replied, "But that's impossible—they were lying there so beautifully."[18] Modigliani did a number of drawings (nude and clothed) of Akhmatova; most of the ones he gave her were lost in the upheaval of the revolutionary period, but she managed to hang on to one drawing that she proudly displayed in every apartment she lived in until her death.

In July, Akhmatova left Paris for the Gumilyov family estate of Slepnyovo, near the town of Bezhetsk, about 150 miles north of Moscow. Owing to the Russian calendar, after spending Bastille Day (July 14) in Paris, Akhmatova arrived in Slepnyovo on July 13. This seeming reversal of the direction of time was appropriate, for the Gumilyov household at Slepnyovo was leading a country-squire existence that to an urbanite like Akhmatova appeared a century out of date. The servant who greeted Akhmatova at the railroad station found her so exotic that she refused to believe the newcomer was Russian and announced, "A French girl has come to visit the Slepnyovo masters."[19] Gumilyov deeply loved his kind and sensible mother, the widowed Anna Ivanovna Gumilyova, but he was visibly out of place amid the various cousins and neighbors, and Akhmatova was even more so. One can imagine the relief the two of them must have felt on returning to the literary life of Petersburg that fall.

In the capital literary battles were raging. The period of 1910–11 is known in the history of Russian poetry as "the crisis of Symbolism." On one level, it was a crisis of self-doubt, as the theurgistic claims that the Symbolists had once made for poetry now seemed increasingly hollow. This self-questioning was reflected in the life of the greatest of the Symbolists, the man whom Akhmatova was later to remember as "the epoch personified" (*chelovek-epokha*) and "the tragic tenor of the epoch," Alexander Blok. Akhmatova's musical metaphor is apt, for Blok's poetry immediately calls to mind Verlaine's dictum, *"de la musique avant toute chose"* (music first and foremost). Sound is so central a feature of Blok's poetry that at times the individual words seem to lose definition, being chosen less for their precise meaning than for their musical suggestiveness, their ability to create a mood. (This trait makes it extremely difficult, if not impossible, to translate Blok's work adequately into English.) Blok's first book of poetry, *Verses on the Beautiful Lady*, was completed in 1902 and published two years later, when he was twenty-four years old. The Beautiful Lady of the title was identified both with Sophia, the mystical Divine Wisdom and Eternal Feminine, and with a specific woman–his idealized beloved, Lyubov Mendeleyeva.When Blok married his Muse, however, he soon found out that she was an all-too-earthly woman, and the rapid breakdown of their marriage shook him to the depths of his soul. He repudiated his youthful dreams in a lyric drama, *The Puppet Show* (1906), a parody of the commedia dell'arte in which Pierrot wins and then loses Columbine against a background of absurdly portentous mysticism and self-unmasking theatricality (when a clown is stabbed, he cries, "Help! I'm bleeding cranberry juice!"). The Beautiful Lady was replaced by the Unknown Woman, whose fallen but still-beautiful figure might be briefly glimpsed, incongruously radiant, amid drunks in a squalid tavern. Blok had lost every shred of faith in his early ideals, but he could not stop loving them, and the contradiction tore him to pieces. At times he threw himself into drinking and womanizing in a search not for pleasure, but simply for some passion, some sensation strong enough to make him forget everything else—the Dostoyevskian intoxication of the blizzard celebrated in his cycle of poems *The Snow Mask* (1907). At other times he was appalled by his debauchery, experienced an unbearable sense of loneliness and the pointlessness of life, thought of himself as a walking dead man forced to go through the motions of living—an agony reflected in such poems as the cycle *Dances of Death* and *The Steps of the Commendatore* (1912).

At the same time that the Symbolist view of art was being shaken from within, it was under assault from without. Whereas Symbolism had once been the upstart, challenging the presuppositions and limitations of nineteenth-century realism, now it was the establishment, and a new generation was challenging it. This new generation, to which both Gumilyov and Akhmatova belonged, was drawn to the slogan proclaimed by the poet and critic Mikhail Kuzmin in 1910: "beautiful clarity." The new poetry was to be a work of deliberate craftsmanship rather than vatic inspiration, Mediterranean rather than Teutonic, neoclassical rather than neoromantic. Every new artistic movement had its journal, and the increasingly vocal anti-Symbolist sentiment found its voice in the aptly named *Apollon* (*Apollo*), which started publishing in late 1909. Gumilyov regularly contributed critical articles. In October 1911, he joined with an older poet, Sergei Gorodetsky, to form a group calling itself the Poets' Guild. Akhmatova was the group's secretary and put out the bulletin of its monthly meetings. In March 1912, her first book of poems, *Evening*, appeared, bearing on its cover the guild's logo of a lyre.

Literary battles could not distract Gumilyov from his wanderlust, and in April and May 1912 he and Akhmatova made a six-week trip overland through Germany and Switzerland to northern Italy, where they toured Genoa, Pisa, Florence, Bologna, Padua, and Venice. Akhmatova, who would not have the opportunity to travel in western Europe again for more than fifty years, spoke of her Italian tour as being "like a dream that you remember for the rest of your life."[20] Her sense of unreality is understandable: more than one sensitive person has been psychologically overwhelmed by intensive exposure to Italian art (a phenomenon described by Stendhal), and she was also experiencing her first pregnancy. Upon the couple's return to Russia, Akhmatova visited her mother and a cousin in Ukraine while Gumilyov went on to Slepnyovo. In July Akhmatova joined him there, and in August they returned to Petersburg.

On September 18, 1912, Akhmatova gave birth to a healthy baby boy, who was given the name Lev. During the first days after Lev's birth, Akhmatova was so strongly attached to her child that she insisted on breastfeeding him, contrary to the practice of women of her social class. As the weeks passed, however, she surrendered more and more of the responsibility of caring for her son to Gumilyov's mother, Anna, and his older half-sister Alexandra Sverchkova. Akhmatova, only twenty-three years old and still discovering her literary abilities, was simply not ready psychologically for the burden of full-time motherhood. Her confidence in her ability as a mother may also have been undermined by Sverchkova, who had never approved of her. In the end, the family reached an arrangement whereby Anna Gumilyova and Alexandra Sverchkova took Lev to live with them in Slepnyovo, and Akhmatova went there to visit her son during holidays and in the summer. It is a measure of how different our expectations are for a man and a woman that while Akhmatova's willingness to be separated from her son surprises us, Gumilyov's equal willingness does not, nor do we assume that he did not care deeply about his child. The conflict between Akhmatova's roles as a poet and as a mother would reemerge years later, as Lev grew up; but for his first years, it seemed she had found an acceptable solution.

In a fragment on Gumilyov's biography, Akhmatova wrote, "Soon after Lev's birth, we tacitly gave each other complete freedom and ceased to be interested in the intimate side of each other's life."[21] From this time on the Gumilyovs had a thoroughly open marriage. In October 1913, the actress Olga Vysotskaya gave birth to Gumilyov's child, a fact that

Akhmatova acknowledged without any anger or jealousy. (In the early 1930s, Lev Gumilyov met his half-brother Orest Vysotsky, and the two young men became close friends.)

Although Gumilyov's and Akhmatova's relationship as husband and wife had essentially ended, their relationship as colleagues remained as strong as ever. By early 1913, the Poets' Guild had given rise to a new literary movement, which came to be called Acmeism (to suggest a period of flourishing or heightened capabilities). Some of the subscribers to the Acmeists' manifestos are now historical footnotes. But in addition to Akhmatova and Gumilyov, Acmeism won the allegiance of one truly brilliant poet, the twenty-two-year-old Osip Mandelstam, who in spring 1913 published his first volume of poetry, entitled *Stone*. In contrast to the Symbolist concept of the poet as an oracle of otherworldly mysteries, Mandelstam was joyously interested in everything human. He wrote poems inspired by Hagia Sophia, Bach, Petersburg landmarks and street scenes, a silent movie, a tennis match; in a seemingly ordinary old man he caught glimpses of Verlaine and "a drunken Socrates." Opponents of Acmeism scoffed that there was, in fact, no such movement and asked what common factor could be found in the highly intellectual poems of Mandelstam, Gumilyov's stern celebrations of warriors and explorers, and Akhmatova's intensely personal lyrics. But the three young poets recognized one another as kindred spirits: seven years after Gumilyov's death, Mandelstam wrote to Akhmatova, "You know that there are only two people with whom I have the ability to carry on an imaginary conversation–Nikolai Stepanovich [Gumilyov] and you. My conversation with Kolya has never been broken off and never will be broken off."[22]

The three Acmeists all were regulars at the Stray Dog, the most famous artists' cafe in Petersburg. The atmosphere of the club was captured in the recollections of another habitué, the painter Sergei Sudeikin:

> The "Stray Dog" was open every evening. Everyone who entered had to register in an enormous book lying on a lectern in front of a tall red lit candle. The public entered from the courtyard and went through a small door, like going through a needle's eye. The main door onto the street was opened only for "our crowd." There were shutters over the windows, and on the shutters fantastic birds were painted. On the wall between the windows I painted Baudelaire's "Flowers of Evil." ... At the door there always stood either Pronin [the proprietor], or Lutsevich, or

Tsybulsky. Poets, musicians, artists, and scholars were admitted free. Everybody else was referred to as "pharmacists," and what they were charged for entrance depended on their appearance and on the mood.[23]

At the Stray Dog, Akhmatova became acquainted with the celebrated beauty Olga Glebova-Sudeikina, a dancer and actress who would become the heroine of *Poem Without a Hero*; the composer Artur Lourie, with whom Akhmatova had a brief affair; and the poet and Assyriologist Vladimir Shileiko, who later became Akhmatova's second husband. In this gifted bohemian company, organized and spontaneous performances of poetry, theater, and music went on till dawn, while arguments raged about the nature of life and art.

In 1913, the great topic of debate was another new literary movement, Futurism. The Futurists, as their name suggests, were an aggressively avant-garde movement (the most prominent of their many factions was briefly known as the Cubo-Futurists, since it included a number of painters attracted to Cubism): their manifestos, with titles like "A Slap in the Face of Public Taste," loudly proclaimed the irrelevance of all previous art and declared themselves the only true artistic representatives of modernity. One of the most conspicuous of the Futurists was the eighteen-year-old poet Vladimir Mayakovsky, who at this stage of his life could be described as a sort of Russian anticipation of the Beat poets, brilliantly violating the traditional canons of Russian poetry with works like "A Cloud in Pants" and "The Backbone Flute." The Stray Dog was exactly the sort of forum the self-dramatizing Mayakovsky enjoyed, and he soon became one of the regulars. He professed a derisive amusement at both the emotional subtleties of Akhmatova's poems and her restrained public demeanor, and when being introduced to her, he grabbed her hand and exclaimed, "What little tiny fingers, oh my God!"[24] But in private, he regularly turned to reading Akhmatova's poems when suffering from yet another of the breakups that punctuated his stormy private life.

If Mayakovsky was unwilling to admit the effect Akhmatova's poetry had on him, there were many readers who were less restrained. In March 1914, Akhmatova's second collection of poems, *Rosary*, was published. It was so popular that despite wartime conditions it was reprinted in June 1915, April 1916, and January 1917. Admiring readers would "tell the *Rosary*," one person starting to recite a poem and another finishing it.[25]

Rosary was both a continuation of and departure from Akhmatova's first volume, *Evening*. As in *Evening*, many of the poems in *Rosary* addressed the theme of "nonlove": the female narrator loves but is not loved, or is loved but does not love in return. This nonlove evokes not the intense emotion that might be expected from a young woman, but a quiet, sorrowful resignation, occasionally mixed with guilt and self-reproach. What is new about *Rosary* is that this mood has become a conscious outlook on life, a belief that the happiness of love, indeed any happiness, is brief and likely to bring suffering in its wake, and as a result an attraction to the path of self-renunciation. Such an outlook, even if not religious in the sense of formally embracing a creed, is emotionally in tune with a type of religious striving; it is also close to the Russian Orthodox tradition of regarding suffering as something to be borne patiently rather than fought against. Early in 1914, the critic Nikolai Nedobrovo wrote an article about Akhmatova that she would later regard as a prophecy of her future. In Nedobrovo's view, the pain reflected in so many of her lyrics was a mark not of weakness, but of an extraordinary passive strength, a capacity to endure: "These torments and complaints, and such extreme humility—is this not weakness of spirit, simple sentimentality? Of course not: Akhmatova's very voice, firm, even self-confident, her very calmness in confessing pain and weakness, the very abundance of anguish, poetically refined,—all bear witness, not to tears over life's trivialities, but to a lyrical soul rather harsh than soft, cruel than lachrymose and clearly masterful rather than downtrodden."[26]

At the time Nedobrovo wrote these words, he and Akhmatova had been lovers for the better part of a year. Apparently they became acquainted at the meetings of the Society of Poets, a group that Nedobrovo founded in spring 1913. Nedobrovo was himself a minor poet but was best known as an arbiter of literary taste. A descendant of an old noble family, he was the embodiment of nineteenth-century aristocratic elegance—"after him, every other man seems like a stablehand," Akhmatova later remarked.[27] His refinement and psychological perceptiveness made it possible for him to enter Akhmatova's inner world in a way that the more conventionally masculine Gumilyov could not. The relationship was profoundly important to Akhmatova: in a private jotting written near the end of her life, she described herself as "¾ made by" Nedobrovo.[28] Their romance would be short-lived, but his sympathetic understanding of her poetic gift and its potential would permanently alter the way Akhmatova viewed herself.

Looking back fifty years after the publication of *Rosary*, Akhmatova wrote, "The book was published on March 15, 1914 (Old Style) and it was allotted a life of approximately six weeks. In early May the Petersburg season was beginning to die down; *everybody* was going away. This time the parting with Petersburg turned out to be forever. We returned not to Petersburg, but to Petrograd; from the nineteenth century we suddenly found ourselves transported to the twentieth, everything had changed."[29] At the end of May 1914, Akhmatova made her regular summer trip to Slepnyovo. She was there on July 15, 1914 (July 28 by the Western calendar), when, in response to a Serbian nationalist's assassination of the heir to the throne of the Austro–Hungarian Empire, Austria declared war on Serbia. Russia had long regarded itself as the protector of all Orthodox Slavs, and the Russian government believed that if it did not defend Serbia it would lose any claim to being taken seriously as a major power. On July 17, Russia declared a general mobilization and defied the demand of Austria's ally Germany that the Russian army stand down. Two days later, Germany declared war on Russia. The war, coming so soon after Russia's humiliation in the Russo–Japanese conflict of 1904–05, terrified the women at Slepnyovo, and the twenty–two–month–old Lyova, knowing something was wrong and not understanding what, kept lisping, "Grandma Ana's cwying, Mommy's cwying, Aunt Khukha's cwying."[30]

This distress was not shared by Gumilyov, who regarded war as a purifying force, an opportunity to test one's courage. He immediately resolved to join the cavalry. On July 23, Gumilyov arrived at Slepnyovo to say good-by to his family, and the next day he and Akhmatova left for the capital, the name of which had been changed from the German-sounding Petersburg to the Slavic Petrograd in a burst of wartime patriotism. Gumilyov's wish for combat was quickly fulfilled. On August 5, Akhmatova saw him off from the Tsarskoe Selo train station to join his unit in Novgorod, and after completing basic training he was sent to the East Prussian front on September 23. Despite the breakdown of their marriage, Gumilyov and Akhmatova maintained a regular correspondence while he was at the front. At Christmas 1914, he was able to obtain a leave from the front, and when he returned to his regiment, Akhmatova accompanied him as far as Vilnius.

Unlike Gumilyov, Akhmatova did not regard the war as glorious, seeing it rather as an ordeal laid upon Russia. In a poem entitled "July 1914," written days after the news of war had come to Slepnyovo, she depicts a stricken countryside, the crops failing for lack of rain, the air smelling of smoke from a burning peat bog, the birds fallen silent; a crippled pilgrim making his way through the village warns of apocalyptic disasters to come. In "May Snow" (1916), a description of an untimely frost destroying the new life of spring in its first flowering becomes a lament for the young men dead at the front: "So terrible is the sight of early death / That I cannot bear to look upon God's world." In "Prayer" (1915), the poet offers to accept freely any affliction God may impose upon her–physical suffering, the loss of her child, of her beloved, of her poetic gift–if at that price "the dark cloud that lours over Russia / Is transformed to a halo of light." In contrast to the emotional dramas that often marked Akhmatova's personal relationships, her love of her homeland was simple and unchanging, and the heightened sense of danger to her country made her more conscious of herself as a Russian and a believer in Russia's age–old faith. Many years later, in a fragment addressed to Gumilyov's memory, she wrote, "But in 1916, when I said something unfavorable about our relationship, he replied, 'No, you taught me to believe in God and to love Russia.'"[31] This new solemnity of emotion, expressed in elevated, hieratic language, became an integral part of Akhmatova's poetic voice, finding its way even into her love poems, as can be seen in this lyric of 1916:

> I yearned for him in vain so many years,
> An empty time, like walking in a doze.
> But then the never–fading light appeared:
> Three years past, on Palm Sunday, it arose.
> My words broke off, there was no need for speech–
> The longed–for bridegroom stood and smiled at me.
>
> Outside the throng unhurriedly processed
> Bearing candles. Oh, that holy time!
> April's thin ice crunched beneath their steps
> While overhead the bells rang out their chimes
> Proclaiming joyous prophecies come true,
> And on the flickering flames a dark breeze blew.

> The white narcissus blossoms in a vase
> And the red wine in a crystal flask
> Seemed lit up by a misty dawn's first rays.
> My hand, white-spotted by the dripping wax,
> Trembled as he raised it for a kiss,
> And my blood sang: Now enter Heaven's bliss!

It was poems like this that made the critic Boris Eikhenbaum speak about the "dual (or, rather, oxymoronic) nature of the lyric heroine's image–half a 'harlot' with stormy passion, half a 'beggar nun' able to pray to God for forgiveness"[32]–a formulation that would later be put to ugly use by Akhmatova's Communist denouncers. The "double image" was, of course, in the eye of the male beholder, who would never have dreamed of describing John Donne as "half Don Juan, half priest" but who was thoroughly unprepared for a woman to combine physical and spiritual love in a similar manner.

It has been suggested that this poem was inspired by Nedobrovo, since he and Akhmatova would have met at the right time, in April 1913. If so, this poem was born of fond remembrance rather than current passion, for although Akhmatova never lost her friendship and esteem for Nedobrovo, by 1916 they were no longer lovers. In a painful irony, Nedobrovo's place in Akhmatova's heart was taken by his best friend, Boris Anrep, an artistically gifted young man who at that time was still seeking his metier (he ultimately became a mosaicist whose works adorn the floor of London's National Gallery). The letters that Nedobrovo wrote to Anrep in 1913 and 1914 are full of praise of the extraordinary Anna Akhmatova, and, naturally enough, Anrep soon wanted to meet her. The first, brief encounter between Akhmatova and Anrep was in August 1914, when Anrep, a reserve officer, was on his way to the front, and it made so little impression on Akhmatova that she later forgot about it altogether. But their second meeting–several days spent together in March 1915 as guests of Nedobrovo–had an effect their host could not have foreseen: the two fell in love. Although Nedobrovo was hurt at being displaced in this manner, he was far too well-bred to show it openly; and Akhmatova continued to value his admiration for her as a woman and as a poet. In February 1916, when Anrep was on leave from the front, Nedobrovo invited both Akhmatova and Anrep to his home, where he read them his just–completed verse tragedy *Judith*. Both listeners politely praised the work, though Anrep later recalled that he had been so absorbed in gazing at Akhmatova that he had hardly heard a word of the play. Such meetings between Akhmatova and Anrep were necessarily infrequent, a fact that may have spurred Akhmatova's imagination: she dedicated more poems to him than to any other person.

In 1915 Akhmatova contracted a severe case of bronchitis, and by 1916 she had developed the chronic cough and low–grade fever of tuberculosis, a disease that ran in her family. As a result, she spent the fall of 1916 in the Crimea, where the mild climate was regarded as healthful. At Bakhchisarai–the site of a ruined palace immortalized for all lovers of Russian poetry by Alexander Pushkin's *The Fountain of Bakhchisarai*–she again met Nedobrovo, who was also suffering from tuberculosis. Their reunion was at once joyous and painful. The guilt that Akhmatova already felt for not loving a man who loved her so greatly was deepened by the awareness that soon they might be parted forever, for Nedobrovo's health was visibly worsening. In fact, he was to die in December 1919, amid the hardships and chaos of civil war, and Akhmatova was never able to learn the details of his final days or where he was buried. By mid–December, however, Akhmatova's health had improved sufficiently so that it was considered safe for her to return to the north, and she went to Slepnyovo. Looking back over almost half a century, she remembered that last winter of tsarist Russia: "It was magnificent. Everything was somehow transposed into the nineteenth century. . . . The sleds, felt boots, bearskin rugs, enormous fur coats, the ringing quiet, the snowdrifts, the diamond–like snow. I greeted the year 1917 there."[33]

CHAPTER 2

Revolution and Civil War, 1917–1922

❧ ❧ ❧

O NE DAY AT THE END OF JANUARY 1917, Akhmatova, who had just returned from the countryside to Petrograd, dined with Natan Altman, an avant-garde painter who had done a well-known portrait of her. After dinner, he presented her with a drawing which he inscribed, "On the day of the Russian Revolution."[1]

Talk of revolution was everywhere in Petrograd in January 1917. The war was dragging on, and the Polish and Romanian fronts had seen slaughter as massive and senseless as any in France. People looked to the top for an explanation of the bloody stalemate, and it was widely assumed that the empress Alexandra (who had been born a princess of Hesse-Darmstadt) was a German spy. In addition, Alexandra's patronage of the dissolute "holy man" Rasputin had severely damaged both her and her husband's reputation. The situation was made even more explosive by the economic hardship caused by the war, which had simply overwhelmed Russia's limited industrial capacity. The workers of Petrograd found their purchasing power reduced as their wages did not keep up with wartime inflation, and the number of strikes and other labor protests jumped dramatically. The overburdened transport system caused delays in the delivery of foodstuffs and fuel to the capital, and workers' wives formed angry lines outside bakeries that did not have enough flour for bread.

By February 25, 1917, the unrest in Petrograd reached a critical mass, as a number of labor demonstrations and protests against food shortages coalesced into a citywide general strike. Troops were called out to disperse the crowds. For two days they obeyed orders to fire on the demonstrators, hundreds of whom were wounded or killed. But on February 27, a mutiny spread through the troops, and they refused to leave their barracks. The government's authority collapsed as crowds of workers, students, and soldiers roamed the streets attacking police stations and other symbols of royal authority.

On the morning of the twenty-fifth, Akhmatova, who was living with her friend Valeria Sreznevskaya in the Vyborg neighborhood on the far side of the Neva, crossed the river to visit her dressmaker. When she tried to return home, hailing a horse-drawn cab, the driver refused to take her, saying, "There's shooting on the bridge, and I have a family." So Akhmatova set off on foot, wandering the city alone, ignoring the risk from stray bullets as she drank in the atmosphere, at once terrifying and intoxicating, of a world that was ending. She was among the crowd that watched as the headquarters of the Okhrana, the hated tsarist political police, was sacked and burned.[2] Boris Anrep had just returned from London, and he did not intend to let anything, even the outbreak of a revolution, stop him from seeing Akhmatova. Because the demonstrators were attacking officers, he removed his epaulets and, as an extra precaution, avoided the barricades set up on the Neva bridges by crossing the frozen river on foot. That night he and Akhmatova went to the opening night performance of Vsevolod Meyerhold's staging of Mikhail Lermontov's *Masquerade*. The play's harsh depiction of upper-class intrigues and their destructive results caught the angry public mood of the moment. As the two walked home after the performance, they caught sight of a Cossack cavalry unit dashing past. Akhmatova told Anrep of her fears of what lay ahead: "It will be the same as it was in France during the Great Revolution, perhaps even worse."[3] The two of them said good-by. Anrep took the next train out of town, then left for England.

Out of this chaos emerged two claimants to power. Nicholas II formally yielded power to a Provisional Government made up of leading members of the Duma (the prerevolutionary Russian parliament). The street demonstrators, however, regarded this body as concerned primarily with the interests of the upper classes and organized their own representative body, the Petrograd Soviet (the Russian word for "council") of Workers' and Soldiers' Deputies.

The class conflict reflected in the existence of these two bodies soon reached the army, where peasant soldiers began to challenge the authority of upper- and middle-class officers. Ordinary soldiers saw no reason why they should get killed in the name of Russia's geopolitical interests, which meant nothing to them, their families, or their villages; many of them took the position that while they would fight if attacked, they would not engage in offensive actions. To the officers, this disintegration of military authority and fighting capability was infuriating. Gumilyov was so disgusted that he decided to leave the front lines and seek service as a military liaison on the Western Front. Alexander Blok's diary mentions seeing him in Petrograd with Akhmatova on May 8; a week later he left for France.

In mid-June Akhmatova left for her regular summer visit to Lyova in Slepnyovo. But here, too, the Revolution was having its effect, as the centuries-old hostility of the peasantry toward large landowners threatened to turn violent. On July 31, Akhmatova ironically wrote to her friend Mikhail Lozinsky, "How I'd like to go to Petersburg and be at *Apollon!* But the peasants have promised to destroy the Slepnyovo estate on August 6, because that's a local holiday and 'guests' are coming. Not a bad way of entertaining guests. I walk around pulling flax and write bad poems."[4]

Had Akhmatova been in Petrograd, she would have found the situation there no better. In June a brief-lived Russian offensive had failed, destroying in the process whatever was left of army morale. The public demand for peace became ever louder. But the government could not make peace. The socialist program of a no-fault peace, with no annexations or indemnities paid by either side, was not supported by either the French or the British government. If Russia broke with its allies to make a separate peace, the weakness of its position meant surrender on whatever terms Germany cared to name. Thus, for lack of any alternative, the war dragged on, while the deep class divisions in Russian society gave rise to assertions that the real reason the Provisional Government did not make peace was that it was under the influence of profiteers whose income depended on continued hostilities. In early July, demonstrations calling for the Provisional Government to step down and yield all power to the soviets turned violent, as pro– and antigovernment soldiers fired on each other. In the end the demonstrations fizzled as the Petrograd Soviet refused to assume sole leadership of the government, but the possibility of civil war still hung in the air. On August 16 Akhmatova wrote to Lozinsky, "Today I got a letter from Valya Sreznevskaya, which starts with: it seems that more butchery is impending. News like that makes everything repellent. . . . Next winter appears equally unattractive to me whether I spend it in Paris or Bezhetsk. The only place where I used to breathe freely was Petersburg. But now that people there have gotten into the habit of washing the bridges each month with the blood of citizens, it's lost a little of its charm for me."

One important reason for the continuing political tension was that the economic problems which had caused the February Revolution had not eased. Breakdowns of the overstrained transport system continued, as did shortages of food, fuel, and raw materials for factories. Workers regarded the ongoing hardships as the result of a plot by the rich to keep them from enjoying the fruits of the Revolution and repeatedly challenged their managers, while managers, who had to deal with steadily falling productivity, were in no mood to negotiate with workers. The number of strikes and layoffs mounted. Crime rose, and a sense of general insecurity prevailed.

In September Akhmatova returned to the capital, where her third book of poems, *White Flock,* was being published. Years later she would recall,

> This collection appeared under even more ominous circumstances than *Rosary.* If *Rosary* [published four months before the start of World War I] was tardy, then *White Flock* simply missed the bus. Transportation was coming to a standstill—it was impossible to ship the book even to Moscow, it was sold entirely in Petrograd. The paper was coarse—practically cardboard.
>
> The journals were closing down, as well as the newspapers. Therefore, unlike *Rosary, White Flock* did not have a sensational press. Hunger and ruin were mounting with each day.[5]

As the continuing crisis brought discredit upon both the liberals of the Provisional Government and the moderate socialists who controlled the soviets, the hard–line left became increasingly popular. The greatest beneficiary of this trend was the Bolshevik Party led by Vladimir Lenin. The Bolsheviks' simple slogan exactly summed up the demands of the soldiers, workers, and peasants: "Peace, bread, and land." Their approach to the problem of government was equally direct: they were the only party to offer unqualified support to the demand for "all power to the soviets." The Bolsheviks had played a role in the violent demonstrations of early July, although it is difficult to say to what extent the party was leading and to what extent following its own grassroots supporters. In any event, after the July Days the government had issued arrest warrants for several party leaders, including Lenin, who went into hiding. This, however, did not hinder the party's rise. In late September, Leon Trotsky, a leading figure in the Revolution of 1905 who had recently joined the Bolsheviks, was elected chairman of the Petersburg Soviet; soon after– ward, the party took control of the Moscow Soviet as well. Lenin took this as a sign that the majority of the people was on his side and argued that the time had come for the party to seize power.

A crucial date was October 25, when the Second All–Union Congress of Soviets would meet. If the program of all power to the soviets were pursued, this body could logically declare itself the sole government. Lenin's scheme was to overthrow the Provisional Government imme– diately before the Congress convened, thereby forcing it to step into the resultant power vacuum and take command. Taking advantage of fears that opponents of the Revolution would try some sort of coup against the Congress, on the twenty–fourth the Bolsheviks summoned their most committed supporters to come to their defense. Red sailors from Kronstadt, the island fortress that guarded the sea entrance to Petrograd, took their vessels up the Neva River to the Smolny Institute, formerly a school for young ladies and now the Bolsheviks' headquarters. The bridges over the river had to be opened to let the ships through, and Akhmatova later remembered her first glimpse of the October Revolu– tion, as she was approaching the Liteiny bridge: "At the moment when I had just set foot on the bridge, something unprecedented occurred: they opened the bridge in broad daylight. Trams, trucks, cabs and pedestrians all came to a halt. Everyone was dumbfounded."[6] Throughout the day, the Bolshevik forces gradually took control of key positions throughout Petrograd. As they easily displaced the forces loyal to the Provisional

27

Government, their boldness increased, and what had originally been described as a defensive move shifted to an offensive one. By daybreak the only part of the city still controlled by the Provisional Government was its own seat in the Winter Palace. While more and more Red forces converged on this lone holdout, the number of defenders steadily decreased, until the defense simply collapsed. Communist propaganda films would later depict "the storming of the Winter Palace," but in fact the Provisional Government fell with a whimper, not a bang.

The more moderate delegates to the Congress of Soviets, members of the Menshevik and Socialist Revolutionary parties, were infuriated with the Bolsheviks' action and fiercely denounced the radicals' presumption for launching an attack which could lead to civil war and the destruction of the Revolution. They walked out of the chamber, followed by Trotsky's taunt, "Go where you belong–into the dustbin of history!" The rump Congress, now consisting only of the Bolsheviks and a minority faction of Left Socialist Revolutionaries, continued its session without the moderates and approved the appointment of an all–Bolshevik government, the Soviet of People's Commissars (Sovnarkom), with Lenin as its chairman. The moderates subsequently challenged this action and demanded that the government be broadened to include members of other socialist parties, but the Bolsheviks refused to compromise, and events had made it clear that the moderates did not have sufficient armed support to make them back down. The losers consoled themselves with the thought that the Sovnarkom was in any case merely a temporary government, which was to hold power only until the convening of the Constituent Assembly in January 1918.

Meanwhile, the Bolsheviks moved quickly to consolidate their hold on power. The peasants' demand for gentry land was met by a decree that declared the abolition of private landownership; all land belonged to the people, and its fruits belonged to those who cultivated it. For the workers, a decree on "workers' control" significantly increased the powers of their factory committees at the expense of management's power. For the soldiers, the fighting came to a stop almost immediately, as a truce for negotiations was declared. The truce would last for several months, until Germany, which needed to transfer troops to the Western Front, threatened to resume the offensive unless Russia met its peace terms: not only all of Russian–occupied Poland and the Baltic states, but also all of

Ukraine were to come under German sovereignty. Since by then the Russian army had completely disintegrated, if Lenin's government wanted to survive it had no choice, and it duly signed the treaty of Brest–Litovsk on March 3, 1918. But the several months' truce meant that at the time the Constituent Assembly met, Lenin could present himself as a peacemaker without yet having to disclose how high the cost of that peace was.

In the elections for the assembly, the Bolsheviks did well in the urban areas of Petrograd and Moscow. But Russia was still primarily a rural country, and the majority of delegates elected were members of the peasant–oriented Socialist Revolutionary Party (SR). On the day the Constituent Assembly convened, January 5, 1918, the SRs elected one of their party leaders as the assembly's chairman and took their party's platform as the basis for the assembly's agenda. The armed Bolshevik sailors who were serving as self–styled guards for the representatives took this amiss and strongly suggested to the chairman that it was time for the session to adjourn. Since the SRs, whatever their strength in the country as a whole, did not control the capital, this adjournment turned out to be permanent. The Bolsheviks–who now renamed themselves the Communists– had successfully seized power, and they intended to hold on to it.

In the winter of 1917–18, while Gumilyov was still in western Europe, Akhmatova became romantically involved with Vladimir Shileiko, a brilliant scholar of the ancient Middle East who was also, to quote a standard history of Russian literature, "a poet of great originality but exceedingly meagre output."[7] In the prewar years, he had frequented the Stray Dog and had formed particularly close friendships with Gumilyov and Lozinsky, who nicknamed him "the Egyptian." At that time, Shileiko and Akhmatova knew each other well enough to engage in an exchange of poems, and after Anrep's departure from Russia, friendship developed into love. In one of her autobiographical jottings from the early 1960s, Akhmatova wrote down the lines she remembered from three of Shileiko's poems and noted, "November 1 (O.S.), 1917, St. P., Fontanka House (Sumerian coffee room)."[8] Shileiko, who had a post as the tutor of Count Sheremetev's grandchildren, lived in a wing of the Sheremetev Palace on the Fontanka Canal. The "Sumerian coffee room" refers to his study, which was crammed with Sumerian cuneiform transcriptions and had a lingering smell of the coffee he loved to drink. One of the three lyrics quoted in Akhmatova's notebook is a love poem, and it seems likely that it was dedicated to her.

But Shileiko did not want to be just another one of Akhmatova's lovers: he wanted an exclusive relationship–marriage. It may seem strange that the somewhat bohemian young Akhmatova would take such a demand seriously; but this ascetic scholar, who had taught himself Hebrew at the age of seven, aroused in Akhmatova a streak of self-abnegation that was the other side of her passionate temperament. Explaining her decision to divorce Gumilyov and marry Shileiko, Akhmatova would later tell Gumilyov's biographer, "I went to him [Shileiko] of my own free will. . . . I felt so impure, I thought it would be . . . like going to a convent, knowing you are going to lose your freedom."[9]

Russia's exit from the war meant that Gumilyov no longer had any official reason to remain in western Europe, and in the spring of 1918 he returned to Petrograd. When he arrived in the city, he took the precaution of discreetly asking Valeria Sreznevskaya, with whom Akhmatova was still living, if Akhmatova was seeing anyone and learned of her affair with Shileiko. But he had no idea of the seriousness of Akhmatova's intentions and was dumbfounded when she asked him for a divorce. Sreznevskaya recalled, "Sitting on my large sofa, Anna told Nikolai she wanted to leave him, forever. Nikolai turned deathly pale and, after a prolonged silence, finally spoke: 'I have always said you were perfectly free to do whatever you wanted!' He stood up and left."[10] Their marriage might be a thoroughly open one–Gumilyov had returned to Russia bearing a cycle of poems to his latest love–but it had a real meaning for him, and he did not want it to end. That May, the couple went together to Bezhetsk to see Lyova, then five and a half years old. One day the two parents sat on a divan as Lyova played between them, seemingly the picture of family harmony, and Gumilyov suddenly asked, "And what did you start all this for?"[11] But Akhmatova was determined, and Gumilyov did not try to stand in her way. The revolutionary regime, which regarded both religion and the family as relics of the old order, had made divorce extremely easy. If it was uncontested, there was not even a need to go to court. As Akhmatova recalled, "I did not . . . go anywhere, I did not speak with anybody, I absolutely do not know how it was done. I simply received a piece of paper that I was divorced from so–and–so."[12]

In August, Shileiko received a commission to go to Moscow and as–

sess the value of a number of artworks that had come into the possession of the new government, and Akhmatova traveled with him as his wife. Marriage had become just as informal as divorce: whereas before the Revolution there had been no civil marriage, now that was the only legally recognized type of union, and the abrupt change had produced confusion as to what exactly a couple needed to do to be legally married and whether it was even worth the bother. Osip Mandelstam's wife, Nadezhda, recalled that they had gotten married in the early 1920s only because they were traveling together from Kiev to Moscow, and a railroad official who was annoyed by the number of female travelers who were "wives" only for the duration of a trip demanded to see a marriage certificate.[13] Shileiko's and Akhmatova's wedding was not legally registered until December 1918, three months after their return to Petersburg, and the required statement was made by Shileiko alone; Akhmatova was not even present.

The forced dismissal of the Constituent Assembly had left the opponents of the Communist government no peaceful means of protest, and in spring 1918, civil war broke out. The government remained in control of the two capital cities and of Russia's heartland, but there was fighting all around the periphery, in Ukraine, southern Russia (the Azov and Black Sea coasts and the northern Caucasus), the Volga and Ural regions, western Siberia, and the far north around Murmansk and Arkhangelsk. By the end of the year, however, the anti-Communist forces had ceased to be a serious threat in any of these regions except Ukraine and southern Russia, an economically vital area containing both the best farmland and the largest coal deposits in the former Russian Empire. The fighting in this area, which went on into 1920, was a particularly ghastly chaos involving at various times not only the newly created Red Army and their opponents, the Whites, but also Ukrainian nationalists, Polish forces asserting Poland's historical claim to sovereignty over western Ukraine, Don and Kuban Cossacks who wanted to preserve or extend their traditional local autonomy, violent anti-Semites (provoked by assertions that the Jews were pro-Communist), and just plain bandits taking advantage of the total breakdown of order.

Aside from the direct economic impact of the war itself, the catastrophic breakdown of transport and infrastructure that had been going on throughout 1917 continued and intensified. The Bolshevik panacea of workers' control, based on the assumption that the problem was merely the fault of counterrevolutionary managers, did nothing to address the actual causes of the steady drop in production. By early 1918, the flow of consumer goods had simply dried up. Peasants who brought grain to market could find nothing to buy with their money. At the same time, reckless government printing of money had led to soaring inflation, so that money not immediately spent on goods became worthless. The peasants' response was simple: if they couldn't get anything for their grain, they wouldn't sell it. Urban food stocks dropped precipitously.

The Bolsheviks, who had little sympathy for what they regarded as a backward rural class, assumed that the disappearance of grain from the markets was an act of ideological sabotage and chose to treat the peasantry as an enemy. Armed detachments were sent into the countryside to confiscate what were officially described as surplus grain supplies. In fact, the armed detachments that descended upon a village would take everything not sufficiently well hidden. The villagers' protests to the "people's government" were ignored. The anger of the countryside exploded in violence. There were 245 of what the government itself characterized as "major anti–Soviet uprisings" in 1918 in the twenty provinces of Central Russia, whose proximity to the central government made them particularly subject to heavy requisitioning.[14] The Soviet response to these rebellions is illustrated by a letter dated August 1918, in which Lenin himself wrote to the Bolsheviks of Penza ordering them to make an example of the local peasant rebels and providing specific instructions on how this should be done: "1. Hang (and make sure that the hanging takes place *in full view of the people*) *no fewer than one hundred* known kulaks, rich men, bloodsuckers. 2. Publish their names. 3. Seize *all* their grain from them. 4. Designate hostages in accordance with yesterday's telegram." Lenin apparently realized that even dedicated Bolsheviks might have qualms about carrying out a mass public hanging, since the final words of his letter were, "Find some truly hard people."[15] Such repression merely led to even wider resistance, and only when the defeat of the Whites enabled the government to turn all its forces against the peasantry was peace of a sort restored to the countryside. In a measure of how much damage was done to the rural economy, in a country in which virtually all plowing was done by horses, the number of horses decreased from thirty-five million in 1916–already a war year–to twenty-four million in 1920.[16]

The civil war years were thus a time of hunger for city dwellers: the government did not have the resources to track down and commandeer enough food for the entire urban population. Food rationing was instituted, workers being entitled to larger rations than members of the former upper or professional classes. Yet only a third of the total urban food supply came from official sources; the rest came from a black market supplied by enterprising peasants who smuggled food past the roadblocks set up to prevent such trade.[17] Given the risks the sellers ran, the prices–paid in goods, not money–were correspondingly high. The formerly rich traded their jewelry and carpets for bread, while factory workers ignored their assigned tasks and worked on handicrafts that they could barter. Anyone who could escape the city did so: workers, many of whom had migrated to the cities within the past generation, returned to their relatives in the villages. The population of Petrograd was 2.5 million in 1917 and one-third of that number in 1919. Educated and professional people, who could not take up peasant labor, were left behind in the dark, cold, empty buildings. Malnutrition took a steadily rising toll among them, undermining health and increasing mortality: the death rate in Petrograd was 25 per thousand in 1917, 44 per thousand in 1918, and 81.5 per thousand in 1919.[18]

In an attempt to prevent Russia's leading intellectuals from literally dying of starvation, the government created work for them by setting up an Institute of World Literature. Its mission was to bring enlightenment to the masses by translating the classics of world literature into inexpensive, high-quality Russian translations. Under the institute's patronage, Shileiko set to work on a translation of the Gilgamesh epic–a task which, coincidentally, was also being worked on by Gumilyov, who, because he did not know the original language, was translating a French version of the work. Gumilyov's translation came out in 1919 with a preface by Shileiko; the manuscript of Shileiko's translation has been lost, and only fragments of it have been published. Akhmatova, who could not get a position of her own, assisted Shileiko as best she could by transcribing his dictated translations. She was also the one who actually stood in the endless lines to receive his rations. Despite the couple's best efforts, however, they lived in stark poverty. They did not even have any pots or pans, and if they wanted to cook something Akhmatova had to borrow a pan from a neighbor.

In August 1920, as the couple's situation became dire–Shileiko's salary had not been paid–they were rescued by an unlikely benefactor. Among the admirers of Akhmatova's poetry was Larisa Reisner, a former mistress of Gumilyov's who subsequently became the wife of Fyodor Raskolnikov, the deputy people's commissar for the navy. Reisner, whose circle of acquaintances did not include the Revolution's dispossessed, arrived at Shileiko's apartment and was appalled to find Akhmatova, emaciated and dressed in rags, boiling soup in a borrowed saucepan. Reisner promptly used her connections to obtain food and clothing for the poet and her husband, arranged for Shileiko to be admitted to a hospital for treatment of his sciatica, and boosted the couple's income by lining up a job for Akhmatova at the library of the Agronomy Institute.

As Russia's civilian population struggled to survive, the war dragged on. The Whites came closest to victory in October 1919, when the monarchist general Anton Denikin led an offensive that started in Ukraine and headed northeast, reaching to within two hundred miles of Moscow, while a separate White force headed by Gen. Nikolai Yudenich marched from the Baltic states to threaten Petrograd. But the Petrograd Red Guards quickly repelled Yudenich's forces, and the Bolsheviks, who controlled central Russia and thus were able to move their troops readily from one front to another, then brought all their force to bear on Denikin's army. By December 1919, the Red Army not only had driven Denikin back, but had established itself in his army's heartland and occupied Kiev. A Polish invasion of Ukraine in 1920 prolonged the war, but inexorably the Communists simply pushed their adversaries further and further out from the country's center until, by November 1920, the White forces under General Pyotr Wrangel were forced to evacuate the Crimea and sail off into exile.

All through this period, Akhmatova was cut off from her family. Poverty made it impossible for her to visit her son in Bezhetsk. The war in the south had broken all communications with the Crimea, where Akhmatova's mother and sister were living. Only in July 1921 was she able to learn of the disasters that had overtaken them. Her mother was indigent because the Soviets would not pay the pension she was due as the widow of a tsarist officer. Her sister Iya was in the final stage of tuberculosis, the same disease that had killed their older sister Inna. Her brother Victor had disappeared, and the family believed he was dead. (In fact, he had safely made his way to the island of Sakhalin in Russia's Far East, an area so remote and untamed that violence there was the old–fashioned kind, criminal rather than political.) And, most terrible of all, her favorite brother, Andrei, had killed himself. He had gone abroad to study and there had married a cousin, Maria Zmunchilla. In 1920, while the couple was living in Greece, their only child died of malaria, and in their isola- tion and despair the bereaved parents made a suicide pact and took poison. When they were found, Andrei was dead, but Maria was suc- cessfully revived, turned out to be pregnant, and gave birth to a healthy child.

By early 1921, although the war was over, privation and misery had risen to such a level that the Soviet government could not count upon the loyalty even of those segments of the population that had originally been its most fervent supporters. In March 1921, the Red sailors at the naval base of Kronstadt–the very ones who had supported the Bolsheviks so decisively in October 1917 and January 1918–rebelled against the regime. They demanded that new elections be held to seat a government that would contain representatives of all left–wing parties. The rebellion was crushed with heavy casualties, but it frightened even the most doctri- naire Communists sufficiently to allow the ever–pragmatic Lenin to push through a series of measures (the New Economic Policy) intended to re- vive the moribund economy by allowing limited amounts of capitalism.

For the countryside, the new policy was too little, too late. To the man–made catastrophe already visited upon the villages was added a natural catastrophe, drought. By summer 1921, peasants in the Volga region were beginning not merely to suffer from malnutrition, but actu- ally to die of starvation. Survivors fled the most devastated villages, looking for places where there was still food. If they found a village with food, they would massacre the inhabitants and seize their supplies– unless, of course, the inhabitants had had the foresight to arm them- selves, in which case the starving refugees were slaughtered instead. Cases of cannibalism were reported. The drought–affected area was the home of some thirty–five million people. The situation was so dire that Lenin overcame his suspicion of capitalists' motives and accepted aid from the American Relief Association, headed by Herbert Hoover. The association was active in Russia from October 1921 to June 1923, and at the height of its activity was feeding ten million people. In spite of even this heroic effort, the famine resulted in five million deaths.[19]

Some ten million people died during the civil war (not counting the famine deaths), the majority as a direct result not of violence, but of typhus, tuberculosis, cholera, influenza, all the diseases that found easy prey in a malnourished, exhausted, cold, dirty, and lice–ridden populace. Death had become commonplace in Russia–not just individual death, but death on a catastrophic scale. Bodies lay unburied by the roadside or were tossed en masse into shallow pits where they might be dug up by scavenging animals. To the extent that any authority existed in this chaos, it belonged to men who had guns and did not hesitate to use them. To the new rulers, such values as compassion and decency were no more than the pathetic shibboleths of a bourgeois culture rightfully swept away by the Revolution. The humanist culture of the old Russian intelligentsia was dying.

Among those who recognized this passing was Alexander Blok, who in a speech delivered in February 1921, on the eighty–fourth anniversary of Pushkin's death in a duel, wrote what would prove to be his own obituary: "Pushkin died. But . . . what killed Pushkin wasn't D'Anthes' bullet. What killed him was lack of air. His culture was dying with him. . . . Peace and freedom. They are necessary to a poet. . . . But peace and freedom were also taken away. Not external peace, but creative peace. Not childish freedom, the freedom of liberal chatter, but creative free-dom, inner freedom. And the poet dies because there's nothing for him to breathe; life has lost its meaning." Blok's last public reading was in April 1921. He was already showing symptons of an exhausting and painful disease that has never been definitively diagnosed. Those who knew him well believed he had simply lost his will to live, and in the cold, hungry, disease–ridden city death came readily for those not pre-pared to resist it. After prolonged suffering, Blok died on August 7, 1921.

For Russians, the funeral of a great writer had a special significance. In nineteenth–century Russia, where social questions could not be ad-dressed directly, it had been common to address them indirectly through literature. As a result, a literary funeral or commemoration frequently acquired overtones of a mass political demonstration. This tradition was so well established by 1910, the year Leo Tolstoy died, that special police measures were taken to ensure that any commemorative speeches praising Tolstoy as the champion of the peasantry did not shade into revolutionary sentiments. Blok's funeral was also the occasion for an outpouring of public emotion, but of a different type. No speeches were made; an immense, somber crowd silently followed the coffin to the cemetery. They understood the unspoken reality that they were seeing the funeral not merely of a man but of an era in Russian culture. One of the mourners remembered seeing Akhmatova in the crowd, dressed in unfashionable gray and making no effort to hide her tears. Blok's death, coming less than a month after she had learned of her brother Andrei's death, had left her stunned. And yet more was to come, for at Blok's funeral she learned that Gumilyov had been arrested on political charges.

Gumilyov had always been disdainful of the Revolution and did not hesitate to proclaim his monarchist convictions in any company, but his form of resistance to the upheaval around him was aesthetic, not political: in addition to his work at the World Literature publishing house, he gave lectures on poetry. He firmly believed that by teaching his students to recognize and appreciate good poetry he was helping to preserve civilized values in the midst of barbarism, a mission more important than any the politicians and soldiers might have. Gumilyov had convinced himself that the new rulers understood his principles and so would not harm him. But Akhmatova's intuition told her he was doomed. The last time he visited her, in July 1921, she led him to the most direct way out of her apartment, which was not the main entrance but a back staircase, dark and winding. As he set off down it, she suddenly said, "You only go down a staircase like that to your execution."[20]

Gumilyov was accused of being involved in a counterrevolutionary conspiracy led by one Nikolai Tagantsev. The evidence against him was weak. Gumilyov's friends, who assumed his arrest was a mistake, the overreaction of some petty functionary that would be corrected once his case was properly reviewed, began making calls to draw the matter to the attention of higher authorities. Akhmatova took no active part in these efforts, since after Blok's funeral she had entered a sanatorium in Tsarskoe Selo, but she was still close enough to Petrograd to learn quickly of any news connected with Gumilyov's case. Two friends of Akhmatova's, the sisters Natasha and Manya Rykova, were living on a nearby farm and visited her regularly. On September 1, their father returned from a trip to Petrograd and found them sitting with Akhmatova on the sanitorium balcony. He called Manya to him, and from the expression on her face Akhmatova guessed that something had happened to a family member. Then Manya returned to Akhmatova and said simply, "Nikolai Stepanovich. . . ." There was no need to say any more. The next day Akhmatova went to the railroad station, where a copy of *Pravda* was posted on the wall. It contained an official statement that on August 25, 1921, sixty–one counterrevolutionary conspirators had been shot without trial. The list of names included that of Nikolai Gumilyov, "thirty–five years old, philologist, poet."

Akhmatova's response to Gumilyov's execution marked the first appearance of what was to become one of the driving forces of her life: the determination to honor the dead and to preserve their memory among the living. As state criminals, Gumilyov and his alleged fellow conspirators had been given a mass burial at an unknown location. Akhmatova was determined to find the grave, and throughout the 1920s she spent hours with Mandelstam and Nadya wandering through the woods around Petersburg and along the shores of desolate Golodai Island looking for the telltale marks of disturbed ground. In 1962, Akhmatova told her friend Lidia Chukovskaya that in 1930 she had found the place:

> I know about Kolya [Gumilyov's nickname]. . . . They were shot near Berngardovka, on the Irininsk road. Some friends of mine had a laundress, and she had a daughter who was an investigator. She, that is, the laundress, told them and even indicated the place based on her daughter's words. They went there at once, and it was clear that the earth had been tromped on by boots. And I found out after nine years and went there. An open field; a small crooked pine tree; next to it another one, mighty, but with its roots exposed. And there was a wall. The ground had sunk, subsided, because they hadn't properly filled in the graves. Pits. Two common graves for 60 people. When I went there, tall white flowers were growing everywhere. I picked them and thought: "Other people bring flowers to a grave, and I'm picking them from a grave."[21]

But this seemingly definitive account has an odd sequel. Irina Punina, Akhmatova's stepdaughter, recollected that in August 1945 the two of them made a trip by taxi to the neighborhood of Rzhevka–Porokhovye:

"The street we went on was like a wagon trail.... There was a place where Akuma [Akhmatova's family nickname] told the driver to slow down, and with a look she pointed out to me a fairly high mound, where burdock, nettles and wildflowers were growing.... When we got back home, she stopped in the hallway, took my hand and quietly said, 'That's the place where they shot Nikolai Stepanovich. A worker came to see me and said that people could hear them being shot that night.'"[22] The two descriptions do not square with each other: although Rzhevka–Porokhovye and Berngardovka are both part of the hinterland of Petersburg/Leningrad, Rzhevka–Porokhovye is less far from the city center; and the persons whom Akhmatova credited with giving her the information are not the same. Apparently Akhmatova, for all her searching, was never entirely certain where Gumilyov's grave was. Only since the fall of the Soviet Union has it been possible to establish that the Tagantsev conspirators were executed in Rzhevka near an area used as an artillery firing range (*porokh* in Russian means "gunpowder").[23]

It was not only through her search for his grave that Akhmatova strove to commemorate her first husband. In early 1924, she dreamed about Gumilyov three times in a row: she then wrote a short biography of him, and the dreams stopped occurring. Soon after, she was approached by the twenty–three–year–old Pavel Luknitsky, who was writing a dissertation on Gumilyov. Akhmatova took his arrival as a fulfillment of her premonition and offered her complete cooperation with his work in return for a biography of Gumilyov that would be largely shaped by her viewpoint. Over the next four years she regularly assisted him in his research, reviewing and commenting on the work he had done, going through Gumilyov's papers with him, introducing him to members of Gumilyov's family, and allowing him to use her name in requesting interviews with Gumilyov's friends. The nature of their work together encouraged Akhmatova to confide in Luknitsky, and soon she came to regard him as a friend. He ran errands for her and worried about her poor health and was rewarded with inscribed photographs of her and autographed copies of her books.

In the end, the political climate made it impossible for Luknitsky's work to be published until after both he and Akhmatova were dead. Indeed, one cannot help but wonder why a young man just starting his career would risk all by choosing a subject presenting such obvious political difficulties, and there is some reason to believe that Luknitsky was submitting reports on Akhmatova to the secret police. But whatever his motives were, the study of Akhmatova is indebted to him for the two volumes of memoirs he left recounting his meetings with and impressions of her in the years 1924–27.

Akhmatova's work with Luknitsky also had a significant effect on her public image. At a time when many people were doing their best to reinvent themselves and to play down their connections with disgraced figures from the past, Akhmatova conspicuously made herself Gumilyov's literary executor and the representative of his memory. Thus even though Gumilyov had remarried and had a daughter by his second wife, in the mind of the public and of the authorities, it was Akhmatova who had the politically risky honor of being Gumilyov's widow.

It was not, however, as a research editor or a memoirist but as a poet that Akhmatova gave her most immediate, personal response to the deaths of Gumilyov and Blok and the destruction of the world of her youth. After the virtual silence of 1920, Akhmatova wrote some thirty-four poems in 1921, eleven of which are specifically dated August 1921. These poems are filled with images of bitter and irreversible separation, violence, and death. They reflect not only Akhmatova's personal agony, but the agony of her country. Thus in one lyric of eight simple and devastating lines she uses traditional folk diction and imagery to evoke the lament of a Russian peasant Everywoman.

> Life is for others, not for you,
> Cold in the snow you lie,
> Bayonets made twenty–eight wounds,
> Bullets–another five.
>
> A garment of new grief I made,
> I sewed it for my love.
> Oh Russian earth, it loves the taste,
> It loves the taste of blood.

But consciousness of the historical catastrophe that had overtaken both Russia and herself was not Akhmatova's only source of inspiration. A purely personal factor was involved as well. By 1921, although she still regarded Shileiko as a brilliant scholar and, in his own way, a good man, she had come to find him impossible to live with. Shileiko was happy to have a wife intelligent enough to assist him in his work, but the idea that she should have an intellectual life of her own was intolerable to him. He was enraged when, in 1919, she signed a contract for a reprint of *White Flock* and used the name Akhmatova rather than Shileiko.[24] He forbade her to write new poems, and, if one is to believe the account of Amanda Haight, who befriended Akhmatova during the last years of the poet's life, after she ignored his prohibition and continued to write, he responded by burning her manuscripts.[25] Their poverty and the tuberculosis from which both were suffering (and which ultimately would kill Shileiko) could not have made their life together any easier. The strain clearly made it difficult for Akhmatova to write: only one surviving poem is dated 1920.

In summer 1921, Akhmatova left Shileiko and moved into the apartment of the composer Artur Lourie, who had gone from being a habitué of the Stray Dog to a brief stint as people's commissar of music. He was living with another friend from the Stray Dog, the dancer and actress Olga Sudeikina. Here Akhmatova found the emotional support of friends with whom she could share her art. Lourie set to music Akhmatova's poem on Blok's funeral, "Today is the feast of Our Lady of Smolensk . . . ," and in the winter of 1921–22, Akhmatova worked on a libretto (now lost) for Lourie's ballet version of Blok's *Snow Masks*. For a time Akhmatova and Sudeikina were almost inseparable, to the point that the threesome gave rise to considerable gossip about a ménage à trois. There may have been some truth to it. During World War II, when the man whom Akhmatova hoped to marry wrote in one of his letters to her about how important his late wife had been to him, she was infuriated and exclaimed, "What if I wrote to him that Lourie had been the most important person in my life?"[26]

The relationship, whatever it was, was broken off in August 1922, when Lourie emigrated. In doing so, he joined a Russian diaspora of perhaps a million people, including a disproportionate number of Russia's most gifted individuals. Diaghilev, Stravinsky, Chaliapin, Pavlova, the artists who had dazzled Paris a decade before–all of them left Russia. So did Marina Tsvetayeva, the brilliant poet who in 1916 had hailed Akhmatova as the "muse of lamentation"; the poet and critic Vladislav Khodasevich, who had once told a minor poet, "If I were the editor of a magazine, I would print [Fyodor] Sologub always, Akhmatova often, myself sometimes and you never";[27] and Alexei Remizov, a writer of elaborately stylized prose who, shortly before his departure, used his power as self-appointed chancellor of the Great and Free Order of Apes to confer upon Akhmatova a calligraphic document recognizing her as a Cavalier of the Order. Some, like Tsvetayeva, whose husband was a White Army officer, left to escape political danger. Others simply realized that their creative work could not be continued in a war-ravaged country that offered no support to any art not justified under the rubric of "public enlightenment." In 1922, for example, the Futurist poet Velimir Khlebnikov, who was known for his brilliant experiments in "transsense" language (*zaum*) and regarded by his friends, including Mandelstam, as a sort of holy fool, died of sheer exhaustion and privation.

A new life abroad–free of terror, typhus, famine–beckoned. But Akhmatova's poems resolutely rejected the very idea of leaving Russia. In the summer of 1917, in a poem addressed to Anrep, she denounced him as an apostate who was destroying his Orthodox soul by preferring the "green island" of England to "our songs, and our icons, and the pine tree above a quiet lake." The poem "When in suicidal anguish . . ." opens with a bitter picture of Russia's national humiliation in late 1917, when no one knew who would next lay claim to power and no resistance could have been offered to the prospect of a German invasion; but when the poet hears a voice urging her to leave her sinful country, she resolutely puts her hands over her ears to block out the unworthy words that defile her grief. In 1922 she wrote,

> I'm not one of those who left the land
> To its enemies to grab and rend.
> I'm not flattered by their clapping hands,
> I offer my songs, but not to them.
>
> Yet for the exile my heart still aches,
> As for those sick or within jail walls.
> Wanderer, dark is the road you take,
> And foreign bread tastes of bitter gall.
>
> But here, as the dark fires blaze around
> And our last youth burns out in their glow,
> We don't ask where refuge can be found,
> Don't try to avoid a single blow.

We know each hour's worth will be made clear
And justified at the end of days . . .
None bear grief like ours with fewer tears,
With a prouder or a simpler gaze.

Akhmatova recognized that emigration would have its difficulties, but that was not what stopped her. Her decision to stay was motivated by a fundamental belief that leaving Russia in the country's time of travail was an act of desertion, of unpardonable disloyalty. Years later, when reading James Joyce's *Ulysses*, Akhmatova would be deeply struck by the sentence, "You cannot leave your mother an orphan." Akhmatova's attitude toward emigration might be summed up by a slight modification of that sentence: "You cannot leave your Motherland an orphan." At a time when it seemed that all civilized values were ceasing to exist, Akhmatova nevertheless was convinced that one day Russia would need her and her poetry.

CHAPTER 3

Outcast in the New Order, 1922–1935

§ § §

I N THE NEW SOVIET RUSSIA that was slowly emerging from the
chaos of the civil war, Akhmatova's position was an ambiguous one.
Many readers regarded Akhmatova as a poet of a now–discredited
social order. The critic Kornei Chukovsky, in a lecture delivered on sev-
eral occasions in 1920 and 1921, pointed to Akhmatova as the outstand-
ing representative of a literary culture rooted in prerevolutionary Russia
and contrasted her with Vladimir Mayakovsky, the self-proclaimed poet
of the new:

> Akhmatova . . . possesses that intellectual refinement and charm that
> are given to those who participate in a long cultural tradition. But May-
> akovsky in every word and every line is the product of the present
> revolutionary epoch. The faith, the cry, the ecstacy, and the failures of
> that epoch are in his work . . . She has long preserved the old Russian
> faith in God. He, as befits a revolutionary, is a blasphemer. For her the
> holy of holies is Russia, the motherland, "our earth." He, as is proper in a
> revolutionary bard, is an internationalist. . . . And while Akhmatova
> knows only the pronoun "thou" that a woman addresses to her be-
> loved, or that other pronoun "Thou" that she addresses to God, May-
> akovsky is constantly shouting "Hey, you" . . . at the top of his voice to
> the many–faced mass.[1]

Chukovsky intended only to describe the difference between two outlooks and styles, not to present one as superior to the other: "I find to my astonishment that I love them both equally. . . . That Old Russia that Akhmatova stands for—so sensitive and so restrained—is very dear to me; as is the riotous and drumbeating element incarnated in Mayakovsky." But the points Chukovsky made would become the basis of the Communist attack upon Akhmatova. In the journal *Na postu* (*On guard*) for September–October 1923, the critic G. Lelevich attacked her for filling her poems with "mysticism and eroticism" while ignoring politics: "The social upheavals which represent the most fundamentally important phenomenon of our time have found only a very feeble and, moreover, hostile reflection in her poetry."[2] In October 1925, V. Pertsov, a critic for the journal *Zhizn iskusstva* (*Life of art*), bluntly relegated Akhmatova to the dustbin of history: "Contemporary language has no common roots with that spoken by Akhmatova, modern, living people are now and will remain cold and heartless towards the laments of a woman who was born too late or did not manage to die in time."[3]

Such violent hostility was, in a sense, a perverse tribute to Akhmatova's genuine popularity. During the civil war years, paper production had dwindled almost to nothing, and publishing virtually ceased to exist. But one of the first books to appear under the New Economic Policy (NEP), in April 1921, was a collection of poems Akhmatova had written during the early years of the Revolution, from 1917 to 1919. The book was entitled *Wayside Herb* (*Podorozhnik*, a plant that grows readily by roadsides). The publisher was operating on such a financial shoestring that it was printed on small sheets of coarse paper about six inches by three inches. Nevertheless, the print run was set at one thousand copies. Early in 1922, this volume was followed by a second one with the significant title *Anno Domini MCMXXI*. A year later, these two postrevolutionary books were combined with the new poems Akhmatova had written in 1922 to produce the volume *Anno Domini*. Her older works also continued to be popular, as *Evening, Rosary,* and *White Flock* were all reprinted during the early 1920s. Years later she would proudly recall that fifteen thousand copies of her books were sold during NEP.[4] In April 1924, Akhmatova gave a poetry reading at the Moscow Conservatory that caused such a furor that its organizers feared it would be regarded as an antigovernment demonstration. By one account, so many people tried to force their way into the auditorium that the police could hardly hold them back.[5]

Not all the literary critics were unsympathetic to Akhmatova. The Formalist critics Boris Eikhenbaum and V. M. Zhirmunsky wrote closely reasoned and admiring studies in which they sidestepped political difficulties by concentrating on the techniques that made her work recognizable as great poetry and not mere versification, independent of whatever message the poems might convey.

The controversy between the critics who bluntly attacked Akhmatova for her "un-Soviet" poetry and those who cautiously defended her by speaking of her place in the ongoing development of Russian literature was a reflection of a larger controversy dominating Soviet cultural spheres in the 1920s. Theoretically, one could claim that the new revolutionary era was such a radical break from all preceding history that every past work of art had become irrelevant, and some literary movements followed the lead of the Futurists and did precisely that. Others, however, argued that older classes and societies had had time to develop superior literary techniques that the proletariat, a new force in history, had not yet mastered, so that technically skilled writers could make a contribution to proletarian culture even if they were not completely pure ideologically. This position, however, certainly did not go as far as the Formalist emphasis on technique above all; it still required that the writer be, if not a revolutionary activist, at least a sympathizer, a "fellow traveler" (to use Trotsky's term).

In 1925, literary activists appealed to the Central Committee to settle the question. The response was a decree affirming that "in a class society there is and can be no neutral art" but adding that the proletariat, although it had successfully seized control of the political and economic spheres, was not yet fully ready for the more subtle, sophisticated tasks involved in the cultural sphere. Thus, until the question of appropriate literary forms could be resolved (appropriate content was regarded as already settled), various literary tendencies would be allowed to coexist.

By the standards of ten years later, this policy was liberal. But it excluded Akhmatova from any place in Soviet literature. Likely an indirect result of the decree, a Central Committee resolution issued that same year indefinitely prohibited any further publication of Akhmatova's works. The resolution was not publicized, and Akhmatova learned of it only two years later in a conversation with the fellow traveler writer Marietta Shaginyan. A planned two-volume collection of Akhmatova's poems, the impending publication of which had already been announced, was not officially canceled, but one difficulty after another was put in its way until the project simply faded out of existence. No work by Akhmatova would be published in Russia again until 1940.

Left-wing critics may have crudely dismissed Akhmatova as having out-lived her time, and her public may have preferred to regard her as the tragic and faithful widow of Gumilyov, but Akhmatova in the 1920s was not ready to declare her personal life ended. The most enduring roman-tic relationship of her life had its beginning on August 10, 1922. Akhma-tova and Lourie, who would leave Russia in a few days, spent that night in conversation with Nikolai Punin, an art critic best known for his de-fense of Vladimir Tatlin and other avant-garde artists. Punin was a close friend of Lourie's but until then Akhmatova had known him only dis-tantly, through common acquaintances. That night was the first occasion on which Akhmatova and Punin had talked at length in a private setting, and apparently each made an immediate impression on the other. A short time afterward, Punin received a note from Akhmatova telling him to come visit her at a poets' workshop. Punin noted in his diary, "I was completely moved . . . since I hadn't expected that An. could condescend to call me."[6] On September 5, the two had a lengthy talk about Lourie. It appears that Akhmatova, wounded by Lourie's departure, had decided to try to put him behind her as quickly as possible. Two years later she would boast to Luknitsky about how Lourie had written letter after letter to her while she coolly refused to respond.[7] Presumably she made Punin aware of her decision in a manner that clearly opened the possibility of a relationship between the two of them, since a copy of *White Flock* in-scribed from Akhmatova to Punin on September 5, 1927, identifies the day as their fifth anniversary. Soon the two were deeply in love.

From the very beginning the relationship was a difficult one–"a dark joy and sweet destruction," in Punin's words.[8] Punin had a wife and an infant daughter, and although he was secretly delighted when, in Febru-ary 1923, his wife guessed what was happening and threatened to leave him, she did not carry out her threat, and he could not summon the ruthlessness to leave her. At the same time, he disliked Akhmatova's

bohemian friends from the Stray Dog period of her life and was fero-
ciously jealous of any possible rivals for her affection. Akhmatova re-
garded such possessiveness with distaste. She told Punin, "I love you
very much, and that's not good," explaining that she felt a person should
not be exclusively reliant on a single relationship.[9] After her experience
with Shileiko, she was more than ever convinced of the danger that too
close a bond to a man could pose to the autonomy and creativity of a
female artist.

In fall 1924, Olga Sudeikina emigrated, and the breakup of the mé-
nage that Akhmatova had shared with her and Lourie was complete.
Akhmatova needed to find a new place to live. Having quit her job at the
Agronomy Institute library, she was no longer entitled to state housing,
and the rentals available on the private market were scarce and expen-
sive. Akhmatova had many claims on her limited resources: she was
sending money to her mother and to her son Lev and his grandmother in
Bezhetsk, and she was helping Shileiko, with whom she had become
friends once the irritations of marriage had ended.

Akhmatova's solution to the problem was to become a permanent
guest. Both Shileiko and Punin, as professors, were state employees and
hence entitled to have an apartment assigned to them—indeed, Shileiko,
whose work required him to spend extensive time in Moscow, had an
apartment there as well as in Leningrad. Akhmatova stayed in Shileiko's
Leningrad apartment during the months he was away and lived the rest
of the time in the Punins' apartment in the former Sheremetev Palace on
the Fontanka Canal. Punin's wife, Anna Ahrens-Punina, put the best face
she could on the matter, treating Akhmatova as if she were a visiting
relative. In November 1926, Akhmatova officially gave up her legal claim
to residence at Shileiko's apartment and was registered as living in the
Fontanka House together with Punin, his now ex-wife, and his daughter.

As outlandish as this situation appears to a westerner, it would not
have been too surprising to a Soviet. As Nadezhda Mandelstam wrote in
her memoirs,

> Who could ever leave his wonderful, precious twelve and a half square
> meters of living space? No one would be so mad. . . . Husbands and
> wives who loathe the sight of each other, mothers-in-law and sons-in-
> law, grown sons and daughters, former domestic servants who have
> managed to hang on to a cubby-hole next to the kitchen—all are wed-

ded forever to their living-space and would never part with it. In mar-
riage and in divorce the first thing that arises is the question of living-
space. I have heard men described as perfect gentlemen for throwing
over their wives but leaving them the living-space.[10]

Although Akhmatova displaced Anna Ahrens as a wife, she never
displaced her as "lady of the house." Akhmatova was resolutely anti-
domestic and lacked even the most basic skills in such household arts as
cooking or sewing (though it is difficult to say how much of her inepti-
tude was genuine and how much a tactic, conscious or otherwise, to
avoid being confined within the traditional feminine sphere). And while
Punin's ex-wife, a doctor, was able to make a significant financial contri-
bution to the household, after publishing opportunities for Akhmatova
vanished, her sole income was a tiny, irregular state pension—a sort of
tacit, half-hearted admission by the government of its responsibility for
depriving her of her livelihood. By the early 1930s, her financial situation
was so difficult that she sold her entire library, including many first
editions with authors' inscriptions to her.

Akhmatova knew perfectly well that if she were to confess her ideo-
logical sins and throw herself on the party's mercy, conditions would be
made easier for her. But in her eyes, that was a price no true poet could
pay. The prosperity of officially favored writers awakened only scorn in
her. Like a nun, she saw herself as having a vocation that required her
either to live on the charity of others or to go without. She consciously
entered the Punin household in the vulnerable position of a dependent.
For the next thirty years, she would have no home of her own.

When Lenin died in January 1924, he left no obvious successor, although
in the collective leadership of the Politburo, Trotsky and Stalin were
more equal than their colleagues. Within four years, Stalin had suc-
cessfully sidelined Trotsky, who was first exiled to Alma-Ata (now Al-
maty, Kazakhstan) and then, a year later, expelled from the Soviet Union.

The great question facing Lenin's heirs was how to transform an in-
dustrially backward agricultural country like Russia into the type of ad-
vanced industrial country which alone, in classic Marxist doctrine, could
prove hospitable to Communism. There were two possible approaches,
gradualist and militant. The gradualists, led by Nikolai Bukharin, argued

that the key was to make agriculture more profitable so that prosperous peasants would demand more consumer goods, which would in turn create more factory jobs. Such a policy described what was happening in Russia in 1921–28, the years of the so–called NEP, and it actually worked, for by 1928 Russia had largely regained the economic level of the pre–World War I years. But it was not a vision to inspire a party of self–described revolutionaries impatient to change the world. And there was still the old Communist fear, dating from civil war days, that prosperous peasants–or, as they were pejoratively called, *kulaks* ("fists")–would be more sympathetic to capitalism than to socialism. The alternative was a return to the requisitioning and heavy–handed state control of the civil war years, regarded by Communists as a heroic period rather than an economic catastrophe. Under this approach, the peasants would be compelled to surrender their grain to the state for export, and the money thus obtained would be used to finance rapid industrialization.

In 1929, Stalin aligned himself with the program of rapid industrialization. That April, the first Five–Year Plan was proclaimed. Its figures called for a 180 percent rise in industrial output, with even higher increases in key sectors. Anyone who doubted that this goal could be reached within such a short time was guilty of "petty bourgeois thinking." Military imagery, never absent since the civil war, became more prominent: "There are no fortresses Bolsheviks cannot storm" was a common phrase among party activists. In November 1929, Stalin announced a new party program that would fundamentally reorganize agriculture. The kulaks were to cease to exist as a class. For those households considered the worst offenders, the head of the family would be shot and all the remaining members, from grandmothers down to infants, deported to barren wastelands in the far north or Siberia. How they were to survive there was not the state's problem. The least noxious kulaks would have their land confiscated, but would be allowed to farm some small plot of the least desirable land in their area. Once the oppressive influence of the kulaks was removed, it was assumed, the remaining middle and poor peasants would happily abandon their inefficient small individual plots and join in more economically viable collective farms (*kolkhozes*). Twenty–five thousand armed party activists–city dwellers with no knowledge of and even less sympathy for the peasants' traditional way of life–were sent to the countryside to "dekulakize" it.

When it turned out that so-called voluntary collectivization did not inspire the peasants to volunteer, it was announced that any peasant, even the poorest, who refused to join the collective would be regarded as a "kulak henchman" and subjected to the same penalties as the kulaks themselves. In a desperate last outburst of resistance, peasant families slaughtered and ate their livestock rather than surrender it to the collective farm. In 1928, the total number of cattle in the Soviet Union was sixty million; during the most intensive period of collectivization, in January and February 1930, fourteen million cattle were slaughtered.[11] The situation was so out of control that it alarmed even Stalin, who in March 1930 denounced the "excesses" of the dekulakization campaign. As a result, collectivization was suspended for a few months, then resumed on terms somewhat less unfavorable to the peasants, who were allowed to keep a limited number of animals and a small vegetable plot for themselves.

In late 1931 a drought hit the Ukraine and the northern Caucasus, key agricultural regions already severely disrupted by collectivization. Both areas produced a poor crop that year, followed by a total failure in 1932. Soon peasants were eating dogs, cats, and rats and were trying to eat tree bark. People with the grossly swollen bellies of severe malnutrition became a common sight. As in 1921–22, cases of cannibalism were reported. But in contrast to 1921–22, no aid was offered. The quotas of grain that collective farms were compelled to deliver to the state were not lowered. Over a million tons of grain were exported in 1932. In 1921–22, hordes of peasants had fled their ruined villages and stormed any available train, and some of them had reached Moscow, only to collapse from hunger and die in the city's railroad stations. This time, urbanites would not have the reality of famine brought home to them by the sight of emaciated bodies: armed detachments were stationed in the countryside to stop any peasant exodus. No mention of the famine could be found in the media. The denial of its existence was so systematic that even city dwellers who were in contact with their village relatives and were fully aware of the suffering in a specific area might fail to grasp the overall dimensions of the devastation. As a result of this policy of concealment, it will never be possible to make an accurate count of the number of deaths in the 1932–33 famine: estimates run from 3.5 million to 7 million.[12]

From Stalin's point of view, the enormous losses, both human and economic, were worth it. The broken and collectivized peasants no longer worked for themselves, but for the state. The government would never have to worry about their wants or fear their resistance again.

The drive to eliminate the limited amount of individualism that the NEP had allowed was not limited to the economic sphere. As already noted, throughout the 1920s there had been a literary conflict between the self-proclaimed proletarian writers and the less ideological fellow travelers. In 1929, official favor shifted sharply toward the proletarians, who had organized themselves into the Russian Association of Proletarian Writers (RAPP). They were given free rein in the press to attack the All-Russian Union of Writers (VSP), the organization to which the fellow travelers belonged. In August and September 1929, a singularly concentratred and vicious attack was directed against the novelists Boris Pilnyak and Yevgeny Zamyatin. As targets they had a strategic value: both were leaders of the VSP—Pilnyak was head of the Moscow branch, and Zamyatin of the one in Leningrad—so that a campaign against them would damage the reputation of the entire organization. Their offense, as cited in the press, was that they had published works abroad (Pilnyak's *Mahogany* and Zamyatin's *We*) which presented the Revolution in a less-than-flattering light. No one bothered to mention that throughout the 1920s copyright considerations had made it common for Russian literary works to be published abroad (notably in Berlin), or that Pilnyak was negotiating to have *Mahogany* published in the Soviet Union. The implication was that the two writers were traitors, sympathizers with the capitalist enemy.

The attack against the VSP in the name of an openly propagandistic approach to literature was successful. On September 30, 1929, the VSP was renamed the All-Russian Union of Soviet Writers, the term "Soviet writer" being understood to refer not merely to a writer living in the USSR, but to a writer willing to follow the Soviet government line. Members of the former union were not automatically granted membership in the new one. Instead, a reregistration of members was conducted throughout October and November, and writers deemed insufficiently Soviet were denied admission.

Pilnyak and Zamyatin were both old friends of Akhmatova's, and in October, while the reregistration was going on, she indignantly wrote a letter of resignation from the VSP. She gave it to Luknitsky to deliver, but he never did so, presumably believing he was protecting her from the consequences of such a protest. In practical terms, the nondelivery of the letter made no difference because by November the VSP had ceased to exist, and its successor organization had no more desire to admit Akhmatova than she had to be admitted.

As for the two impugned novelists, Pilnyak recanted his supposed sins (although had his accusers not been deaf to irony, they surely would have wondered how seriously they should regard the extravagant and paradoxical language of his apology) and issued a revised version of *Mahogany*. Zamyatin refused to recant, and when, in 1931, he was granted permission to leave the country for a year, he departed and never returned.

It was not only conscious ideological dissenters like Zamyatin who suffered as Russian literature fell increasingly under the sway of Soviet bureaucrats. The new ruling class was repugnant even to an impassioned Communist like Mayakovsky, who satirized their crudity and opportunism in his plays *The Bedbug* and *The Bathhouse*. Needless to say, such works did not improve Mayakovsky's position, and as various literary factions jostled for official favor he found himself an outsider. His growing sense of isolation, intensified by difficulties in his personal life, became intolerable. In April 1930, Mayakovsky shot himself.

Mayakovsky had been no friend to Akhmatova, but he was a fellow poet. Five years earlier, when the peasant poet Sergei Yesenin had committed suicide, Akhmatova had told Luknitsky, "Every year another poet dies. . . . It is horrible when a poet dies."[13] On the day she heard of Mayakovsky's death, Akhmatova paid tribute to him by visiting the building he had mentioned in his poem "Man" (1916), in which he imagined himself returning to earth in the far distant future, ages after his death:

> The lamps over there—yeah, the ironwork's the same,
> line goes straight down the street.
> Houses look like they did.
> There's the same
> horse's head
> sticking out
> of its niche.
> "Hey, you there!

Is this street Zhukovsky?"
He gives me a look
like a kid seeing a ghost,
he's got eyes big as this,
tries to slip past,
"It's been Mayakovsky for thousands of years,
he shot himself here, right at his love's door."

As she walked down Zhukovsky Street toward the building in front of which Mayakovsky had so often waited in hope and despair, Akhmatova saw workers gathered and heard the sound of hammering. With a sudden sick feeling, she realized they were knocking down the horse's head.

The increasing repression took a visible toll on Akhmatova. After visiting her in August 1929, the young fellow traveler writer Konstantin Fedin (who would become one of the pillars of the Soviet literary establishment) wrote in his diary, "There's something about her that's pitiful in a childlike way, very unhappy and at the same time inaccessible, like a great tree drying up. She talks about literature willingly, at length and passionately, but never for a minute forgets about 'that,' as if someone inside her was keeping watch on her every glance, on every word. And she suddenly breaks off, falls silent, turns into her own portrait."[14] During what would turn out to be one of Luknitsky's final visits to her, on December 31, 1929, Akhmatova told him simply, "Genuine literature cannot exist now."[15]

In this period Akhmatova almost ceased to write poetry. Precise counts of how many poems she wrote in a given year are difficult because some of her poems may be lost or misdated, but it is safe to say that she wrote fewer poems between 1923 and 1935 than in the single year 1921. Inability to write was not unusual: Mandelstam wrote no poems between 1926 and 1930, Boris Pasternak published no work other than translations from 1933 until World War II. This "genre of silence," as Isaac Babel called it at the Congress of Writers in 1934, reflected the strain on writers whose Muses stubbornly refused to comply with party policy and who, in their solitude, could not help but torment themselves with the question, What if the party really does know what society needs, really is the wave of the future, and I am the one who is out of step? How could one judge a regime that claimed to be unprecedented in history?

For Akhmatova, the answer lay precisely in history, in remaining in spiritual communion with the values that Western art and civilization had built up over centuries. In the 1930s, when Mandelstam was asked what Acmeism was, he answered, "Nostalgia for world culture."[16] Akhmatova would have wholeheartedly endorsed that reply. In the 1920s, she taught herself Italian well enough to be able to study Dante in the original; she later discovered that Mandelstam was doing likewise. She also began studying English, and although she never learned to speak it, she read it well enough that in 1933 she was able to undertake a translation of *Macbeth*—a choice of work that can certainly be seen as a comment on the times.

But the writer from the past to whom she gave the most thought and from whom she drew the most strength was Russia's greatest poet, Alexander Pushkin (1799–1837). Pushkin is more central to Russian literature than even Shakespeare is to English literature or Goethe to German. His position is not merely the result of his poetic genius; he lived at a moment when the relation between the Russian writer and the Russian state was being defined, and his work, his life, his death became a template of that relation.

Throughout his creative life, Pushkin was in conflict with the state. In the early 1820s, the brilliant young poet burst upon the consciousness of the Russian reading public with his Byron–influenced narrative poems *The Prisoner of the Caucasus* and *The Gypsies*, both of which featured as protagonists men who are in rebellion against the conventions of their society and who try to escape into a primitive, exotic culture they see as free and natural. In such a protagonist, every intelligent, frustrated young Russian man could see himself, and Pushkin was quickly recognized as the spokesman for the aspirations of society against state repression. Pushkin's obnoxiousness to the authorities resulted in his being confined to his family estate, Mikhailovskoe, in the rural province of Pskov. He was there in December 1825, when in the confusion following the unexpected death of the childless Tsar Alexander I, a group of liberal army officers tried to intervene in the succession, with the ultimate goal of converting Russia to a constitutional monarchy. When their efforts failed, five of the leaders were executed and more than a hundred other participants were exiled to Siberia. Many of the Decembrists (as the rebels came to be known) had been personal friends of Pushkin's, and the new tsar, Nicholas I, marked him down as an enemy. Responsibility for ensuring that his writings stayed within acceptable bounds was assigned to Alexander Benckendorff, the chief of gendarmes. In the 1830s, Pushkin's already difficult position was further complicated by an ill–advised marriage to a young beauty, Natalya Goncharova. Natalya began carrying on a public flirtation with a handsome young horse guardsman, George D'Anthes. In all probability, Natalya was guilty only of indiscretion, not infidelity, but Pushkin's enemies gleefully assumed the worst, and gossip proclaimed him a cuckold. After years of humiliations inflicted by the court aristocracy, Pushkin was furiously glad to have a specific target for his retribution. He challenged D'Anthes to a duel in defense of Natalya's honor. The duel took place on January 27, 1837. Pushkin was mortally wounded by his adversary's shot and died two days later. In the days following his death, the twenty–two–year–old Mikhail Lermontov made his reputation with a poem entitled "Death of a Poet," an impassioned outburst against all the slanderers who had poisoned Pushkin's last years, all those whose "black blood," as the poem ominously concluded, "cannot pay for the poet's pure blood." The work could not appear in print, but every educated Russian knew it. Russia's greatest writer, whose position made him the spokesman of all Russians who yearned for freedom and personal dignity, had become a martyr, destroyed by an oppressive regime.

In the 1930s, Akhmatova started work on a series of studies of Pushkin which she would continue at intervals for the rest of her life. Her first article, "Pushkin's Last Fairy Tale," written over the two–year period 1931 to 1933, was a study of Pushkin's "The Tale of the Golden Cockerel." It established that Pushkin's tale was derived from Washington Irving's *The Alhambra*, but that Pushkin had significantly modified his source to make the tsar who was the central character appear significantly more foolish and more despotic. Pushkin, by deriding a fictional monarch, had indirectly gibed at the real monarch who was making his life miserable. This technique of using what Russians call Aesopian language, that is, indirect or oblique references to difficulties that could not be discussed openly, was one that Akhmatova also adopted. For example, in "Flip Side," the second part of *Poem Without a Hero*, she achieves a memorable paradox by openly pointing out her use of concealment. Her article "Pushkin's Death," which was not published until the 1970s but was largely written in the 1930s, is a defense lawyer's speech on Pushkin's behalf, summarizing all the slanders put forth by his enemies in the last months of his life, pointing out their inaccuracies and inconsistencies, revealing the unworthy motives of his attackers, assembling a picture that vindicates Pushkin's reputation and ruins that of his enemies. Surely, as Akhmatova sat in the archives poring over the letters and diaries of Pushkin's contemporaries, she reflected on the New Testament dictum that the disciple can expect no better than the master: if Pushkin, the greatest of all Russian poets, had been subjected to such hounding, how could she expect any mercy?

Yet, as subsequent events in Akhmatova's life would show, the relationship between a Russian poet and the Stalinist regime was not quite as straightforward as the writer–prophet being persecuted by the oppressive regime. To be sure, the Communists had no scruples about silencing dissent. Nevertheless, they still had some remnant of the nineteenth–century Russian intelligentsia's respect for the moral authority of the writer. The regime saw literature as a possible source of prestige, a confirmation of its legitimacy, much as other totalitarian states have regarded successful sports programs. To obtain this support, the government controlled rank–and–file writers through the Union of Soviet Writers, which provided rewards such as a larger apartment or a car to politically compliant authors, while making life difficult for the more independent–minded. The most prominent artists, those of Akhmatova's stature, were the subject of Stalin's personal attention.

Perhaps the most extraordinary example of Stalin's direct intervention in a writer's fate befell Akhmatova's close friend, the poet Osip Mandelstam. By the early 1930s, Mandelstam had reached the conclusion that it was his duty, as a poet, to speak of the ever–lengthening shadow of repression and the prison camps where he sensed he would meet his end. In a poem from December 1930, he wrote of still having the addresses "where I'll find the voices of the dead"; in another, written a month later, he prayed simply to survive and not be arrested that night: "Living in Petersburg is like sleeping in a coffin." Soon after, the Mandelstams moved to Moscow, but the situation there was no better. In 1962, Akhmatova remembered a walk she and Mandelstam had taken through Moscow when she was visiting him in February 1934: "We turned [from Prechistenka Street] onto Gogol Boulevard and Osip said, 'I'm ready for death.' Twenty–eight years have gone by and I recall that moment every time I pass that spot."[17]

Mandelstam was afraid, as any human being would be, but he was also defiant. During another conversation from this time, he told Akhmatova, "Poetry must be civic now."[18] The Russian concept of "civic" (*grazhdanskaya*) poetry is close to that of *littérature engagée*, a denunciation of the injustices of power. In the words of the nineteenth-century poet Nikolai Nekrasov, it was poetry inspired by a "Muse of wrath and sorrow." Mandelstam then illustrated the type of poetry he had in mind by reciting for Akhmatova a verse he had written on the subject of Stalin himself:

> We live, deaf to the land beneath us,
> Ten steps away no one hears our speeches,
>
> But where there's so much as half a conversation
> The Kremlin's mountaineer will get his mention.
>
> His fingers are fat as grubs
> And the words, final as lead weights, fall from his lips,
>
> His cockroach whiskers leer
> And his boot tops gleam.
>
> Around him a rabble of thin-necked leaders—
> fawning half-men for him to play with.
>
> They whinny, purr or whine
> As he prates and points a finger,
>
> One by one forging his laws, to be flung
> Like horseshoes at the head, the eye or the groin.
>
> And every killing is a treat
> For the broad-chested Ossete.[19]

Creating such a poem ("writing" would be the wrong word, since Mandelstam realized that it was much too dangerous to commit to paper) was itself an act of extraordinary courage. Yet Mandelstam went further and recited it to some dozen people. Under Soviet law, each listener who did not denounce such anti-Soviet propaganda to the OGPU became liable to a charge of counterrevolutionary activity. Inevitably, someone who knew the work was not strong enough to bear the potentially dangerous position created by Mandelstam, and the poem came to the authorities' notice.

The dreaded midnight knock on the door came on the night of May 16–17, 1934.[20] As it happened, Akhmatova was in the Mandelstams' apartment when the OGPU operatives arrived: Mandelstam, who had sensed the noose tightening around him and wanted the comfort of a friend's presence, had sent Akhmatova one telegram after another begging her to come, and she had arrived in Moscow that very day. The search of Mandelstam's apartment went on through the rest of the night. It was not until 7:00 a.m. that the agents took Mandelstam away, together with a relatively small quantity of his papers. The intensity of the search, combined with the fact that most of the poet's papers were not seized, led Nadya and Akhmatova to deduce that the searchers must have been looking for something specific—something that had not been found because it had never been written down. This suggested that Mandelstam was in extreme danger: while his other poems would probably have gotten him a term in a prison camp, the anti-Stalin poem was a death sentence.

More precisely, it was a death sentence under any ordinary circumstances. But the arrest of a major poet was not an ordinary case. Nadya and Akhmatova turned to Boris Pasternak, who a quarter century later would himself become the center of a political–literary controversy as the author of *Doctor Zhivago*, but who at this point was favorably regarded by the authorities as a highly gifted poet, too abstruse and modernistic for the masses, to be sure, but basically loyal. At Nadya's request, Pasternak went to visit Bukharin, who had assisted Mandelstam in the past. Although by 1934 Bukharin's political star had waned, he was not completely disgraced and still had some influence. Bukharin in turn wrote a carefully phrased letter to Stalin, warning, "Poets are always right, history is on their side."[21]

Stalin, who knew his Russian history as well as anyone, was well aware of the opprobrium that had attached itself to Tsar Nicholas I for his persecution of Pushkin. From the point of view of the Leader's public image, this was a great opportunity for a display of magnanimity, and Stalin issued instructions to the OGPU to "isolate but preserve" Mandelstam. On May 26, a special tribunal found Mandelstam guilty of "composing and distributing counterrevolutionary works" and gave him what by the standards of the time was a ludicrously light sentence: three years of exile in Cherdyn, a small town in the Urals. Contrary to all precedent, Nadya was allowed to visit her husband at the Lubyanka prison, where she was told of his sentence and offered the chance to accompany him. She immediately accepted.

Mandelstam was to leave Moscow no later than May 28, meaning there was very little time to prepare for the journey. Thus while Nadya packed, a number of her friends, including Akhmatova, went to ask everyone they could think of for money—a political exile was not going to find a job waiting for him in his new residence. Akhmatova would never forget the generous response of Yelena Bulgakova, wife of the author Mikhail Bulgakov, who "burst into tears and emptied her purse into my hands."[22] The night the Mandelstams left Moscow for the Urals, on a train in a special compartment with three guards accompanying them, Akhmatova also left the capital to go back to Leningrad.

Nadya had been allowed to accompany her husband because he was in no condition to look after himself. Mandelstam had not been tortured, in the strict sense of the word, but he had been subjected to a great deal of physical and emotional pressure, as a result of which he was psychologically disoriented. While the couple and their three guards were traveling, he told Nadya he would be taken off the train and executed somewhere along the route, and the sight of a peasant carrying an ax to cut wood seemed to him a threat of beheading. He was also convinced that Akhmatova had been killed and scanned the ditches looking for her body. On the evening he reached Cherdyn, Mandelstam tried to commit suicide by jumping out a window but only succeeded in fracturing his shoulder.

Nadya sent a telegram to Mandelstam's brother in Moscow, who brought the suicide attempt to the attention of the OGPU. Since this organization had been instructed to preserve Mandelstam, it had to find a way to dissuade him from making any more attempts. Accordingly, his sentence was hastily commuted to "minus twelve"—exile in a place that Mandelstam himself was to be allowed to choose, excluding only the twelve largest cities. Mandelstam more or less randomly named Voronezh, a city on the Don River some three hundred miles south of Moscow. By the time the Mandelstams, still under special convoy, reached this city, the most acute of the poet's symptoms had passed. Ironically, it was the very government that ultimately would kill him which also, by its intervention on his behalf, enabled Mandelstam to survive long enough to write the poems of his *Voronezh Notebooks.*

Soon after Mandelstam's arrest and exile, an amazing story was cir-
culating in Moscow—all the more amazing for being true. One day in July,
utterly unexpectedly, Pasternak received a call from none other than
Stalin. The Leader assured Pasternak that Mandelstam's case had been
reviewed and that everything would turn out all right. He asked Paster-
nak why he hadn't done more for Mandelstam: "If I were a poet and a
poet friend of mine were in trouble, I would do anything to help him." (A
touching sentiment coming from a man who would pass death sentences
on most of his close colleagues—but Stalin knew the line would be re-
peated by every hearer of the story.) Pasternak replied, "The writers' orga-
nizations haven't bothered with cases like this since 1927, and if I hadn't
tried to do something, you probably would never have heard about it."
Then, with a poet's love of accuracy in the use of language, he tried to
describe his relationship to Mandelstam, which was not exactly friend-
ship. Stalin interrupted with the question, "But he's a genius, he's a ge-
nius, isn't he?" Pasternak replied, "But that's not the point." Pasternak then
asked for a personal meeting with Stalin: he wanted to have a talk with
him "about life and death." At this point Stalin hung up. Pasternak then
called the Kremlin; he was not put through to Stalin but, significantly,
was told that he could discuss their conversation with anyone he wished.

When he heard about the conversation, Mandelstam remarked, "Why
is Stalin so afraid of genius? It's like a superstition with him. He thinks we
might put a spell on him, like shamans."[23] The simple fact was that Stalin
respected power, and in the Russian tradition the poet possessed a form of
power, albeit one singularly dangerous to its wielder. As Mandelstam
remarked, "Poetry is respected only in this country—people are killed for
it. There's no place where more people are killed for it."[24] Soon Akhma-
tova, like Mandelstam, would have to pay the price for that respect.

From a Bolshevik point of view, the year 1934 had started off well. The
drive for rapid industrialization, despite all its wastefulness and chaos,
had produced some real successes; collectivization had been completed,
and the famine had run its course; urban living standards, which had
been declining since 1928, were beginning to rebound. The Seventeenth
Party Congress joyously proclaimed itself "the congress of victors" and
fervently lauded the brilliant leadership of Stalin. Yet behind the scenes,
all was not adulation. Among many delegates, there was a feeling that

Stalin was taking too many risks, going too far too fast. Some of them made an effort to limit his dominating role in the party by promoting Sergei Kirov, the Leningrad party secretary, although Kirov himself was apparently too prudent to encourage such moves on his behalf.

On December 1, 1934, a disgruntled party member named Leonid Nikolayev walked into Kirov's office and fatally shot him. In the atmosphere of the times, no one would have believed this was the act of a lone gunman. In terms of who stood to benefit from such a crime, the obvious suspect was Stalin himself, but no proof can be offered. Certainly, if Stalin was guilty, it was in his interest to establish someone else's guilt; and if he was not guilty, the thought that a leader could be attacked in the seeming safety of his office would have roused all the suspicious and vindictive tendencies of Stalin's nature. Since Nikolayev was a party member, and since before Kirov's tenure the head of the Leningrad party organization had been Grigory Zinoviev, who had been a supporter of the archfiend Trotsky, by Stalinist logic it was clear where the real guilt lay. In January 1935 Zinoviev and his close associate Lev Kamenev were tried for "moral and political responsibility" for Kirov's death. Zinoviev was sentenced to ten years in prison, Kamenev to five.

Obviously, if appointees of an enemy like Zinoviev had been in charge of the Leningrad party organization, there was no telling how many socially dangerous elements they had allowed to flourish. Accordingly, a roundup of the usual suspects (called by the Communists "former people")—members of former gentry families, children of merchants, Orthodox priests, supporters of any former political party—was ordered. Estimates of the number of people arrested range from one thousand to forty thousand.[25] A scene described by a friend of Akhmatova's helps put a human face on these numbers:

> In 1935 Akhmatova and I went to the Paveletski station to see off a frail woman with three small boys who was being exiled to Saratov. They were not, of course, going to be given a permit to live in the town itself—people as helpless as this were expected to make out as best they could in the country somewhere. The station presented the usual sight—it was impossible to move in the milling throng, but this time the people were sitting not on bundles, but on quite respectable–looking trunks and suitcases still covered with old foreign travel labels. As we pushed our

way through to the platform, we were constantly greeted by old women we knew: granddaughters of the Decembrists, former "ladies" and just ordinary women. "I never knew I had so many friends among the aristocracy," said Akhmatova.[26]

It was not only Akhmatova's friends who were in danger. She also felt the threat closer to home. In 1935, her son Lev was a student at Leningrad University. He had some experience of the obstacles confronted by a son of an executed counterrevolutionary. His aunt Alexandra Sverchkova had favored the modest goal of trying to enroll Lev at the local Pedagogical Institute in Bezhetsk, but Akhmatova felt that her son, who was unquestionably very gifted, was entitled to aim higher. She wanted Lev to study at Leningrad University, although she hoped he would choose some relatively safe field of study such as ethnography, rather than literature. Such a goal would require a higher level of scholastic preparation than Lev could achieve in Bezhetsk. Punin's brother Alexander was the director of one of the best high schools in Leningrad and was able to use his influence to get Lev admitted there in 1928–29.

Lev's position in the Punin household was a difficult one. The urban population, unlike the peasants, did not actually have to starve to support the Five-Year Plan, but its living standard dropped significantly. At the same time Punin had numerous obligations to his own and his first wife's relatives. He did not always deal well with the resulting financial stress, and Akhmatova told a friend that he complained, "Too many people eat with us"–a remark that could hardly have made Lev feel welcome.[27] While Akhmatova felt that her dependent position in the Punin household made it impossible for her to demand better treatment for Lev, Lev suspected that she did not care about him enough to do so. In a culture in which traditional sex roles were still very strong, Lev couldn't accept that his mother had an intense creative life in which he had no place, and he was left with deep–seated feelings of neglect. Once his aunt Sverchkova asked young Lev what he was doing, and he replied, "I'm figuring out what percentage of time Mama thinks about me."[28] As a result of the discomfort he felt with both his stepfather and his mother, Lev spent as little time in the Fontanka House as possible, preferring to stay with Lev and Sara Ahrens (Anna Ahrens–Punina's brother and sister–in–law) or with his friends. After he was denied admission to Leningrad University in 1930, he joined a geological expedition to the Lake Baikal region and spent two years in Siberia.

In December 1933, Lev, back in Leningrad, was arrested for the first time. In connection with his ethnographic and linguistic studies, he was visiting a professor who specialized in Arabic culture, and while he was there the police suddenly showed up and arrested the professor, his wife, and Lev. The times, however, were still comparatively "vegetarian" (to use Akhmatova's expression). Lev convinced the authorities that his presence at the apartment was a pure coincidence, and after being held for nine days he was released. Nevertheless, he found it prudent to avoid drawing further attention from the Leningrad OGPU by leaving the city and went to stay with the Mandelstams in Moscow. Recalling those days, Nadya Mandelstam described a brighter side of the often–strained relationship between Akhmatova and her son: "When his mother met him at our place, they found it hard to tear themselves from each other's embraces. Punin could not stand Lev and at the mere sight of him always began a 'Punic war' against him. But we liked him just as much as his mother, and they were able to enjoy their meetings in our apartment without anyone disturbing them."[29] But the Mandelstams' apartment was not a safe haven for anyone, let alone a man under suspicion. By a stroke of pure luck Lev was not present when Mandelstam was arrested—he had decided to spend the night with friends to reduce the crowding in his host's tiny apartment. When he returned the following morning, Nadya's first words to him were, "Go away at once. Osip was arrested last night." Lev understood the danger implied in her words and unquestioningly obeyed.[30]

Even when he finally gained admission to the history department of Leningrad University in September 1934, the triumph was short–lived. In mid–October 1935, when Lev passed through Moscow on his return from an archeological expedition on the Don, he told Mandelstam's friend Emma Gershtein, "When I go back to Leningrad, they'll arrest me."[31] His premonition proved all too correct, for on October 23, 1935, Punin, Lev Gumilyov, and a group of Leningrad University students were arrested on charges of "creating a counterrevolutionary terrorist organization." The denunciation of a fellow student had led to their arrest—a common phenomenon, as Lev later explained:

At that time in Leningrad they were hunting down students from intel-
ligentsia families, students who did good work and knew their subject
well. . . . [E]verybody who was arrested was charged with being mem-
bers of an anti–Soviet group or organization. I don't know exactly how
they classified us then. True, at that time they didn't torture people, just
interrogated them. But since there were conversations held in youth
circles on, among other things, political themes, and the students also
told each other anecdotes, there really was something for the interroga-
tors to ask us about.[32]

To say that people were "not tortured" merely meant that, in contrast to
what was to come, they were not actually beaten to make them confess.
However, tactics such as questioning a prisoner for nights on end while
refusing to let him sleep in the day and threatening to arrest fam-
ily members as coconspirators were standard interrogation techniques.
And this was a case in which no investigator would have risked appear-
ing less than zealous in his work, since, as Lev noted, the prisoners had
truly committed the crime of holding unacceptable opinions: one of the
charges against Lev, for example, was that he had recited Mandelstam's
anti–Stalin poem.

Akhmatova knew what she had to do for her husband and her son.
Once again, as at the time of Mandelstam's arrest, she went to make the
rounds of her friends and possible intercessors. On October 29, she went
to Moscow. Her first stop was Emma Gershtein's apartment. Her first
words to Emma were: "They've been arrested." "Who are they?" "Niko-
lasha and Lyova." Gershtein gave up her bed to Akhmatova and watched
her as she slept: "Her eyes were sunken and triangles had formed around
the bridge of her nose. They had never been there before. She was chang-
ing right in front of me."[33]

The next day Akhmatova went to see Bulgakov. She had heard how
Bulgakov had saved himself from a difficult position in 1929, when he had
come under attack at the same time as Pilnyak and Zamyatin. In despera-
tion, in March 1930, Bulgakov boldly wrote an appeal to Stalin, and three
weeks later Stalin personally called him and asked him if he wished to
emigrate. Bulgakov replied that he believed that a Russian writer be-
longed in Russia, but that he could not live without employment. Stalin
told him to reapply for work at the Moscow Art Theater, where he was
promptly hired as an assistant director. Akhmatova planned to take the

same route of a direct appeal to the Leader and presumably hoped that Bulgakov could give her guidance on what she should write.

The next day Emma Gershtein picked Akhmatova up at Bulgakov's apartment, and the two women set out to see Lidia Seifullina, a writer and journalist best known for her short story "Virineya," depicting a peasant woman who has embraced the new Soviet ideals and struggles against the traditional patriarchal mores of the countryside. This streak of Bolshevik feminism made Seifullina relatively sympathetic toward Akhmatova, and she also had good contacts in official circles. Gershtein remembered the nightmarish taxi ride:

> The driver started the car and asked where to. She didn't hear. I didn't know where we were going. He repeated the question twice, and she came to: "To Seifullina's, of course." "Where does she live?" I didn't know. . . . I took a guess: in the Writers' House? . . . Somehow we worked it out: yes, on Kamergersky Lane. We set out. The whole way there Anna Andreyevna was crying out, "Kolya [Nikolai Gumilyov's nickname] . . . Kolya . . . blood." I decided that Anna Andreyevna had lost her wits. She was raving. I led her as far as the apartment door. Seifullina herself opened it. I left.[34]

Seifullina agreed to help and was able to use her contacts with the Central Committee to arrange for Akhmatova to deliver a letter to Alexander Poskryobyshev, Stalin's personal secretary, at the Kremlin.

From there Akhmatova went to see Pasternak and asked him to write a letter in support of her appeal. Pilnyak, who happened to be at Pasternak's, added his voice to Akhmatova's. He would have been willing to write a letter himself but felt that one from Pasternak would be more effective. While at Pasternak's apartment Akhmatova showed signs of heart trouble, and she ended up spending the night there resting while Pasternak composed his letter.

The next day, November 1, Pilnyak, who enjoyed the rare luxury of owning a private car, drove Akhmatova to the Kremlin, where she delivered the two letters in the prearranged manner.[35] Akhmatova's letter has been preserved in the archives:

> Dear Iosif Vissarionovich,
>   Knowing of your attentiveness to the cultural forces of our country and particularly to writers, I have resolved to address myself to you

with this letter. On October 23 in Leningrad, the NKVD arrested my husband Nikolai Nikolaevich Punin (a professor at the Academy of Arts) and my son, Lev Gumilyov (a student at Leningrad State University). Iosif Vissarionovich, I do not know what they are accused of, but I give you my word of honor that they are neither Fascists, nor spies, nor members of any counterrevolutionary societies. I have lived in the Soviet Union since the beginning of the Revolution, I have never wanted to leave the country with which my heart and mind are bound up. Despite the fact that my poems are not printed and the critics' reviews have given me many bitter moments, I have not lost heart; in very difficult moral and material circumstances I have continued to work and have already published one work on Pushkin, another is being printed. I live a very solitary life in Leningrad and am frequently ill for long periods of time. The arrest of the only two people who are close to me is a blow that has fallen so heavily on me that I cannot bear it. I implore you, Iosif Vissarionovich, return my husband and son to me, and I am convinced that no one will ever regret it.

While maintaining her dignity, Akhmatova carefully presented an unthreatening image of herself not as the heiress of Pushkin, but as a poor, sick woman patiently enduring a difficult fate—in short, a worthy recipient of the royal alms. As he had with Mandelstam, Stalin took the opportunity to display his magnanimity. On the margin of Akhmatova's letter is a note: "C[omrade] Yagoda. Release both Punin and Gumilyov from arrest and report on implementation. I. Stalin."[36]

At 10:00 p.m. on November 3, Punin and Lev Gumilyov were released with all charges against them having been dropped. Akhmatova, still in Moscow, received a telegram from her husband and son the next day. Too exhausted by the events of the past two weeks to join in the rejoicings of her friends, she returned to Leningrad.

As it had at the time of Nikolai Gumilyov's execution, terror spurred inspiration. Sometime during those nightmarish days in Moscow, Akhmatova wrote a poem starting with the lines, "Arrest at dawn. Like a funeral rite / They bore you off, I followed in back." This was the beginning of the work that would become *Requiem*.

CHAPTER 4

Terror and the Muse, 1936–1941

❧ ❧ ❧

VEN BY THE DRAMATIC STANDARDS OF Akhmatova's bi-
ography, the years 1936–41 are an extraordinary period. These
were the years of the Great Terror that decimated the Russian in-
telligentsia, years that Punin later recalled as being like a war, "when
each person thought, 'Tomorrow, maybe it'll be me.'"[1] Many of Akhma-
tova's friends did not survive these years. Her son was rearrested, and
there was no guarantee that she herself would not follow him into the
Gulag. And yet it was during this catastrophic period that the poetic
inspiration that had almost abandoned her for so many years returned
with overwhelming force. The period of silence turned out to have been
a period of transformation: the young woman whose terse yet deeply
moving lyrics of unhappy love had dazzled Silver Age Petersburg had
been replaced by a woman who had survived the destruction of her
world and emerged from the ruins with a deepened consciousness of
herself as a poet and of the price exacted by her vocation. As Akhmatova
herself described it:

> My name was struck off the list of the living. . . . And after accepting the
> experience of those years–terror, weariness, emptiness, deathly isola-
> tion–in 1936 I began to write again, but my handwriting had changed,

my voice sounded different. . . . *Requiem* arose (1935–1940). There could be no return to my earlier manner. Which is better, which worse–it's not for me to say. 1940 was the apogee. Poems sounded uninterruptedly, stepping on each other's heels, hurrying and out of breath. . . . In March *Requiem* was finished with the "Epilogue." Those same days saw *The Way of All the Earth* (*The Woman of Kitezh*), which was my own great requiem mass for myself, and in the fall there was . . . my poor Olga ("You came to Russia out of nowhere") [the first fragment of what was to become *Poem Without a Hero*].[2]

A number of the first poems Akhmatova wrote in this new phase were about poets and poetry. In January 1936, she wrote "The Poet," a tribute to Boris Pasternak; in February and April 1936, "Didn't he send a swan for me . . ." and "Incantation," both associated with the memory of Gumilyov; in March 1936, "Voronezh," inspired by a visit to Mandelstam at his place of exile that February; in August 1936, "Dante"; in November 1936, "Creation," a description of what might be called the experience of being pregnant with a poem. Each of the poems to a poet refers to the social tragedy of which the poet was a witness, if not a victim. "The Poet" is filled with imagery from Pasternak's own nature poems, but it also describes him visiting "a Daryal gravestone, cursed and black / Coming again from someone's funeral," an image which was to prove prophetic: in 1931, when Pasternak traveled through the Caucasus, he not only admired the spectacular Georgian scenery–including the Daryal Gorge–but also became friends with two Georgian poets, Titian Tabidze and Paolo Yashvili, both of whom perished in the purges the year after Akhmatova's poem was written. "Didn't he send a swan for me . . . " and "Incantation" both echoed her separation from Gumilyov through untimely death; "Incantation" was written on what would have been Gumilyov's fiftieth birthday. "Voronezh" shifts abruptly from a vivid description of the city to "the room of the banished poet" where "terror and the Muse take turns keeping watch." "Dante," evoking the poet whom Akhmatova and Mandelstam both deeply loved, celebrates his choice to remain in exile rather than to accept public humiliation as the price of return to his beloved Florence.

Facing her own grim prospects, Akhmatova drew courage from the long-ago words of Nikolai Nedobrovo, who had seen her as a woman suffering "griefs, giving rise to fatal torments without bringing death, but by their extreme intensity, calling forth the miracle of creation–their instant antidote."[3] In a poem of November 1936 dedicated to his memory, she wrote,

> Some meet a glance and know themselves adored,
> Some drink a toast while watching the sun rise,
> I spend my nights in endless back and forth
> With conscience that won't hear of compromise.
>
> "How many years, how weary I have grown
> From carrying your burden," I appeal.
> But earthly time is something it doesn't know;
> For it, the three dimensions are unreal.

At the same time Akhmatova was preparing to accept the burden of her calling, ever more intense attacks were being made, not merely against every dissident voice, but even against every dissident thought. Stalin had already succeeded in destroying any effective opposition to him by the Old Bolsheviks, the one-time companions of Lenin. The most fortunate among them, like Bukharin, had been sidelined in relatively unimportant positions; others, like Zinoviev and Kamenev, who had been found guilty of moral responsibility for Kirov's assassination, were in prison; Trotsky had been exiled. Although Stalin had decisively defeated them, however, the Old Bolsheviks continued to believe in private that they were right and he was wrong, that some unforeseen turn of events might restore them to what they saw as their rightful position in the party, and that it was prudent to put out occasional feelers to one another about how to maintain a common front. By the summer of 1936, some information about these abortive efforts had reached Stalin. It was second nature to him to see enemies everywhere, and now a shred of evidence seemed to confirm that belief. His response was massive retaliation. In August 1936, Zinoviev and Kamenev were produced for a show trial, accused of responsibility for the death of Kirov and of having planned to kill Stalin next. In response to a private promise that they would not be put to death, they made the required public confession, after which they were executed anyway.

In September 1936, Genrikh Yagoda, the head of the NKVD, was dismissed and subsequently arrested on the grounds he had not shown sufficient vigilance against enemies of the people. Nadezhda Mandelstam recalled how "the press unleashed a flood of abuse against Yagoda, accusing him of being soft on all the scum in the camps and in exile. 'Who would have thought that we have been in the hands of humanists!' we said to each other."[4] Yagoda was replaced by Nikolai Yezhov, an up-and-coming figure who had recently presided over a nationwide review of the qualifications of all Communist Party members and had distinguished himself by his zeal in finding class enemies, spies, and "wreckers" (Soviet jargon for the alleged perpetrators of a broad range of industrial and agricultural sabotage) who had infiltrated party ranks.

In early 1937, a second show trial was directed against several important secondary figures among the Old Bolsheviks. The defendants were strongly encouraged to implicate Bukharin in their "Japanese–German–Trotskyist" plots to restore capitalism, and the Party Central Committee plenum of February–March 1937 resolved that at the least Bukharin must have had sufficient guilty knowledge to justify expelling him from the party and to warrant further investigation by the NKVD. The inevitable result, a year later, was yet another show trial, which sentenced both Bukharin and Yagoda to death. By May, the wave of arrests reached the armed forces: the highest-ranking officer in the Red Army, Field Marshal Mikhail Tukhachevsky, was arrested along with a number of generals.

To the paranoid Stalin, there was a logical deduction: if he could not trust the party and he could not trust the army, then he could not trust anyone. In the summer of 1937, quotas were sent out to the various regional branches of the NKVD, indicating how many arrests they were to carry out in their area, and of those arrested how many were to be executed and how many sent into exile. Local initiative was encouraged: regional NKVD branches could request that Moscow increase their quota (needless to say, nobody asked for a decrease), and such increases would be readily granted. According to Soviet figures declassified after the collapse of the Soviet Union, the number of people executed in 1937 was more than three hundred times the number executed the previous year.[5] The same source gives the total number of executions in the years 1937–38 as 681,692, a figure that may be incomplete. An equal number of deaths may have occurred in those two years among the newly arrived inmates of Gulag, many of whom were unable to adapt to a regime of extremely demanding physical labor and near-starvation rations.

Political arrests were typically made under Article 58 of the Soviet law code, which forbade, among other things, "propaganda or agitation, containing an appeal for the overthrow, subverting, or weakening of the Soviet power . . . and equally, the dissemination or possession of literary materials of similar content." This vaguely written law was interpreted so generously that a factory worker's grumbling about his supervisor (a representative of Soviet power) or a person recording a political joke in his diary ("literary materials") could be charged with a crime. Truly absurd arrests occurred: one prison memoirist shared a cell with an uneducated peasant woman, sixty-five years old, who couldn't understand why she was accused of being a "tractorist" (her version of "Trotskyist")—surely everyone knew that a woman her age wouldn't be riding one of those newfangled machines.[6]

When such obscure and harmless figures were arrested, they were, in a sense, the victims of bad luck. Unless half the population was put to work spying on the other half—something which, no matter how much it might have appealed to Stalin, was simply not feasible—there was no way to keep a close watch on everyone in the country. Instead, the security organs paid only perfunctory attention to ordinary workers and collective farmers, while directing intense surveillance against everyone considered a possible threat, either because they held a prominent position or because they fit a demographic profile of supposed enemies. The highest ranks of society were devastated: of the Central Committee's seventy-one members in 1934, only sixteen were still alive by the purge's end in 1939; similarly, 90 percent of the Red Army's generals and 80 percent of its colonels were purged.[7] Also prone to arrest were anyone who had lived in a foreign country (including Communists from Fascist countries who had fled to Moscow, Russian veterans of the Spanish Civil War, and members of the USSR's own espionage service) or who showed an interest in international organizations (including Esperantists and stamp collectors); members of smaller ethnic groups who were active in preserving their cultural traditions (these were charged with "bourgeois nationalism"); engineers, who were the obvious scapegoat for every industrial accident or shortcoming; and, of course, anyone who had been previously arrested.

Given the traditional prerevolutionary role of the Russian intelligentsia as social critics, it was to be expected that the NKVD would turn its attention to writers, especially those who had politically compromised themselves in the past. In October 1937, Akhmatova's old friend Boris Pilnyak, who had driven her to the Kremlin two years before with her petition for clemency for her son and husband, was arrested. Pilnyak had never entirely escaped the shadow of his disgrace in 1929, even though he had disavowed his novel *Mahogany* and published the politically acceptable *The Volga Flows to the Caspian Sea*, the plot of which centered on the socialist construction of a giant dam on the Volga. Pilnyak was accused of being a Japanese spy (presumably on the basis of his trips to the Far East in 1926 and 1932) and of having been a member of a conspiracy to assassinate Yezhov. After a trial that lasted fifteen minutes, from 5:45 to 6:00 p.m. on April 20, 1938, he was sentenced to the "highest measure of punishment"–death. The sentence was carried out immediately.[8]

In the same month as Pilnyak's arrest, October 1937, the poet Nikolai Klyuyev was executed. His first collection of poems had come out in the winter of 1911–12, at the same time the young Akhmatova was writing the lyrics that would go into her first book, *Evening*. Klyuyev had briefly been a member of the Poets' Guild but had soon realized it was no place for him: while the members of the developing Acmeist movement looked to the heritage of the West for inspiration, Klyuyev, who grew up in the remote northern town of Olonets, based his poetry on traditional Russian folklore and mores. The Bolsheviks' attacks on his beloved Old Russia, culminating in the brutalities of collectivization, gave rise to his long poem "The Burned Ruins," in which an idealized Russian village is attacked by infidels (referred to as both Tatars and Saracens) who pillage it and kill the inhabitants. In another long poem, "To the Slanderers of Art," he denounced those whom he described as clipping the wings of the Pegasus of Russian poetry and reducing it to a beast of burden. One passage of the poem specifically referred to the silencing of Akhmatova, whom Klyuyev described as a jasmine blooming amidst the gray asphalt of the hated city. In the winter of 1932–33, when both Klyuyev and Mandelstam were living in Moscow, Klyuyev recited "To the Slanderers of Art" to Mandelstam, who learned it by heart and recited it to Akhmatova; a modified citation from it appears as an epigraph in *Poem Without a Hero*. Like Mandelstam, Klyuyev was arrested in 1934 and sent into exile, but in the harsher conditions of the town of Tomsk, in Siberia. His subsequent fate was clarified only after the end of the Soviet Union, when the opening of the archives revealed that in June 1937, while still in Tomsk, he was rearrested as a supposed leader of a counterrevolutionary organization taking its orders from Paris (exactly how these orders made their way to Siberia was not explained). He was sentenced to death on October 13, 1937, and was shot ten days later.[9]

In May 1937, Mandelstam's sentence of exile in Voronezh came to an end. He was duly released and allowed to return to Moscow, but it was clear to him that his days at liberty were numbered. On March 3–5, 1938, he and Nadya paid their last visit to Akhmatova in Leningrad. Akhmatova recalled those days as "an apocalyptic time. . . . Osip had great difficulty breathing and gasped at the air with his lips. I went to see them, but I don't remember where they were staying. It was all like a terrible dream."[10] Two months later, on May 2, Mandelstam was rearrested. He was in no condition to face a labor camp, as poverty and persecution had physically worn him down, and his heart was failing. Photographs of him taken in the 1930s show a man who looks twenty years older than his actual age. On December 27, 1938, he died in a transit camp.

Amid the epidemic of arrests, Akhmatova's greatest fear finally came to pass. On the morning of March 11, 1938, Lev Gumilyov's half-brother Orest Vysotsky came to Akhmatova with the news that Lev had been arrested at his apartment the previous night. This was the beginning of a long ordeal not only for Lev, but for his mother. The family of an arrested person was not told where he was taken.Family members would go from one prison to another bearing money to be paid over to their missing relative, but the money would be accepted only if the addressee's name was found on the list of inmates of that particular prison. Similarly, no information was provided to the family on the status of the investigation, which might last for months. Families learned of a conviction indirectly: once a prisoner was convicted, he was transferred out, which meant that a relative delivering a parcel to the prison would reach the window only to have the package refused on the grounds that the addressee was no longer there. Occasionally some additional information, such as the length of term or the camp's name, would be provided. Because the number of arrests grew steadily but the number of prison bureaucrats did not, the progress of the Terror could be measured by the increasing number of hours relatives had to stand in line before reaching the window. The ever-lengthening lines were made up almost exclusively of women, both because the responsibility for holding families together traditionally fell upon them and because, in a male–dominated society, people who attracted the attention of the NKVD were overwhelmingly likely to be men (although in the case of prominent figures, their wives and daughters might also be arrested).

Akhmatova did not have far to look for Lev since he was being held at Leningrad's central prison, Kresty–Russian for "the Crosses" (the name referred to the building's shape, but its symbolism could hardly have been lost on the poet). At the height of the Terror, this prison–colloquially referred to as the Big House (*Bolshoi dom*) by those bold enough to speak of it at all–held about thirty thousand prisoners, with sixteen men sharing a cell that in tsarist times had been meant for a single inmate.[11]

As a veteran of arrest, Gumilyov would have been in a position to recognize how much worse Soviet prisons had become during the Terror, even by the low standards of the earlier 1930s. In 1935, his interrogator had focused on a "crime" (conversations criticizing Stalin and the party) that had actually occurred. In 1938, NKVD agents were expected to uncover more spectacular offenses, and Lev was thus confronted with the fantastic accusation that he had planned to assassinate Andrei Zhdanov (who had replaced the murdered Kirov as Leningrad party secretary) to avenge the execution of his father in 1921. Akhmatova supposedly had urged this course of action upon him. Interrogators were expected not only to extract confessions to such preposterous charges, but to do so quickly because the vastly increased number of inmates meant that less time could be spent on an individual case. Accordingly, starting in August 1937, interrogators turned to "simplified methods of interrogation"–beating a prisoner until he admitted whatever was required. Lev saw cases in which people had been beaten so severely that their ribs or collarbones were broken; he himself, when he refused to confess, was beaten for eight nights.[12]

On September 27, 1938, Gumilyov was found guilty of membership in a "counterrevolutionary terrorist organization" and sentenced to ten years' forced labor at the Belomor (White Sea) camp. After the sentence was passed, Lev was transferred to a prison in Moscow, where Akhmatova was allowed to visit him. He told her, "Mama, I spoke like Dimitrov, but no one listened to me."[13] Georgi Dimitrov, the representative of the Communist International in Germany in the early 1930s, had defended himself so ably during a Nazi show trial that to minimize the damage to

Germany's public image the judges were forced to acquit him. But, as Gumilyov had learned, such a defense could make a difference only in a public trial, not in the closed door, rubber–stamp proceedings that were the fate of millions of Soviet citizens.

In fact, the prosecutor thought a mere ten years in a concentration camp was too lenient a sentence. He lodged a formal appeal that the sentence be upgraded to execution, and in November 1938 the case was officially reopened. Gumilyov, who by this time was felling trees on the White Sea Canal, was duly transported back to Kresty prison in Leningrad for further investigation.

By this time, the absurdity of the Terror was becoming unsustainable. As already noted, the arrests fell heavily upon people with managerial and technical expertise, and these people, when they were tortured, naturally incriminated the people they knew, that is, their professional colleagues. As the circles of arrests grew ever wider, inevitably the point was reached where the Soviet Union's relatively shallow pool of experienced specialists was so depleted as to cause obvious economic damage. By Stalinist logic, there had to be someone to blame for this, and since it could not possibly be the Leader himself, the obvious candidate was Yezhov, the head of the NKVD. On November 25, 1938, he was dismissed from his position and replaced by the supposedly more moderate Lavrenty Beria. In early 1939, at the Eighteenth Congress of the Communist Party, Stalin accused Yezhov of allowing the security forces to get carried away, so that while many class enemies had indeed been dealt with appropriately, some innocent people had gotten caught up as well. A few days after this denunciation, Yezhov was arrested.

Interestingly, precisely at the time of Yezhov's fall, Akhmatova was once again in Stalin's thoughts. In February 1939, at a reception in honor of prizewinning writers, Stalin unexpectedly asked what had become of Akhmatova.[14] Obviously he knew the answer to that question, but by asking it he was able to present himself in the traditional Russian role of the "good tsar," the benevolent ruler unaware of the wrongs done by his malignant subordinates–the same role he was playing in his denunciation of Yezhov.

This shift in the political wind had a direct effect on Lev Gumilyov's fate. On July 26, 1939, his earlier terrorist conviction was replaced by a conviction under Article 58, Sections 10 and 11. Section 10 was "anti–

Soviet agitation or propaganda," and Section 11 was the aggravating factor of having performed the criminal act as a member of a group. As a result, his sentence was changed to five years in a mining camp at Norilsk–a remarkably short term for a political prisoner (his original sentence of ten years would have been much more common).

On August 15, 1939, a few days before Lev was sent off to the north, Akhmatova was allowed to visit him in prison and to bring him a parcel. She was told of the visit only the day before it was to take place. On such short notice, one could not hope to find any warm clothing in the notoriously ill-supplied Soviet stores, even if Akhmatova had had the money to buy it. So she called her friend Lidia Chukovskaya, and the two women hastily made the rounds of friends to beg for warm clothes for Lev, getting a hat from one person, a scarf from another, gloves from yet a third. The following day, Akhmatova had to wait in the prison line for so long before she was admitted that she could barely hobble home on her swollen feet. It was immediately after this visit that she composed "To Death," poem 8 of *Requiem.*

Akhmatova knew that, in the harsh conditions of Gulag, even a light sentence was life-threatening. In the hope of protecting her son, she set out to present the literary authorities–and through them, the political authorities–with as conformist an image of herself as her nature and conscience would allow. Thus on September 11, 1939, Akhmatova finally petitioned to be admitted to the Union of Soviet Writers. There was no thought of denying her, since in the expression of Alexander Fadeyev, the secretary of the union and a master of finding the appropriate political formula, "For all the unsuitability of her poetic gift in our time, nevertheless she was and remains a major poet of the prerevolutionary period."[15] She was officially received into the union on January 5, 1940, and a speech in her honor was delivered by her friend of Acmeist days Mikhail Lozinsky, who compared her early lyrics to those of Catullus.

Her apparent willingness to conform was rapidly rewarded. In January 1940, she was offered a contract for a one-volume edition of her selected works, which was published with unusual rapidity, coming out at the end of May. The volume was entitled *From Six Books* (Akhmatova had in fact published only five books; the sixth book was a small selection of her post-1922 poems). In a lingering sign of official mistrust, only a small edition was allowed to be printed, ensuring that most of the copies never reached ordinary readers but were instead diverted to those with good connections in the literary world. Nevertheless, the mere fact that the book existed and that reviewers expressed qualified approval was encouraging to the more politically cautious among Akhmatova's sympathizers. Fadeyev and Alexei Tolstoy, both talented and influential novelists within the constraints of Socialist Realism, canvassed for the book to be awarded a Stalin Prize. Fadeyev even offered his services on Lev's behalf by arranging for Akhmatova to meet with an official from the procurator's (state prosecutor's) office in Moscow.

The meeting, which took place in August, turned out to be a nightmare. Emma Gershtein recalled:

> When they called her into the procurator's office, I waited for her in the hall. Very soon, too soon, the office door opened, and Anna Andreyevna appeared. And in the doorway stood a man much shorter than she who, looking up at her, shouted crude and abusive phrases right in her face. Anna Andreyevna walked down the corridor, looking around with unseeing eyes, fumbling at various doors, unable to find the exit. I rushed after her. I don't remember how and where I led her away. She set out for Leningrad immediately.[16]

Further, Akhmatova's nomination for a highly prestigious competitive prize made her a conspicuous target. In September an official report on Akhmatova's book was submitted to none other than Zhdanov, the Leningrad Communist Party boss, who had become a Politburo member and one of Stalin's closest associates (as well as being the alleged target of her son's murderous intent). The report noted, "This collection has no poems about revolutionary or Soviet themes or people of Socialism. . . . Two sources give rise to Akhmatova's rubbishy verses, and her 'poetry' is dedicated to them: God and 'free' love, and 'artsy' images for this are borrowed from church literature." Zhdanov was duly indignant and wrote to the Leningrad party organization, "How could this 'harlotry to the glory of God' of Akhmatova's be printed? Who's behind this?"[17]—the latter question being a hallmark of the Stalinist mentality. The Leningrad officials timidly defended themselves, noting that Stalin had asked why Akhmatova was not being printed and that Fadeyev, who was present, had conveyed the Leader's remark to them. This did not save them from being censured by a resolution of the Secretariat of the Communist Party, which ruled on October 29, 1940, that the book was to be withdrawn from bookstores and libraries.

Agonizingly, Akhmatova blamed herself for revisions made to the book's contents during its production, revisions that she believed had resulted in a book that was not what the authorities had originally approved. "And if I had not done this," she told Chukovskaya, "Lyova would now be at home."[18] Chukovskaya tried to argue her out of this belief, pointing out that the only revisions Akhmatova had made were the ones demanded by her Soviet editors. Akhmatova refused to listen. One wonders which view would have been more painful: that she had, however unwittingly, failed to do something to alleviate her son's sufferings or that there was nothing she could do to alleviate her son's sufferings.

The year 1938 saw not only the arrest of Akhmatova's son, but also the final breakdown of her marriage to Punin. By the mid–1930s, Akhmatova's and Punin's relationship had become a hollow shell: the two of them were leading emotionally independent lives. Yet from sheer inertia the marriage drifted on.

In September 1938 Akhmatova finally left Punin—left, that is, in a manner of speaking. Faced with the continuing housing shortage, Akhmatova found she could leave only to the extent of exchanging rooms with Ahrens–Punina. Punin, whom neither woman had bothered to consult, watched silently as the two Annas rearranged their meager personal belongings. Only when Anna Ahrens was out of the room did Punin remark to Akhmatova, "You could have stayed with me for just one more year." Then he quoted a line from a well–known Lermontov poem–"Long, long the king's daughter will stay in his mind!"–and left the room.[19]

Akhmatova's wish for putting a definite end to the relationship was presumably linked with her growing feelings for Vladimir Garshin, a physician whom she first met in February 1937 when she was hospitalized for treatment of a thyroid condition called Basedow's disease. Although Garshin enjoyed considerable respect in his field, he was no narrow specialist. His uncle, Vsevolod Garshin, a contemporary of Chekhov, had been a writer, and although his output was small and uneven, his best short stories were known to every literate Russian. In the harsh Soviet world, Vladimir Garshin preserved the spiritual qualities of the old Russian intelligentsia: Akhmatova's stepdaughter Irina Punina remembered him as "a dear and touching man, with such unusual delicacy that it already seemed like a museum piece."[20] He was a collector of medals, coins, and icons, and he loved poetry. Certainly, when he was called in on Akhmatova's case, he could appreciate just who his patient was. He and she readily found a common language, and by September 1937 he was visiting her at the Fontanka House.

Although the small size and thin walls of the apartment made privacy impossible, once Akhmatova had separated from Punin she could at least close a door when she was with Garshin. Emma Gershtein was present at one such visit: "In 1939 I first saw Vladimir Georgievich Garshin at Anna Andreyevna's. He arrived about seven p.m., carrying a package of tea and food of some sort. Anna Andreyevna sat with her feet on a soft chair and ate a little, and he solicitously asked her about her health. There was a sense of a haven, as sometimes happens in misfortune when the most crushing burdens have been alleviated to some degree through the warmth of a human heart.

"When he left, Anna Andreyevna said that he always came to her like that." [21] Yet Garshin's position was not an easy one. He was married, and although he no longer loved his wife, he knew she was emotionally dependent on him, and he was not ruthless enough to divorce her. At the same time, he knew how much Akhmatova needed him and blamed himself for not being able to be with her more. And, although his compassionate nature encouraged others to look to him for their needs, he was not a strong individual. Garshin's family was characterized not only by emotional sensitivity and love of art, but also by a tendency to manic depression, and his famous uncle had died at the age of thirty-three as the result of a jump or fall. Indeed, the situation the nephew found himself in—suffering from pain and guilt as the result of shouldering a responsibility beyond his strength—is very reminiscent of the characteristic atmosphere of the uncle's stories. But though at times he poured out his grief to others, he never breathed a word of it to Akhmatova, and she continued to regard him as utterly steadfast. In one poem from 1940, Akhmatova imagined herself walking toward the abyss; when everyone else accompanying her had stopped, he alone continued with her up to the very edge of the pit and called after her as she fell.

Throughout 1939 and 1940, Akhmatova's domestic situation was an extremely difficult one. Since she was clearly no longer a member of the Punin family, the other members of the household wanted her to move out. The small apartment had become even noisier and more crowded when Irina Punina got married in September 1938: her husband, Genrikh Kaminsky, moved in with his wife's family, and in May 1939, Irina gave birth to a daughter, Anna Kaminskaya. (Punin also got married, to an assistant of his named Marta Golubeva, but she had more sense than to move into an apartment with two ex-wives and continued to live with her parents.) During Akhmatova's brief interval of official favor in 1940, the writers' union submitted a petition to the Soviet of People's Commissars and the Literary Fund on her behalf, asking that she be granted a pension of 750 rubles a month and a room of her own. Akhmatova's friends urged her to seize the opportunity, but she did not want to move: for all her difficulties with the Punins, she saw life with them as preferable to living in a communal apartment amid strangers, and in view of her deep love of the classic architecture of prerevolutionary Petersburg, she felt she belonged in the Fontanka House.

A rare window into Akhmatova's day-to-day life during this period is offered by the indefatigable diarist Chukovskaya. Akhmatova and Chukovskaya met for the first time on November 9, 1938, in a manner befitting the times: Chukovskaya's second husband, the theoretical physicist Matvei Bronstein, had been arrested in August 1937 and in February 1938 was sentenced to ten years' imprisonment without the right of correspondence. Chukovskaya was the daughter of Kornei Chukovsky, the literary critic who had lectured on Akhmatova and Mayakovsky back in the early 1920s, and as someone who moved in literary circles Chukovskaya had heard how Punin and Lev Gumilyov had been released from prison in 1935 after Akhmatova had written to Stalin. Hoping to learn what formulas were successful in placating the authorities, Chukovskaya visited Akhmatova to ask for a copy of the letter, although the news of Lev's rearrest could not have given Chukovskaya much encouragement. It was not until December 1939 that Chukovskaya learned through indirect channels that her efforts had been in vain: Bronstein had already been secretly executed. Still later she came to realize that a sentence of imprisonment without right of correspondence was regularly used to cover up executions.

Although Akhmatova could not help save Bronstein, she could help make Chukovskaya's suffering bearable. As the daughter of a writer, Chukovskaya had been brought up to revere poetry and those who created it. In the crushing conditions of the Terror, she found herself regarding life as a prolonged and meaningless ordeal, and her association with Akhmatova was the one thing in her life that kept her from experiencing a slow spiritual death, that still affirmed humanity's higher nature. She kept a diary of her meetings with Akhmatova, using abbreviations and literary allusions to remind herself of what was said when the conversation turned to topics too sensitive to write down. As she recalled years later,

> Day by day, month by month, my fragmentary notes became less and less a re-creation of my own life, turning into episodes in the life of Anna Akhmatova. . . . I was drawn to writing about her because she herself, her words, her deeds, her head, shoulders and the movements of her hands were possessed of such perfection, which, in this world, usually belongs only to great works of art. Before my very eyes, Akhmatova's fate–something greater even than her own person–was chiselling out of this famous and neglected, strong and helpless woman, a statue of grief, loneliness, pride, courage.[22]

Just as Chukovskaya needed to draw courage from Akhmatova, so Akhmatova needed a listener like Chukovskaya. The poems Akhmatova was writing had only a tenuous claim on existence. It was not merely that they could not be published. Given the risk involved, Akhmatova would not write them down, for herself or anyone else. The paranoia of the times made her see dangers everywhere, and she refused to recite her poems aloud even in her apartment. But unless she could find some way of communicating her poems to another person, if anything happened to Akhmatova, her poems would die with her. Chukovskaya, like many Russian intellectuals, had a gift for memorizing poetry, and Akhmatova turned it to advantage:

> Anna Andreevna, when visiting me, recited parts of "Requiem" also in a whisper, but at home in Fontanny House did not even dare to whisper it; suddenly, in mid-conversation, she would fall silent and, signalling to me with her eyes at the ceiling and walls, she would get a scrap of paper and a pencil; then she would loudly say something very mundane: "Would you like some tea?" or "You're very tanned", then she

would cover the scrap in hurried handwriting and pass it to me. I would read the poems and, having memorized them, would hand them back to her in silence. "How early autumn came this year," Anna Andreevna would say loudly and, striking a match, would burn the paper over an ashtray.

Chukovskaya was not the only person to be granted this dangerous privilege: in October 1962, when Solzhenitsyn's *One Day in the Life of Ivan Denisovich* was on the verge of being legally published in Russia and it seemed only a matter of time before *Requiem* would follow, Akhmatova looked back on the dangers both she and her work had surmounted and told Chukovskaya proudly, "Eleven people knew *Requiem* by heart, and not one of them betrayed me."[23] This sense of solidarity found a reflection in the "Dedication" and "Epilogue" of *Requiem*. The two sections play a crucial role in *Requiem* in that they provide the framework holding together what previously had been a number of individual lyrics written at different times over a period of more than a year. And a key idea in both the "Dedication" and the "Epilogue" is that of the link between the poet and the people: while the poet has the greater responsibility of being the one who speaks for her people, the people also have a responsibility, that of ensuring that the poet is not forgotten:

> And once more the hour of remembrance draws near,
> I see you, I hear you, I feel you all here . . .
>
> Every day, every place, I'll remember them all,
> I'll never forget, though new terrors befall,
>
> And if torturers silence me, through whose one mouth
> A nation of one hundred million cries out,
>
> Let them all speak for me, mention me when they pray
> Every year on the eve of my burial day.

The theme of these lines written in March 1940—memory and commemoration of the dead—was to dominate the poems Akhmatova wrote in that extraordinarily fruitful year. Between March 3 and 10 she wrote "Mayakovsky in 1913," which ignored the ill-fated poet's Soviet accolades to honor his prerevolutionary "stormy youth"; on March 9, she visited Chukovskaya and recited to her the poem "All this you alone will

guess," written in memory of Pilnyak; the news that her friend Mikhail
Bulgakov had died on March 10 after a long illness called forth the poem
"To the Memory of M. A. Bulgakov"; between March 10 and 13 she wrote
The Way of All the Earth (the title is a medieval Russian phrase expressing
the transitory nature of all earthly life, equivalent to the English "the way
of all flesh"). After years of silence, the need to write was so great that the
physical strain was at times almost too much for the fifty–year–old Akh-
matova to bear. She told Chukovskaya, "I don't sleep at all. And all night
long I write. Everything is dying off–I can't walk, can't sleep, can't eat, but
this for some reason remains."[24]

The sense of doom that fed this all–consuming artistic drive to per-
petuate the memory of the dead was driven by more than Akhmatova's
personal losses and her sense of obligation to Stalin's victims. Terrifying
as the shadow of the Gulag was, it lay only upon Russia. Rising beyond
Russia's borders was the Nazi threat–a mortal danger not merely to any
one country, but to Western civilization itself, that civilization of which
the Acmeists had proudly regarded themselves as members.

In March 1939, Germany brought Czechoslovakia under its direct
control, and Great Britain and France responded by declaring they would
regard an attack on Germany's obvious next target, Poland, as tanta-
mount to a declaration of war. It was clear that, if such a war were to break
out, Great Britain and France alone would not be a match for Germany,
but in combination with the Soviet Union they might well have made
Hitler hesitate. Russia, however, carried on noncommittal talks with both
sides until August 23, 1939, when it signed a pact with the Nazis. The
treaty, publicly announced as a nonaggression pact, secretly provided for
the partition of Poland and the Baltic states. On September 1, Germany
invaded Poland, and on September 17, Russian troops occupied the east-
ern portion of Poland, an act for which the public justification offered was
that Russia was there to protect the ethnic Ukrainian and Belorussian
populations in the area. Faced with a hopeless two–front war, organized
Polish resistance collapsed by the end of the month.

In the months that followed, the Soviet Union continued to take the
official position that there was no real difference between the Fascists
and any other capitalist oppressors and to claim the spoils granted by the
Nazi–Soviet pact. Following the stationing of Soviet troops in the still
nominally independent Baltic republics of Lithuania, Latvia, and Estonia,

rigged elections were held to produce pro-Soviet national legislatures. These bodies then "freely" petitioned that their countries be annexed by the USSR, a request to which the Soviets graciously acceded. In the case of Finland, however, this scenario did not unfold so neatly. In October 1939, the USSR presented Finland with demands for an exchange of territories, a measure designed to move the Russian frontier further from Leningrad, and for the stationing of Russian troops at bases in Finland. The Finns recognized the danger of the latter demand to their national independence and refused. On December 1, 1939, the USSR recognized and signed a treaty with the so-called Democratic Republic of Finland, that is, with a self-proclaimed Communist government-in-exile, which the Soviets then proceeded to try to install by force. Given the disparity in the size of the combatants, Russia assumed that the war would be over in two weeks. But the Russian army was in chaos after the purges and unprepared to fight in the harsh northern winter. The Red Army suffered horrendous casualties: two hundred thousand by Moscow's official (and, needless to say, understated) count, including fifty thousand killed. In addition, the David and Goliath aspect of the war was giving the USSR a black eye in international public opinion. Had Stalin chosen to prolong the war, ultimately the force of Russian numbers would have prevailed, but at what from his perspective was an unacceptably high cost. He decided to cut his losses and, in March 1940, agreed to make peace on the basis of a border readjustment favorable to Russia. Unlike the Baltic republics, Finland kept its independence (and would continue to do so throughout the Cold War).

During this conflict, which came to be known as the Winter War, Leningrad, as a frontline city, experienced food shortages and wartime blackout conditions. Aside from the extra burden this added to the already difficult day-to-day existence of the average Leningrader, for those people who, like Akhmatova, were able to look beyond their immediate circumstances it was a disturbing glimpse of what might lie ahead. How much the war was on Akhmatova's mind may be judged by the fact that she referred to the most intense phase of work on *The Way of All the Earth* as having occurred "on the night that Vyborg was stormed and a truce was declared" (March 13).[25]

Meanwhile, after six months of inactivity among the combatants in Western Europe, Hitler suddenly and spectacularly took the offensive. In

April 1940, Germany invaded Denmark and Norway. On May 10, it at-
tacked the Low Countries and France. That same day Neville Cham-
berlain resigned as prime minister of Britain and was succeeded by
Winston Churchill. By the end of June, France was defeated and the Vichy
regime installed. The British had turned a military defeat into a moral
victory with the successful evacuation of their expeditionary force from
Dunkirk, but no one seriously believed that Britain alone would be capa-
ble of standing indefinitely against the power that now dominated the
Continent. Summer, with its long days and mild weather, was the best
season for a cross-channel invasion, and as the Luftwaffe dropped its
bombs on London, the world held its breath, waiting for a German fleet
to land on the English coast. In August 1940, Akhmatova wrote the grim
poem "To the Londoners":

> Time is now writing with impassive hand
> The twenty-fourth of Shakespeare's dramas . . .

But as the best sailing weather passed and the days grew shorter and
colder, still the invasion did not come. The values of European civiliza-
tion were in grave danger, but they were not yet lost. In November 1940,
after the withdrawal from print of Akhmatova's *From Six Books*, Pasternak
wrote an extraordinary letter to her:

> Dear, dear Anna Andreevna,
>   Can I do anything to cheer you up even if only a tiny bit and to
> interest you in further existence in this darkness that has once more
> come over us, whose shadow I feel with a shudder every day over
> myself? How can I do enough to remind you that to live and to want to
> live (not according to someone else's rules, but in your own way) is your
> duty to the living. . . .
>   I don't read newspapers as you know. And now lately when I ask
> what's new in the world I learn of one happy thing and one sad: the
> British are holding out; Akhmatova is being abused. Oh, if only be-
> tween these two bits of news, both equally close to my heart, could exist
> some sort of reciprocity and the sweetness of the one could weaken the
> bitterness of the other![26]

Pasternak had a personal reason to be anxious over the fate of England
because his sisters, who had emigrated after the Revolution, were living

in Oxford. But the first paragraph of his letter makes clear that just as his public concern for Britain had a private aspect, so his private concern for Akhmatova had a public one: like Britain, she was defending something precious to humanity, performing a "duty to the living."

As catastrophe unfolded in Europe, Akhmatova's memories turned to the earlier catastrophe that had destroyed the world of her youth. Nineteen forty awoke the ghosts of 1913, the last year of that era which had gone heedlessly to its end. At the time she was writing "To the Londoners," she also wrote the poem "A Shade," evoking the memory of one of the celebrated beauties of her youth, Salomeya Andronikova, the addressee of a well-known poem by Mandelstam. (Andronikova was in fact not "a shade," being very much alive, but, since she had emigrated, Akhmatova's only image of her was in the vanished past.) Both of these poems would ultimately be included in the cycle "In 1940," which also contained the following lines:

> And what's that distant blurred vision–
> Is it Denmark, Normandy, or
> My own former self arisen,
> And is this a new edition
> Of hours forgot forevermore?

In this frame of mind Akhmatova turned her attention to something she had long neglected–the trunk containing the personal effects and papers that her friend Olga Sudeikina had left behind when she emigrated. Sudeikina had been especially close to Akhmatova in the early 1920s, when they shared an apartment, but they had known each other since the prewar days of the Stray Dog. Olga, who at one time was the wife of the painter Sergei Sudeikin, was celebrated in Petersburg's artistic bohemia not only for her beauty, but also for her gifts as an actress and dancer. If her talent was not of a type that would last through the centuries, it was nevertheless intensely characteristic of its era, and her contemporaries recognized and admired it as such. As Akhmatova looked through Sudeikina's papers, the faded past assumed a vivid reality. Akhmatova wrote years later, "Olga's things . . . suddenly demanded their place under the poetic sun. They came to life for a moment, as it were, but the sound that was left continued to vibrate over many long years."[27]

The first expression of that sound was a verse fragment that Akhmatova read to Chukovskaya on November 13, 1940:

> You came to Russia out of nowhere,
> O my wonder with flaxen hair,
> The Columbine of the nineteen–teens!
> Why show such a troubled and keen–eyed gaze,
> You Petersburg doll, acclaimed on stage–
> You're one of my doubles, another me.
> That's one more title you must append
> To the others. O poets' beloved friend,
> The fame you once had is now my own . . .
>
> Circus wagons pale beside your home,
> Around the altar of Venus go
> Cupids with features pitted and gouged.
> You made your bedroom a garden retreat,
> The people living on your street
> Back home in Pskov wouldn't know you now.
> Golden candlesticks form a glittering line,
> Upon the walls saints in sky blue shine,
> These goods aren't quite stolen, but it's close . . .
> Like Botticelli's "Spring," flower–bedecked,
> You received your lovers in your bed,
> And anguish filled the sentry Pierrot . . .

Chukovskaya enthusiastically declared the fragment to be unlike anything Akhmatova had written before, the start of a new period in her creative life. In fact, it proved to be the beginning of a work that would occupy Akhmatova for more than twenty years: *Poem Without a Hero*. A few weeks later, on the night of December 26–27, Akhmatova wrote the first draft of "The Year 1913," which incorporated the lines cited above; this was to become the first and longest part of the *Poem*. A week later, on January 3–5, 1941, she added the first draft of the *Poem's* second part, "Flip Side."

In the spring of 1941, another figure from the past unexpectedly resurfaced. While Akhmatova was in Moscow pursuing her efforts on Lev's behalf, she received a phone call from Pasternak. He told Akhmatova that Marina Tsvetayeva was in the city and would like to meet her.

Tsvetayeva (born in 1892) was the youngest member of the poetic quartet composed of Akhmatova (born 1889), Pasternak (born 1890), and Mandelstam (born 1891) that dominated twentieth-century Russian poetry. In 1916, Tsvetayeva, a Muscovite, had written a cycle of poems hailing Akhmatova as "the Muse of Tsarskoe Selo." Despite Tsvetayeva's ardent wish to meet Akhmatova, their paths never crossed, and after the Revolution Tsvetayeva had emigrated to rejoin her husband, Sergei Efron, who had fought for the Whites and had left Russia after their defeat.

The years of emigration had been difficult for Tsvetayeva. Neither she nor her husband was well equipped to earn a living, and their daughter Ariadna and son Georgy grew up in poverty and with the consciousness that they were exiles. Of course, had the family stayed in Russia, their situation would have been no better and might have been much worse; but given the mostly positive coverage that the Soviet Union received in the Western press during the 1930s, the émigrés could not know that. A Soviet-sponsored repatriation movement sprung up, Efron being one of its leaders. The Soviets demanded that he prove his loyalty, and he did so by taking part in September 1937 in the murder of Ignace Reiss, a Soviet intelligence agent who had been planning to defect. French police traced the crime to Efron, but by the time they came to arrest him he had fled to the USSR. The twenty-five-year-old Ariadna had established herself in Moscow a few months earlier and had written glowing letters to Paris. Georgy, whom Tsvetayeva idolized and spoiled, constantly nagged at his mother for depriving him of his heritage. And so Tsvetayeva overcame grave doubts, set her literary affairs in order, and in June 1939 returned to the Soviet Union with her son.

Tsvetayeva's life in Russia soon proved more terrible than her worst forebodings. She had hoped to see her younger sister Anastasia, but a year and a half earlier Anastasia had been arrested and sent to the Gulag. In August 1939, Ariadna was arrested, and she spent the next seventeen years of her life in a series of labor camps and remote settlements in Siberia. In November, Sergei Efron was arrested. Tsvetayeva, like Akhmatova, learned what it was to stand in a prison line with a parcel for a family member and to rely upon its acceptance as the only evidence that the addressee was still alive.[28] Many of Tsvetayeva's acquaintances shunned her, fearing that the taint of counterrevolutionism attached to her family might incriminate anyone associated with her. She and her teenage son were reduced to poverty, and it was only through the intercession of Pasternak, who used his connections to help her get work as a translator, that she was able to survive.

Akhmatova had learned of the catastrophe that had overtaken Tsvetayeva and in March 1940, almost a quarter century after Tsvetayeva had dedicated a cycle of poems to her, she responded in her "A Belated Answer," which ended with the lines

> On this day, you and I, Marina,
> Walk the midnight capital together,
> And millions follow upon our trail,
> Marching in a somber, silent line
> As the bells toll a funereal tale,
> As the Moscow blizzard's hollow wail
> Wipes out any trace we left behind.

Now, finally, Akhmatova had the chance to meet her sister–poet and sister–sufferer. Two meetings were hastily set up for June 7 and 8, 1941.

The two poets, unfortunately, were not equipped to understand each other. By temperament, Tsvetayeva was a Romantic, an extremist who held nothing back; Akhmatova, by contrast, valued form, restraint, laconicism. In the years since the Revolution had separated them, their differences had become increasingly pronounced. Following the end of the Russian Civil War, at a time when Akhmatova was writing almost nothing, Tsvetayeva was creating a dazzling body of work much closer in spirit to such poetic innovators as Mayakovsky and the young Pasternak than to the tradition–conscious Akhmatova. As a result, Tsvetayeva's youthful admiration of Akhmatova had been replaced by a much more ambivalent attitude, combining respect for Akhmatova's past achievements with a belief that Akhmatova was repeating herself rather than continuing to develop as a poet. Akhmatova, of course, knew none of this when she and Tsvetayeva met. She was amazed by Tsvetayeva's brilliant and torrential monologue describing her life abroad as well as by her recitation of the poems she had written in emigration. To the friend who hosted the two poets' meeting, Akhmatova confessed that Tsvetayeva made her feel like "a cow" by comparison.[29] Akhmatova, who was slow to reveal her deepest feelings to new acquaintances, did not recite *Requiem* or "A Belated Answer" for Tsvetayeva. Instead, she read *Poem Without a*

Hero, a work whose central theme—the attempt to reclaim and come to terms with a deliberately forgotten past—reflected a historical experience that Tsvetayeva had not shared and did not readily grasp. Akhmatova was disheartened by the meeting, believing that she had proved a disappointment to Tsvetayeva, but she consoled herself with the thought that for Tsvetayeva bitter disappointment was as great an inspiration as passionate admiration. Years later, imagining how Tsvetayeva might have described their meeting, Akhmatova wrote, "Perhaps it would have been the lamentation of a twenty–five–year–old love that turned out to be in vain, but in any case, it would have been magnificent."[30]

Soon after the anticlimactic meeting with Tsvetayeva, Akhmatova returned to Leningrad. She was there, at the Fontanka House, on June 22, 1941, when Foreign Affairs Commissar Molotov made a speech that neither Akhmatova nor anyone else who heard it would ever forget. Hours earlier, Nazi Germany had attacked. Russia was at war.

CHAPTER 5

War and Late Stalinism, 1941–1953

§ § §

FOR RUSSIA, THE SUMMER OF 1941 was catastrophic. Stalin had so thoroughly convinced himself that Hitler would not attack that on the brief midsummer night of June 21–22, when the first desperate phone calls from units actually being fired upon were put through to the Kremlin, Stalin initially assumed the German troops were either firing by mistake or staging some sort of provocation. The failure to respond during those first hours had a terrible cost: by midday on June 22, twelve hundred Soviet planes had been destroyed, eight hundred of them on the ground.[1] The dawning realization that he had a real war on his hands so unnerved Stalin that he was incapable of delivering a public address (Molotov had to make the public announcement of the war's outbreak). With the central government paralyzed, a strong response at the local level was all the more necessary; but the purges had fallen heavily upon those regional leaders, whether civilian or military, who had shown signs of being capable of taking any independent initiative. As a result, the Nazi blitzkrieg at first met essentially no resistance.

Leningrad, like Moscow, was one of the targets of the lightning advance. In the second week of July, a hastily assembled Russian force managed to stop the Germans near the town of Luga, some sixty miles from Leningrad. The Luga defenses held for a month, then crumbled. The

Russians had nothing left to throw into the breach. By the last week of August, the Germans had reached the outlying areas of Leningrad. The imperial summer towns of Pushkin (the former Tsarskoe Selo) and Pavlovsk were seized, their palaces gutted. On August 30, the Nazis took Mga, a small railroad station that acquired a sudden ominous distinction: it had been the one remaining land link between Leningrad and Russian-controlled territory. The city was now completely blockaded by the Germans.

As the enemy approached, Leningrad's civil defenses were prepared. Earthworks were dug in building courtyards to serve as crude bomb shelters. Gas masks were issued. Civilian volunteers were recruited to watch for fires started by German bombing. Akhmatova took part in this duty, standing with her gas mask in hand. Luknitsky, who rarely visited her any more, went to see her on August 25, the twentieth anniversary of Gumilyov's execution. He found her physically unwell but calm and resolute, conscious that she was a participant in a great common ordeal. Yet, she could not be brave indefinitely. She described to her friend Nadezhda Chulkova how during a bombardment she had sat in the trench in the Fontanka House courtyard, holding and comforting a neighbor's young son while trying to control her own terror: "I thought about how badly I had lived my life and that I was not ready to die."[2]

Akhmatova was so unnerved by the shelling that she asked her friends Boris and Irina Tomashevsky if they would take her in, since their apartment building had a proper bomb shelter. On August 31, Tomashevsky came to pick her up and escort her to his apartment. The two were near Mikhailovsky Palace when the air raid siren started up. They ducked into the closest building, found a flight of steps leading downward, and headed for the basement. Then they paused to catch their breath and look around at their refuge and recognized the painted decorations on the walls. The fifty-two-year-old Anna Akhmatova was paying her final visit to the Stray Dog.

In September, to demonstrate the continued defiance of Leningrad's embattled citizens, a series of radio broadcasts was organized. Among those asked to participate was Dmitri Shostakovich, who spoke of his ongoing work on his seventh symphony as proof that the city's life and work were continuing normally. Akhmatova also proudly accepted an invitation to speak, and as one of the most famous women in Russia, she addressed the feminine contribution to the war effort: "I, like all of you now, live in the single unshakeable conviction that Leningrad will never be Fascist. This conviction is strengthened in me when I see the women of Leningrad who simply and courageously defend Leningrad and keep up its ordinary human life. Our descendants will give her due to each mother of the time of the Fatherland War, but their gaze will be especially fixed on the Leningrad woman standing on a roof while bombs are falling, boat–hook and tongs in hand, to defend the city from fire, the Leningrad girl volunteer who gives first aid to the wounded among the still–burning ruins of a building.. . . . No, a city that has bred such women cannot be conquered."

On September 16, the newspaper *Leningradskaya Pravda* carried the headline, "THE ENEMY IS AT THE GATES." The final German assault on the city was expected at any moment. But as the days passed and the attack did not come, the inhabitants of Leningrad began to realize that what Hitler had planned for them was both simpler and more terrible than a direct assault. They were under siege. When the city was blockaded on August 30, it had only limited food reserves available. These had been further reduced during the great air raid of September 8, when incendiary bombs had destroyed the main food warehouses. There was no way to resupply the city. The German army had merely to hold its position and wait for Leningrad to starve to death. The city government desperately tried to stretch its supplies by cutting food rations on September 2 and again on September 12. After the second reduction, the bread ration was 500 grams a day (454 grams is one pound) for a factory worker, 300 grams for office workers and children under twelve, and 250 grams for other dependants. Occasionally food could be found either in state stores or in farmers' markets, but the bread ration was the only food supply people received regularly. On September 25, Nikolai Punin noted in his diary that some of his acquaintances had grown so thin he barely recognized them, and many seemed to have become old and gray within days.

Faced with this catastrophe, the Soviet leadership decided to save at least the city's most prominent cultural figures by flying them out on military planes. Alexander Fadeyev, the secretary of the Writers' Union, was ordered to draw up a list of those writers who should be evacuated. The list was then reviewed by Stalin personally. Among the writers thus chosen to be spared the city's doom was Akhmatova. She flew out of the city—the first time in her life she was on an airplane—on September 28, carrying with her Shostakovich's manuscript of the seventh symphony (the composer himself was evacuated on the next flight). She left behind both Punin, who fatalistically made no effort to flee, and her beloved Vladimir Garshin, who felt that as a doctor his place was in the front lines.

The flight to Moscow was only the beginning of a lengthy journey. The capital itself was in danger from the advancing Germans, and both refugees and crucial industries were being evacuated well behind the lines, to Central Asia and Siberia. On October 15, a day of panic in Moscow, when many feared that the city's fall was inevitable, Akhmatova joined a group of writers, including Pasternak, who were being evacuated by train to Chistopol, a town on the Kama River in the Urals.

In Chistopol, Akhmatova was met by the faithful Lidia Chukovskaya, who had been living in Moscow when the war broke out and had been evacuated earlier. Chukovskaya told Akhmatova about the last days of Marina Tsvetayeva, who had been evacuated to the small nearby town of Yelabuga. After being subjected to one humiliation after another, including poverty so dire that she applied for a position as a dishwasher at the Writers' Union mess hall and was turned down, Tsvetayeva finally could not bear any more. On August 31, 1941, she hung herself from a hook near the entrance of the hut in which she was staying. She was hastily buried in the local cemetery in a common grave.

Akhmatova had no wish to stay in such an ill-omened place, and because Chukovskaya and her daughter were preparing to evacuate to Tashkent, where her father Kornei Chukovsky was living, it was arranged that Akhmatova would accompany them. The journey was a slow one since refugee trains were frequently sidelined for days to allow passage of troops and military supplies, and the two women did not reach the city until November 9.

In Tashkent, Akhmatova joined in literary activities supporting the war effort. Together with other evacuated writers, she regularly visited hospitals and gave poetry readings for the wounded soldiers. Often she would recite the love lyrics of her youth—poems that at first could seem a strange choice to recite to men who had seen comrades die and themselves had lost arms or legs, but that brought comfort precisely because they spoke of a world in which people could still experience emotions other than fear and horror. Eduard Babayev, a Tashkent teenager whose love of poetry drew him to Akhmatova, recalled overhearing a sergeant with his arms in traction telling his friends, "Hey, guys, it's too bad you came late. There was a sister here . . ." "What kind of sister?" "Not from here. . . You don't know her. She told stories in song. . ." Babayev passed the sergeant's compliment on to Akhmatova, who was delighted.[3] She also participated in official functions, such as benefit evenings to raise funds for refugee children. On these occasions, she was more likely to read new poems evoking the war effort, such as "The First Long–Range Shelling of Leningrad" and "A deed of glory, with glory begun . . . " The latter poem was inspired by the Russian counteroffensive that stopped the Germans just outside Moscow on December 6, 1941, and then, over the next six weeks, proved the enemy could be defeated by pushing them back.

In February 1942, Akhmatova wrote the most famous of all her patriotic works, "Courage":

> We know what's at stake, and how great the foe's power,
> And what now is coming to pass.
> Every clock shows the same time—it's courage's hour,
> And our courage will hold to the last.
> The bullets can kill us, but cannot deter;
> Though our houses fall, yet we will stand—
> Through it all we will keep you alive, Russian word,
> Mighty language of our Russian land.
> Your sounds will remain pure and free on our tongues,
> To be passed on unfettered through ages to come,
>   Forever!

A correspondent from the capital named Frida Vigdorova quickly picked up the poem, and on March 8, 1942, "Courage" was printed in *Pravda*.

Ironically, this much–heralded poem had nothing Bolshevik about it. It preaches the courage not of "storming fortresses," but of patient endurance—the strength not of the irresistible force, but of the immovable object. This type of courage is traditionally Russian and traditionally feminine (the classic image of Russia is, after all, "Mother Russia"). Equally unrevolutionary is the poem's emphasis on the generational continuity of language and culture—the Russian speech received from the ancestors must be transmitted undefiled to children and grandchildren. The trial of battle had shown that Russian patriotism ran far deeper than any appeal to defend Communism, and "Courage" struck the right chord at a moment when such great tsarist commanders as Alexander Suvorov and Mikhail Kutuzov were once again openly referred to as national heroes, when the old Bolshevik hostility to organized religion was dropped so that Stalin could receive the blessings of the Russian Orthodox Church, and when the most famous military recruiting poster (as well known to Russians as Uncle Sam is to Americans) showed a stern, gray-haired woman, her face filled with just wrath, and the slogan "The Motherland calls!"

With the publication of "Courage," Akhmatova was in favor. In particular, she developed a friendship of sorts with Alexei Tolstoy, whose historical novel *Peter I* had gained him recognition as a "Soviet classic." Tolstoy valued Akhmatova's work insofar as it was politically safe to do so. Akhmatova regarded him as a scoundrel, but a charming one, and valued his connections with the authorities. Tolstoy's efforts to get Akhmatova to move from the tiny room where she was living into the Tashkent Academics' House failed because she could not afford the rent there, but he was able to get her permission to eat in the dining hall of the Union of Writers. He told her not to be discouraged by the fiasco of *From Six Books* and to try once again to publish a volume of her older poems. The result was *Selected Poems*, which came out in Tashkent in May 1943 in an edition of ten thousand copies.

On March 17, 1942, Akhmatova received a telegram from Nikolai Punin notifying her that he and his family had been evacuated from Leningrad and would be passing through Tashkent en route to Samarkand. What they had experienced was beyond imagining. By November 1941, dozens of people in the blockaded city were dying every day from hunger and hunger-related illnesses; by December, hundreds; by January 1942, several thousand. People collapsed and died on the street, and nobody had the strength to take the bodies away. People died in their dark, unheated apartments, and their surviving relatives wrapped their bodies in sheets, loaded them onto children's sleighs, and hauled them off to mass graves. The city's suffering was intensified by a winter that even by Russian standards was exceptionally harsh, the first snowfall coming in mid-October. But the harsh winter was also the city's only hope. By the beginning of December, the ice on nearby Lake Ladoga, which was still in Russian hands, was thick enough to support the weight of a truck convoy. Food began to be trucked in, and the sick and dying to be taken out. The Road of Life, as this improvised and risky supply line came to be called, could not possibly meet the needs of a city of some two million people and could barely keep the city supplied even at starvation levels. Nevertheless, without it no one in Leningrad would have lived through that winter.

On February 19, 1942, Nikolai Punin, Anna Ahrens–Punina, and Irina Punina and her two–year–old daughter, Anna Kaminskaya, were evacuated from Leningrad on the Road of Life. (Irina's husband, Genrikh Kaminsky, had gone to the front early in the war, and Punin's third wife, Marta Golubeva, chose not to join the household.) Punin's brother Alexander had died of starvation eleven days before, and Punin himself was dying of dystrophy. The long, slow trek of the evacuation was an added ordeal. Three times little Anna's fur overcoat caught fire from the stoves that passengers on the train used to cook and keep themselves warm.[4]

By the time the evacuees reached Tashkent, the Central Asian spring was in bloom. As their train pulled in, they saw Akhmatova waiting for them on the platform, holding a bouquet of white flowers. After everything that the household had been through, their former quarrels were put aside: Punin remembered Akhmatova at that moment as "kind and tender, as she never had been before."[5] The train was scheduled to stay in Tashkent for three days, and Akhmatova insisted that the Punins come to her home. Punin was too sick to walk, but Anna Ahrens and Irina Punina accepted the invitation. Without any announcement, however, the train's departure time was moved up, and the two women found themselves stranded in Tashkent without any ration coupons. It was only through Akhmatova's efforts that they were able to obtain food and tickets to Samarkand.

During Punin's long convalescence in the hospital in Samarkand, he wrote to Akhmatova. The letter read in part,

> Hello, Anya,
>
>   I am infinitely grateful for your concern and touched by it–I have not deserved it. . . . The realization that I am still alive brings me to a rapturous state and I call this–the feeling of happiness. Moreover, when I was dying . . . I also felt that rapturous happiness. At that time particularly I thought a lot about you. This was because in the intensity of

the spiritual experience I was going through there was something . . .
akin to the feeling alive in me in the twenties when I was with you. It
seemed to me, that for the first time I understood you so fully and
comprehensively–and it was just because it was so completely un-
selfish, as I, of course, did not expect ever to see you again. It was really a
meeting and farewell before death. And it seemed to me then that I
knew of no other person whose life was so whole and therefore so
perfect as yours, from your first childish poems . . . to the prophetic
murmur, and at the same time, roar, of the *Poema.* I thought then that this
life was perfect not through will, but–and this seemed to me to be
particularly precious–through its organic wholeness, that is, its inev-
itability, which seems somehow not to have anything to do with you.
Now I cannot express all that I thought then, but a great deal of what I
could not forgive in you stood before me, not only forgiven, but some-
thing right and wonderful.[6]

Akhmatova kept the letter as one of her most cherished possessions.

The experience of evacuation and the ordeal of Leningrad formed the
background for the final part of *Poem Without a Hero*, the first draft of
which was completed in Tashkent on August 18, 1942. The wartime evac-
uation had transformed Tashkent from a backwater into an intellectual
capital, and Akhmatova had no difficulty finding sympathetic listeners.
One of them was Jozef Czapski, a Polish reserve army officer who in
September 1939 found himself in the eastern, Russian–occupied part of
Poland, where the entire Polish officer corps was promptly arrested by
the Soviet secret police. Many of them were never seen again; the sur-
vivors wound up in labor camps in Siberia, from which they were re-
leased after the Nazi invasion of Russia so that they could join a Polish
army being formed in Central Asia to serve with the British forces in Iran.
Czapski's translations of Polish resistance poetry into Russian impressed
Akhmatova, and she responded by reading *Poem Without a Hero* to him.
Czapski, who was familiar with officially sponsored Soviet propaganda
poetry, was stunned by the difference between its clichés and Akhma-
tova's work: "Akhmatova's poem was the only work that deeply moved
me and made me feel the true meaning of the defense of the crushed,
starving, heroic city."[7]

Akhmatova's contacts with Czapski, however, were limited because he
was still under supervision by the NKVD and did not wish to compromise
her. A friend whom she was able to see more freely was Bulgakov's widow,

Yelena, who allowed Akhmatova to read *The Master and Margarita,* the brilliant, disturbing novel her husband had finished in the last months of his life. Other companions were Nadezhda Mandelstam, who from mid–1943 on lived in a room directly under Akhmatova's; and a new acquaintance, the actress Faina Ranevskaya. Ranevskaya had a genius for black comedy, a genre not encouraged in Soviet film but one that Akhmatova was fully equipped to appreciate, and the two women became almost inseparable. Ranevskaya's flamboyant temperament and bohemian lifestyle evoked the disapproval of the deeply earnest Chukovskaya, and, sadly, the resulting friction led to a breach between her and Akhmatova that would not be healed for years. Mandelstam, too, felt that Akhmatova was perhaps enjoying her new popularity a bit too much, but she was more able to reconcile herself both to it and to Ranevskaya.

But there was one person dear to Akhmatova about whose fate she knew nothing–Vladimir Garshin. Throughout the entire blockade winter, she received no letters from or news of him, and she became increasingly convinced that he had died. Not until May 1942 did she finally get a postcard from him. Garshin was in relatively good health physically, at least by Leningrad standards, but had suffered psychologically. As a specialist, he had been made the city's chief coroner, a job that put him at the very center of the city's agony. On February 19, 1942, he told Akhmatova's friends the Tomashevskys that his office had registered 650,000 reported deaths from hunger (no one knew how many unreported ones there were).[8] Garshin had simply been too overwhelmed and depressed to write, and throughout the summer of 1942 his letters came infrequently.

In October 1942, Garshin's wife, Tatyana Vladimirovna, collapsed and died on the street. When her body was found, her husband had to identify it by her clothing, as her face had been gnawed by rats. Garshin was deeply shaken and sent a telegram to Akhmatova. A month later, Akhmatova became seriously ill with typhus and was admitted to a special official ward of the Tashkent Medical Institute. When the news reached Garshin, he responded with several telegrams expressing concern for Akhmatova's health, and after her recovery the two began a regular correspondence. In April 1943, Garshin wrote to his son at the front, "I am greatly comforted by the letters of my dear friend A. A. Akhmatova. . . . You and she are the only ones I write to."[9]

Sometime in the first part of 1943, Garshin sent Akhmatova a letter proposing marriage. He wrote to a friend, "Don't pass judgment on me, I can't live without Anna Andreyevna, I'm inviting her to Leningrad, don't pass judgment that so soon after Tatiana Vladimirovna's death I want to be united with Anna Andreyevna."[10] Garshin, who was living at the hospital where he worked, had been promised a new apartment in a building under construction. There he hoped to find a domestic haven after the ordeal of war, to start a new life with Akhmatova. In a gesture emphasizing his desire for the emotional comfort of a traditional family life, Garshin made his proposal conditional on Akhmatova's legally taking his name (which she had not done for either Shileiko or Punin). Akhmatova not only agreed, but was even pleased by the idea. She was over fifty and had never experienced ordinary domestic happiness; it would not be surprising if the wish for it suddenly proved irresistible.

But in the Soviet Union one could not simply pack one's belongings and travel where one wanted. Akhmatova could not return to Leningrad without a permit, and since she had been evacuated through Moscow, she also needed a permit to return there. In October, while waiting for the paperwork to come through, she came down with scarlet fever and was seriously ill for three weeks. She recovered and then, in December, became ill again with a severe case of flu, no doubt complicated by her weakened condition and her tuberculosis-damaged lungs. Akhmatova was still in Tashkent on January 27, 1944, when a 324–cannon salute was fired over Leningrad to celebrate the end of the blockade, 880 days after it had begun with the fall of Mga.

At the end of January, Akhmatova was summoned once again to the Tashkent train station to meet the Punin household, now returning from Samarkand to Leningrad. Of the four who had been evacuated, only three were returning. Punin, who had been near death when he reached Samarkand, had actually recovered after a long stay in the hospital there. But Anna Ahrens–Punina, who had been steadfast and hardworking through all the family's ordeals, finally reached the end of her strength and in August 1943, after a brief illness, died of sheer exhaustion. The family had also suffered the loss of Irina Punina's husband, Genrikh Kaminsky, who had been arrested at the front as the result of a political denunciation and had died in the camp of Taishetlag in 1943. Punin later described the meeting in Tashkent in his diary: "On the 16th [of January] we got on the train. For four days and nights we sat in Samarkand due to every kind of problem. In Tashkent we stopped again; Anya (An.) came in a car. In a fur hat. Gray hair; kind. She gave Anichka a little dog, gave Ira soap, gave me cigarettes."[11]

In March 1944 Akhmatova received a letter from her son Lev, whom she had not heard from in seven months. The previous year his prison term at Norilsk had ended, and although he had not been allowed to return to European Russia, he had been able to obtain work as a technician on a geological expedition in Siberia. He was in good spirits and hoped to be allowed to go to Tashkent to continue his formal education.

While Lev was trying to get to Tashkent, his mother was still trying to leave. Her Moscow permit had finally come through, but that for her ultimate goal, Leningrad, was still delayed. Finally, in mid–May 1944, Akhmatova flew from Tashkent to Moscow, where she spent two weeks with friends before returning to her beloved city. For that brief period, everything seemed hopeful: the war would soon be over, Lev was alive and safe, and she and Garshin would be united. One acquaintance of Akhmatova's wrote that she had never seen Akhmatova so happy as she was then.[12]

Akhmatova took the train from Moscow on May 31 and arrived in Leningrad the next day. Garshin was waiting for her at the station, but the romantic reunion was cut short by his awkward question, "Where shall I take you?" The promised apartment, he explained, was still under construction. It was agreed that she would stay with their mutual friends, the Rybakov family. Garshin visited her there every day for two weeks. Then one day, Olga Rybakova recalled, "I heard Anna Andreyevna give a shriek. The conversation broke off. Garshin quickly emerged from her room, dashed across the dining room and made a hasty exit."[13]

Akhmatova never saw Garshin again. Memoirists who knew Akhmatova wrote with awe of her capacity for fury, and her conduct toward Garshin fully justifies their description. She refused every effort of his to contact her, destroyed his letters to her, then sent Lidia Rybakova to Garshin to ask him to return the letters she had written him, which she also destroyed. She revised the dedication to the epilogue of *Poem Without a Hero*, "To my city and my love," so that subsequent versions were dedicated only "To my city." The lines of the epilogue that were addressed to

Garshin were not removed, but their earlier positive sense was revised to a negative one. To explain the breakup, Akhmatova told her friends that Garshin was suffering from mental illness, and in a poem from 1945, she imagined him wandering Leningrad's back streets "stupefied by insanity, teeth bared like a wolf." At the time he was actually working as a respected professor of pathology.

Akhmatova never displayed such implacableness toward any of her other ex-lovers (or, for that matter, her ex-husbands). One can conclude only that, from her perspective, Garshin had failed her in some remarkably drastic way. A story sprang up that Akhmatova had returned to Leningrad only to find that in her absence Garshin had married a young nurse. In fact, Garshin did not remarry until early 1945, and his new wife, Dr. Kapitolina Volkova, was the same age as Akhmatova. The Garshin of 1944 "betrayed" Akhmatova not by being unfaithful to her, but by no longer being the man she remembered from the prewar years. In the late 1930s, whenever she needed him, he had always been there, ready to offer his unconditional support. But in 1944, Garshin no longer had the strength to help Akhmatova; he was in need of help himself after his experiences during the blockade. He told two of his friends that he had experienced hallucinations in which he saw his dead wife, who forbade him to marry Akhmatova. To a modern westerner, such hallucinations would seem an understandable manifestation of survivor guilt, but in Soviet Russia psychological trauma was not a subject of study or discussion, and if Akhmatova had learned of these visions, they could have been the basis for her assertions that he was mentally unbalanced. Even if Garshin did not speak to Akhmatova about his psychological turmoil, she must have realized that their relationship was not the same as it had been. She took his inability to cope with her needs as a deliberate insult and broke off the relationship once and for all. After a difficult later life, Garshin died, still unforgiven by Akhmatova, in 1956.

The breakup with Garshin also meant the end of Akhmatova's hopes for a home of her own. There was nowhere for her to go except back to the Punin household at the Fontanka House. The awkwardness of her resumed life there was somewhat mitigated by the presence of five-year-old Anna Kaminskaya. In urban Soviet families, grandmothers often played a significant role, assisting their working daughters with child care. Because little Anna's maternal grandmother was dead and because

Akhmatova had no children of her own, she wound up assuming a quasi-grandmotherly role in the little girl's life.

About her own child Akhmatova had no news until February 1945, when a visiting friend of hers, the painter Alexander Osmyorkin, passed on a story he had heard secondhand that Lev had joined a penal battalion. Such battalions were sent to the most dangerous positions on the battlefield with the understanding that any survivors would be rewarded with a legal clean slate. Punin noted in his diary how horrified Akhmatova was by this report:

> She sat on the bed and began bitterly to lament her fate. I had not seen her in such grief in a long time. "What do they want from me, from me, and from Leva . . . they won't be happy until they kill him and me. The penal battalion is execution, for the second time he has been sentenced to execution. . . . What did my boy see? He was never a counterrevolutionary . . . He is capable, young, full of strength. They envy him, and now they're using the fact that he is the son of Gumilev . . . As they made me Gumilev's widow . . ."[14]

The rumor proved true: in late 1944, Gumilyov, tired of the legal disabilities that seemed likely to bar him permanently from taking up residence in any major city or attending any university, enlisted in a penal brigade. As his participation in geological expeditions had shown, Lev was inclined to a physically active life and was not readily put off by hardships. Like his father, he developed a taste for war, and in a letter of April 1945 wrote to Emma Gershtein, "So far I've been successful at soldiering: I've been in attacks, taken cities, drunk hard liquor, eaten chickens and ducks, I especially liked the jam; the Germans, trying to stop me, fired their artillery at me a few times, but missed. I like fighting, it's a lot more boring in the rear."[15] Fortune, in this case, favored the brave: Lyova made it alive and well to Berlin. There he waited with mounting impatience until September 1945, when he was demobilized. It took him two more months to get home. The night he arrived at the Fontanka House, Punin noted, Akhmatova was seized by "a strange excitement; she ran all around the apartment and wept noisily."[16]

As a returning frontline soldier, Lev could legally claim a living space of his own. The prewar inhabitants of the apartment adjoining the Punins' were no longer there, and Akhmatova had been able to get one of their rooms added on to her part of the Punin apartment. This room was now turned over to her son. At age thirty-three, Lev was in a hurry to make up lost time. He enrolled in the history department of Leningrad University as an external student and within ten months had passed the exams for his fourth and fifth years of study (Soviet universities typically conferred a diploma after five years). This peaceful period in his life–a peace that, sadly, was not destined to last long–was also one of the times when he was closest to his mother.

Lev's return was not the only significant event in Akhmatova's life that November. On the night of November 15–16, she formed a brief but profoundly influential relationship with Isaiah Berlin, the "guest from the future" of *Poem Without a Hero*. In the second half of 1945, Berlin, who had been born in Riga in 1909 and whose family had emigrated to England after the Revolution, was serving temporarily at the British embassy in Moscow. He was not a diplomat by training, but an intellectual who before the war had been a lecturer at Oxford. He was thus able to converse as an equal with Russian intellectuals, who during the increasingly paranoid 1930s had been cut off from virtually all contact with Western cultural life and were avid to hear a Western perspective. The isolation had worked both ways, and Western knowledge of the fate of those Russian literary figures who were not in favor with the Soviet regime was equally fragmentary. When, during a visit to Leningrad in November 1945, an acquaintance offered to introduce Berlin to Akhmatova, he was astonished to learn that a figure whom he thought of as a writer from the World War I period was still alive. "It was," he recalled, "as if I had suddenly been invited to meet Miss Christina Rossetti."[17]

A meeting was promptly set up at the Fontanka House. The conversation between Berlin and Akhmatova had barely gotten past the pleasantries when Berlin realized, to his astonishment, that he could hear someone in the building courtyard repeatedly shouting his name. The person calling him in so conspicuous a manner turned out to be none other than Randolph Churchill, the prime minister's son, whom Berlin had known at Oxford. Churchill, who was working as a journalist, had just arrived in Leningrad, and when he had learned that his acquaintance Isaiah Berlin was also there, had decided to track him down. Apparently it never occurred to the young Churchill that in Stalin's Russia the son of the prime minister of a foreign country would be followed by agents of the secret police and thus would draw extremely unhealthy attention to any Russian unlucky enough to be in his path.Berlin left Akhmatova's apartment as quickly as possible–though not quickly enough, as it would later appear.

After telephoning Akhmatova and explaining what had happened, Berlin returned that night. Akhmatova, realizing that Berlin had grown up in the Russian emigration, asked him what he knew of the fate of her friends from prerevolutionary days who were living abroad. He did indeed know some of the important figures from her past. They talked about Artur Lourie, with whom she and Olga Sudeikina had lived a quarter century ago, and the former Petersburg beauty Salomeya Andronikova Halpern, the inspiration for the poem "A Shade" in Akhmatova's cycle of poems *In 1940*. And, although Berlin did not actually know Boris Anrep, who almost thirty years before had crossed the frozen Neva on foot so that he could avoid the revolutionary patrols while visiting Akhmatova, nevertheless the visitor could give Akhmatova some information about her former lover, since after leaving Russia for England, Anrep had gone on to become a celebrated mosaicist.

One can only imagine the emotional impact on Akhmatova as her guest spoke of people dear to her who now belonged to a past so far off, so unlike her present, as to seem almost a dream, and by his words affirmed that she had not imagined it, that all of them really existed, that all of it had really occurred. And in return Akhmatova opened her heart to him, telling this man whom she had just met about things that she otherwise would mention only to her oldest and most trusted friends. She read *Poem Without a Hero* and *Requiem* to him, told him about her life with Gumilyov and his execution as well as about the fate of Mandelstam, whom she considered the greatest poet of her generation. She asked Berlin about his personal life. Feeling he did not have the right to hold himself back from the woman who had revealed herself to him so completely, Berlin answered without hesitation. The words flowed unceasingly, going from the most intimate details of both his and his wife's lives to discussions of art and literature and back again. It was late the following morning when Berlin finally left.

For Berlin, that night was an unforgettable experience, but also an isolated one. He felt the deepest respect and sympathy for Akhmatova both as a great artist and an extraordinarily dignified and courageous woman–"like a princess in exile," he would write later[18]–but he certainly had no sense that his life had been fundamentally changed because of their meeting.

For Akhmatova, however, the meeting had far greater significance. The fact that through no effort of her own she had suddenly and completely unexpectedly come into contact with someone who was a total stranger to her yet intimately connected with the seemingly lost world of her past–to Akhmatova, such an improbable, unsought-for turn of events had the aura of Fate. She and Berlin were destined for each other. Believing in the prophetic power of her poetry, she was convinced that she had foreseen his coming, that he was the awaited guest mentioned in the first lines of "The Year 1913." Indeed, she came to believe that their meeting was of world-historical significance, that it was one of the causes of the Cold War. While a westerner is likely to find such a belief implausible and seek the causes for historical events in politics or economics rather than literature, Akhmatova's perspective is understandable as that of a writer in a country in which poetry was a matter of state– in which, as Mandelstam said, people were killed for it.

Berlin did not see Akhmatova again until he was leaving the Soviet Union, which he did by way of Leningrad and Helsinki. The second meeting, on the afternoon of January 5, 1946, was a brief one, a simple good-by. Akhmatova presented her guest with a book of her poetry which had a new poem inscribed on its flyleaf. The inscription was from *Cinque*, a cycle of five poems inspired by their meeting. It would be ten years before the two would have any further contact.

Initially, it appeared that Akhmatova's meetings with Berlin, however imprudent (from a Soviet citizen's point of view), would have no serious consequences. For Akhmatova, the first half of 1946 was a period of literary triumph. In March, she signed a contract for the publication of a new volume of her selected poems, which would include a number of her recent works. In April, she was part of a delegation of Leningrad poets invited to Moscow to give public readings. On April 3, her readings in the Hall of Columns received a prolonged standing ovation. A similarly enthusiastic response occurred on August 7, 1946, when as part of the observance of the twenty-fifth anniversary of Blok's death, Akhmatova gave a reading at the Bolshoi Dramatic Theater in Leningrad. An ominous sign was noted by Nadya Mandelstam, who was visiting

Akhmatova at that time: not only did the police agents "tail" them when they went out on walks, but on one occasion, as they entered the court-yard of the Fontanka House, they were photographed in a manner that made no attempt to be covert. But Akhmatova took it all in stride, offering a one–word explanation–"Magnesium"–to her friend, who was temporarily disoriented by the brightness of the camera flash.[19]

Then the thunderbolt fell. On August 14, the Central Committee announced a resolution "on the magazines *Zvezda* (*Star*) and *Leningrad*" that attacked the two magazines for printing "ideologically harmful" works, specifically those of Anna Akhmatova and Mikhail Zoshchenko, a satirist well known for his short stories on the absurdity of everyday Soviet life, many of which were told in the first person by a semieducated philistine, a sort of Russian cross between Babbitt and Archie Bunker. The reasoning (if that word can be used) behind the resolution was further expounded in a speech by Andrei Zhdanov, the Politburo member whose hostile reaction to the publication of Akhmatova's *From Six Books* in 1940 had led to the book being withdrawn from circulation. After Zhdanov derided Zoshchenko at some length as vile and vulgar, he turned to Akhmatova. His outrage was particularly aroused by the concluding lines of a poem Akhmatova had written in the summer of 1921, at the time she left Shileiko:

> But by the angels' garden I swear,
> By the icons that show grace to men,
> By the black fire of the nights we shared–
> I will never come to you again.

After quoting the first three of these lines, Zhdanov borrowed Eikhen-baum's unfortunate description of Akhmatova's lyrical protagonist as "half–nun, half–harlot," then added, "or rather both nun and harlot, mingling fornication and prayer." Akhmatova's poetry was the work of "a half–crazed upper–crust lady running between the boudoir and the chapel."

Party literary critics, of course, had been making this type of attack against Akhmatova since the 1920s. Its renewal in 1946, after her wartime popularity, was due to political considerations. At a time when the anti-Fascist alliance between the USSR and the West had come to an end and the Cold War was beginning, Zhdanov's denunciation was directed against magazines and writers associated with Petersburg/Leningrad, which since its founding had been Russia's "window on the West." And in addition to the abuse directed toward individual writers, *Leningrad* was accused of having shown a "spirit of servility before everything foreign" and of having failed to properly recognize the superiority of Soviet literature. In this context, Akhmatova's meeting with a British diplomat, a friend of the son of the archfiend Churchill himself, might well have roused Stalin's anger. Soviet cultural policy was also involved: during the war, cultural repression had been eased somewhat in a conscious effort to rally as many sectors of society as possible behind the war effort. From Stalin's point of view, such a temporary liberalization needed to be quashed as publicly as possible lest any intellectuals start hoping it represented a permanent change.

Akhmatova's popularity may also have been taken as a personal affront by Stalin, whose megalomania was increasing over the years. Akhmatova herself understood that it would not do for anyone besides the Leader to be too publicly conspicuous: in response to the crowd's demands for encores at her Hall of Columns reading, she fumbled with her glasses, shuffled her manuscript pages, and finally refused altogether, saying, "I don't know my poems by heart and I have no more with me." Her self-effacing behavior, however, had not been enough to deflect official wrath, if one is to believe a story that went the rounds at the time, claiming that Stalin had asked, "Who organized this standing ovation?"– a question that, as Pasternak noted, would have been completely in character. Akhmatova herself later remarked on a photograph that had been taken of her and Pasternak at that time, "Here I am earning the Central Committee Resolution."[20]

Immediately following Zhdanov's attack, the entire printing of a new collection of Akhmatova's poems that was awaiting distribution to the bookstores was seized and destroyed. The only copies that survived were a few that had been pilfered by press workers, leading Nadezhda Mandelstam to observe, "One can regard it as having appeared in an edition of twenty copies. We live in a country where editions can be fabulously large or fabulously small."[21] On September 4, Akhmatova was expelled from the Union of Soviet Writers. Because now she was officially not a writer, she was no longer entitled to a writer's ration cards for bread and other foodstuffs (which were still difficult to obtain in the postwar years), although ultimately she was allowed to have a single ration card. Years later, remembering that time, Akhmatova jotted in a notebook, "I clinically starved four times: I–1918–1921, II–1928–1932 (rationing, food shortages), III–the war, in Tashkent, IV–after the C[entral] C[ommittee] decree of 1946."[22]

In this crisis, although many of Akhmatova's acquaintances literally crossed the street when they saw her to avoid compromising themselves, her true friends rallied around her. Nina Olshevskaya collected money for Akhmatova from her friends in Moscow, while Irina Tomashevskaya did the same thing in Leningrad. Pasternak visited Akhmatova and slipped one thousand rubles under her pillow. Slowly, as it became clear that no worse measures were contemplated against her and that she could survive this danger, her spirits rose. An acquaintance of hers who was also a secret police informer submitted this report:

> The subject, Akhmatova, took the Resolution hard. She was sick for a long time: neurosis, heart problems, arrhythmia, furunculosis. But outwardly she was courageous and cheerful. She says that unknown people send her flowers and fruits. No one turned away from her. No one betrayed her. "It only increased my fame," she said, "the fame of a martyr. . . . Even those who never heard of me before will read me. . . . They should have given me a dacha, my own car, special rations, but quietly prohibited the publishing houses from printing my work, and, I swear, in a year the government would have gotten the results it wanted. Everybody would have said: 'Look, she's started pigging out [*zazhralas'*], thinks she's so special.' . . . Then they would have stopped reading my poems, and I would have been pursued to the grave and beyond by contempt and oblivion."[23]

As she had done in the 1930s, during her earlier period of banishment from officially recognized literature, Akhmatova turned to her studies of Pushkin for inspiration and comfort. In April 1947, she finished an article on Pushkin's "little tragedy" *The Stone Guest*, a treatment of the Don Juan legend. She also worked on a study of Pushkin and Dostoyevsky that she destroyed in 1949, fearing that in the wrong hands it would serve as incriminating evidence.

As the months passed, slowly the amount and volume of anathema directed against Akhmatova by the press, whether in the form of attacks by literary critics or letters to the editor supposedly written by outraged factory workers, began to diminish. In the summer of 1948, through Pasternak's intercession, Akhmatova was quietly granted a sick benefit of three thousand rubles from the Literary Fund. The following winter she was commissioned to translate into Russian the letters of Alexander Radishchev, a late eighteenth-century intellectual who, like many educated Russians of his era, habitually wrote in French. The choice of Akhmatova for this task had a certain piquancy, since Radishchev had also experienced official disgrace, including six years of exile in Siberia. But since he was posthumously claimed by Russian revolutionaries as an intellectual ancestor, this was, from a political point of view, a thoroughly safe assignment. Its successful completion opened the door for further work in this field. For the next decade, Akhmatova would earn her living as a translator, concentrating on the poetry of the smaller Soviet nationalities (including Ossetian, Armenian, Georgian, and Tatar) and of other Communist countries (including Korean, Chinese, Rumanian, and Czech). Needless to say, Akhmatova did not know all of these languages. She followed the common Soviet practice of relying upon a linguist to give her a word-for-word translation and using her own poetic sense to turn this into a literary rendition. Even in the humble capacity of translator, however, the name of Akhmatova could not be allowed to sully Soviet literature: until 1956, her translations were published anonymously.

The resolution against Akhmatova and Zoshchenko turned out to be the opening sally in a new campaign to enforce cultural conformity. Soviet composers, among them Dmitri Shostakovich and Sergei Prokofiev, were denounced for writing music inaccessible to the masses. Propaganda paintings depicting heroic builders of socialism were declared by party critics to be superior to anything being produced by decadent Western art.

Punin, whose specialty as a critic and professor was modern art, found himself in an increasingly precarious position. In March 1949, he was dismissed from his position as professor of art history at Leningrad State University "as someone who could not ensure the ideological-political education of the student body."[24] On August 26, 1949, the sixty-year-old Punin was arrested. When the arrest was made, Akhmatova was the only other person in the apartment; Punin's daughter and granddaughter were out of town on vacation. He was allowed to leave them a brief note: "I kiss you, all three of you. I haven't lost hope. Papa." They would never see him again.

On November 6, 1949, Lev Gumilyov was rearrested, once again the victim of official displeasure with his family. In August 1946, he had been on the verge of receiving his university diploma when the Central Committee resolution against Akhmatova and Zoshchenko was announced. As a result, he was not allowed to continue his graduate work and was officially reprimanded by the university's party organization for indifference to social concerns. To get this black mark off his record, he took community service jobs in a mental hospital and a library. By the end of 1948, when the furor over the resolution had died down somewhat, he was allowed to defend his dissertation. But before he could receive his degree, Punin's arrest struck another blow against him. In addition to being accused of "grovelling before the bourgeois art of the West," Punin was charged on the basis of the old case of 1935. There was some awkwardness about this in that Punin had been released on the direct intervention of Stalin himself. By a convenient fiction, however, the intervention was ascribed to Yagoda, the then-minister of internal affairs who was subsequently proclaimed an "enemy of the people" and whose dismissal of the case could thus be ignored. But since Lev had also been involved in the 1935 case and had been released at the same time Punin had, it naturally followed that if Punin's release had been inappropriate, so had Lev's.

When the agents showed up at the Punins' apartment to arrest Lev, Akhmatova was so distraught she collapsed in a faint. Irina Punina helped Lev to gather up the few necessities he was allowed to take with him to jail. This time, instead of being imprisoned in Leningrad, he was taken to Lefortovo Prison in Moscow. Even by the standards of Stalinist prisons, Lefortovo had an especially evil reputation: interrogators at other prisons used the threat of a transfer to Lefortovo as a way to obtain confessions. Lev's experiences there started with his interrogator shouting at him, "You're guilty! In what form would you like to confess it?"[25] Once an interrogator seized him by the hair and banged his head against the wall while demanding that he admit his mother had spied for England—another consequence of Isaiah Berlin's visit.[26]

As Lev's interrogation continued, once again Akhmatova found herself waiting in prison lines to hand in money for her son, reminding herself that by prison rules as long as the money was accepted, its desig-nated recipient was still alive. Because money could be submitted only at the prison in which the recipient was being held, once a month Akhma-tova made the trip from Leningrad to Moscow and back.

In *Requiem*, she had written of "kneeling at the hangman's feet" to beg for mercy for her son. Now, with her duties as a poet–witness and a mother in hopeless conflict, she chose the latter. In hopes of helping her son, Akhmatova undertook to write a cycle of verses on the politically acceptable topic of postwar Socialist reconstruction. These verses, en-titled *Hail to Peace*, appeared in the magazine *Ogonyok* (*Little flame*) from May to July 1950. *Hail to Peace* did not save Lyova, who was duly sentenced to ten years' imprisonment. It may well, however, have saved Akhmatova herself. Such, at least, was the opinion of Punin, expressed in a letter from a labor camp.[27]

One of Akhmatova's few comforts in this difficult period was her increasingly close friendship with Nina Olshevskaya–Ardova. For years, Olshevskaya and her family had served as Akhmatova's hosts when she was in Moscow, and now Nina also took it upon herself to look after the increasingly fragile Akhmatova, who in May 1951 suffered a heart attack. Olshevskaya suggested even that Akhmatova move permanently to Moscow. But too much of Akhmatova's life was bound up with Peters-burg/Leningrad, and she did not want to leave. When she was in Len-ingrad, Akhmatova was largely dependent on her stepdaughter, Irina Punina. At the end of 1951, Akhmatova and Punina were told they would have to move out of the Fontanka House because the Arctic Institute, which occupied part of the building, wanted to expand. Punina, her second husband, and her daughter were offered an apartment of their own, an arrangement that would have left Akhmatova in a vulnerable position, isolated among strangers (which may have been an underlying motive for the eviction). Punina refused to break up the household, and after a prolonged bureaucratic struggle an apartment for all of them was found on Krasnaya Konnitsa (Red cavalry) street, near the Smolny Cathedral.

One day in early March 1953, a part-time houseworker for the Punins entered and announced, "They said on the radio that Stalin's sick." Akh-matova, no doubt suspecting that the woman was an informer testing how she would react, promptly replied, "What rubbish! Our old woman's gone out of her mind. It can't be, and what's more, they wouldn't say that on the radio. Stalin never gets sick and nothing can ever happen to him."[28] Nevertheless, the radio was immediately turned on, and what Akhmatova and Punina heard was enough to make them leave it on for the next several days. As the Leader's condition worsened, the medical bulletins became increasingly explicit, in an attempt to prepare the population for the previously unimaginable event of his death. The final bulletin before Stalin's death, announcing that there was albumen in his urine, called forth Akhmatova's sarcastic rejoinder, "It's unbelievable: a divinity, a being who dwells in some heaven on high–and suddenly he's got urine, there's albumen in his urine!"

On March 5, 1953, Stalin died, and an era came to an end.

CHAPTER 6

Late Fame and Final Years, 1953–1966

§ § §

T HE SURVIVING MEMBERS of the Politburo, simply by the fact that they had outlived Stalin, had proved two things: they were not overly burdened with scruples, but they were also no fools. They understood that a relaxation of the Stalinist terror was necessary, not on any humanitarian grounds but simply because the terror was squandering the nation's economic and intellectual resources. Yet such a change of course was not so simple. They owed their positions to Stalin and feared that any serious attack on his reputation would weaken their own legitimacy.

Their first move was a characteristic one: in July 1953, Lavrenty Beria, the head of the MGB (the secret police, formerly the NKVD), was arrested. From the viewpoint of the other members of the Politburo, this killed two birds with one stone. Not only did it remove someone who, by the nature of his position, was a potential threat to all of them; it also allowed them to heap blame upon him as the person supposedly responsible for the worst policies of Stalin's later years and thus provided political cover for them to change those policies. In December 1953, Beria's execution was announced. He was the last figure of his rank to be executed. The political elite had tired of fratricide, and in future those of its members who fell into disgrace would merely be forced into retirement.

The slight but perceptible easing of repression encouraged Akhmatova to undertake a new round of meetings with literary, cultural, and political figures in the hopes of bringing sufficient influence to bear on Lev's behalf so that his case would be reopened. During these efforts, in May 1954, she was exposed to a deeply painful humiliation. Some twenty British students who were visiting the Soviet Union decided to test for themselves the rumor that Russian writers did not have complete freedom of speech and accordingly requested an interview with Akhmatova and Zoshchenko. The two writers were duly summoned to answer the students' questions and were asked what they thought of the resolution against them in 1946. (The thought that a Soviet citizen might have good reason not to proclaim his or her opinions in the presence of Soviet officials never occurred to the students.) Zoshchenko tried to save some shred of his dignity by giving a qualified answer, but Akhmatova, thinking of Lev, simply announced that she agreed completely with both the party resolution and Zhdanov's speech. Such public submission on Akhmatova's part was sufficiently noted that she was chosen as a delegate to the Second All-Union Congress of Soviet Writers in December 1954, which enabled her to make further valuable contacts. But with Zhdanov's speech still being required reading in every Soviet literature course, it would require powerful patronage indeed to help Akhmatova's son. Lev's health was beginning to break from the rigors of the prison camp, and in 1955 he was in and out of the hospital. Punin had lived to see Stalin's death but had died in a camp in August 1953. Akhmatova must have wondered if the same fate would befall her son.

Then, in February 1956, a thunderbolt fell. For the past two and a half years the first secretary of the Communist Party, Nikita Khrushchev, had been steadily placing his allies in key positions and consolidating his power. Now he was ready to make a bold move. At the Twentieth Congress of the Communist Party, Khrushchev gave his famous "secret speech" denouncing Stalin. The criticisms of Stalin that Lenin had made during the last months of his life and that had been suppressed after his death were finally disclosed; it was admitted that torture had been used against arrested party members to compel them to confess, and some of their final appeals to Stalin (who they still pathetically believed was being misled by those around him) were read out; Russia's ghastly losses in the first months following the German invasion of 1941 were declared to be the result of Stalin's military ignorance and incompetence. In Khrushchev's version of party history, good Communists had been aware all along of Stalin's wrongful actions but were powerless to stop him because the party's role in setting policy had been completely subordinated to what Khrushchev delicately called "the cult of personality"—the constant public glorification of Stalin as the greatest genius in human history. As a result, Stalin had not faced the strictures placed upon Lenin, who (though not answerable to the population at large) had been required to justify his policies to his party comrades.

Although Khrushchev's speech was originally given at a closed gathering, its contents were too sensational to be kept secret for long; and in any event some form of justification would have to be offered to the general public for what was clearly becoming a massive shift in public policy. Throughout 1954 and 1955, a number of political prisoners had been released after their cases had been reopened and they had been declared wrongfully convicted. After February 1956, this stream became a flood. When Akhmatova or her friends visited the prosecutor's office to ask about Lev's case, instead of the arrogance or hostility with which they had previously been received, they were greeted politely and given to understand that they could hope to have a favorable response soon. On May 9, 1956, Akhmatova was informed that her son's case would be taken up in about two weeks.

On May 14, Akhmatova went to Moscow, where she stayed with her friends the Ardovs. The next day, there was a knock on the Ardovs' door. It was Lev. He had just arrived in Moscow after his release and had simply intended to stop off at the Ardovs' before continuing to Leningrad; he had not known his mother was there.

Chukovskaya wrote later of her own first meeting with Lev:

A sense of hugeness and littleness at the same time. It's like that when you're in love. Signs appear in poems, dates have strange coincidences; your heart sinks to your feet each time the phone rings or the postman knocks; the pages of a letter tremble; and then it turns out—this is just a *human being*: no more and no less; a human being—a head, hands, feet. Such an enormous and such an utterly ordinary and trifling thing: a human being. Here he is, right in front of me—a five-letter word—Lyova. Not mine, hers—all the sleepless nights, the dreams, the nonmeetings and meetings, the [reception] windows above spittle-stained floors, the red cloths on the tables, the applications, the notifications, the parcels, the hair that she put in her notebook of poems [to see if her papers were examined while she was out], and the poems that were burned. . . . Two decades of her life. Materialized time—decades—and materialized space—thousands of kilometers. And this, it turns out, is just a human being—and he's here, in this room. You can touch him with your hand or call him by name.

"Mama." "My darling son. My sweet boy."[1]

Akhmatova would have liked Lev to live with her, as he had after returning from the war. But in the Fontanka House there had been a room available for him, whereas the smaller apartment on Krasnaya Konnitsa Street where she now lived had no space for another resident. Thus Akhmatova offered her son the one place that was at her disposal: the little dacha, so tiny that she had nicknamed it Budka (Russian for a sentry booth), that she had recently been granted in the village of Komarovo, just outside Leningrad. Lev, however, preferred to stay with friends.

The little dacha was not the only sign of official favor Akhmatova received at this time. That same year of 1956 Akhmatova was allowed to abandon her previous anonymity and sign her name to a volume of her translations of classical Korean poetry. The bolder editors of literary magazines began to request poems from her, and she was invited to contribute to an anthology in honor of the fortieth anniversary of the Revolution. Finally, in 1958, a book of Akhmatova's poems was published. It was a small volume, and a disproportionate amount of it was taken up by her early lyrics and translations, but it marked the first time since the resolution of 1946 that a collection of Akhmatova's poems had been printed in the Soviet Union.

However much she might welcome the "Thaw," Akhmatova did not automatically assume that it represented any change in the long-term political climate. In the summer of 1956, she received a phone call from Boris Pasternak informing her that Isaiah Berlin was again visiting Russia and wanted to know if he could see her. Akhmatova reacted to this news warily. She refused to see Berlin but did agree to talk with him on the phone, not despite but because of the fact that her line was bugged: let the authorities hear for themselves that in her dealings with this foreigner she had nothing to hide. So unprivate a conversation, after so many years, between two people who had lived in such different worlds would have been awkward at best. The fact that Berlin had recently married could not have helped. To Akhmatova, the brief and limited renewal of their contact–the "nonmeeting," as she would call it–painfully underscored the hopelessness of any real-world relationship between them and the limitations that still existed on what was and was not possible for her.

Pasternak, by contrast, fully believed the party proclamations that a new era was beginning and was prepared to seize the moment. He had recently finished his first novel, *Doctor Zhivago*. Set during the revolutionary and Civil War period, the novel has as its central figure a doctor and poet, a member of the old intelligentsia among whom Pasternak had grown up. By the standards of the Stalin period, which required that the hero be a man of action unhesitatingly leading the way to the bright Communist future, *Doctor Zhivago* was unprintable. But by the standards of the early Soviet years, the novel might well have been accepted. The attitude toward the Revolution and Civil War that underlies *Doctor Zhivago* is, in fact, very reminiscent of the position of a typical fellow traveler of the 1920s: while the novel unflinchingly describes the destructive nature of the forces that had been let loose, nevertheless those forces are regarded as something like an earthquake or a tidal wave, something so incomprehensibly vast as to be beyond mere human judgment. Since Khrushchev had pointed to the pre-Stalin years of the Soviet regime as the ideal, Pasternak did not think he was taking any significant risk when he submitted his manuscript to several Soviet publishers.

By May 1956, people in literary circles knew of the work's existence. Word of the novel reached a visiting representative of the Italian Communist publisher Giangiacomo Feltrinelli, who made Pasternak an offer to publish an Italian translation. Pasternak was initially nervous about the idea. Ever since the Pilnyak and Zamyatin affair of 1929, the publication of Soviet literary works abroad had been handled by official bodies, not individual authors. Yet the fact that Feltrinelli was a pro–Moscow publisher was reassuring, and in the end Pasternak handed over the manuscript of *Zhivago*.

Unfortunately for Pasternak, the course of reform did not proceed smoothly. A conservative faction of the party feared that Khrushchev's attacks on Stalin were delegitimizing the entire idea of Communism, and

many in the leadership saw the 1956 uprisings against the Soviet oc-
cupiers in Poland and Hungary as a confirmation of those fears. The
Stalinist "us versus them" mentality resurfaced, making any unconven-
tional work of art look threatening. In August 1957, when the prospects
of publishing even an abridged Soviet edition of *Zhivago* were appearing
ever more remote, Pasternak publicly sent a telegram to Feltrinelli telling
him not to proceed with publication of the Italian edition. But through
private channels he stated that the telegram should be disregarded. Pas-
ternak was sixty-seven years old, and he regarded the novel as the crown
of his life's work, a summing up of his thoughts and experiences. After so
many years of caution under Stalin, he would not remain silent any
longer.

As the novel's publication date of November 1957 approached, the
Soviet government resorted to increasingly shrill denunciations and
clumsy attempts to quash it. The result was inevitable: a novel that oth-
erwise would have attracted the attention of a small number of readers
of serious literary fiction instead became an instant best-seller. Ulti-
mately even the Soviet authorities came to realize their contribution to
Pasternak's new fame and tried, too late, to ignore the matter. But the
announcement, in October 1958, that Pasternak had been granted the
Nobel Prize pushed his enemies over the edge. The result was an out-
burst of official vitriol in which the most memorable contribution was
made by Vladimir Semichastny, head of the Komsomol (Communist
Youth League), who compared Pasternak to "a pig that fouls its own sty."
There was talk of expelling Pasternak from the country, a measure last
used some thirty years before against Trotsky. Aside from the serious
personal complications exile would have caused Pasternak, he shared
Akhmatova's belief that a writer's fate was necessarily tied to that of his
country. In an attempt to quiet the storm, he renounced the Nobel Prize
and issued a vaguely worded public apology.

This concession somewhat blunted the attacks but left Pasternak still
publicly disgraced and in a difficult position. His health began to fail.
Chukovskaya, who knew him well, wrote that at age sixty he had the
bearing of a young man, as if he were going to live to be a hundred.[2] Now,
at age seventy, time was rapidly catching up with him. On the night of
May 7–8, 1960, he suffered a massive heart attack, and after being admit-
ted to a hospital he was also diagnosed with an advanced case of lung

cancer. Pasternak knew he was dying and was prepared to do so. On May 30, he said farewell to his family, and that night he died in his sleep.

Akhmatova's relationship with Pasternak during his final years was a complex one. He had helped her many times over the years, and she was grateful. But at the same time she had long believed he did not take her poetry as seriously as that of some of their contemporaries. That thought rankled, making Akhmatova quick to take offense at Pasternak's offhand remarks. Her outbursts of anger toward him, however, were something like family quarrels, always ending with Akhmatova's acknowledgement of his stature as a poet.

Her opinion of him as a novelist, however, was something else altogether. While Akhmatova greatly admired the nature descriptions in *Zhivago*, she considered the work as a whole a failure comparable in magnitude to the second volume of Gogol's *Dead Souls* (which was burned by its author, apparently out of despair). As a result, she complained, "he had put his friends and those close to him in a very difficult position."[3] Presumably the difficulty she had in mind was not that of official persecution, but rather the private awkwardness involved in trying to offer emotional support to a beleaguered artist while refusing to praise his art. In November 1958, Akhmatova told Chukovskaya that she was going to pay Pasternak "a visit of condolence, but without expressing any condolence"; they would talk "about the weather, about nature, about anything," only not about the topics that must have been uppermost on Pasternak's mind.[4] Akhmatova also could not escape some bitterness at the thought that the Western world, which had been silent when she was under attack and her son in prison, was now raising a clamor over the comparatively less harsh treatment Pasternak received.

But when Pasternak was dying, Akhmatova went to visit him at his dacha in Peredelkino, just outside Moscow. Although she was not allowed to see him, her realization of how he was suffering awoke her underlying affection and pity for him, and she left feeling there had been a reconciliation between the two of them. On the day Pasternak died, Akhmatova herself was in the hospital as a result of heart problems. Her old friend Maria Petrovykh undertook to break the news of the death to Akhmatova. Petrovykh was struck by the fact that although Akhmatova found it difficult to cry freely after so many years of having to control her emotions in public, on this occasion tears visibly welled up in her eyes.[5]

121

At Pasternak's funeral, Chukovskaya overheard a conversation between two young people: "Now the last great Russian poet has died." "No, there's still one left—Anna Akhmatova."[6] The speakers' admiration of Pasternak and Akhmatova, members of their grandparents' generation, was common among the young. In contrast to the many comfortable middle-aged people who found de-Stalinization disorienting, for those in their teens and twenties it was like a breath of fresh air. In their opinion, their parents' generation was discredited by its craven surrender to dictatorship. The most intelligent and sensitive among them hoped to root themselves in an alternate past, a more humane one, and found it in the achievements of Russian culture. To them, Akhmatova was a living link to that past, and they eagerly sought her out. She became the mentor of four young poets, Josef Brodsky, Anatoly Nayman, Dmitry Bobyshev, and Yevgeny Rein. Her status as the matriarch of Russian literature was tacitly acknowledged even by the regime, which in 1961 allowed a new collection of her poetry to be published under the title *Poems, 1909–1960.* Like all her previous books, this one sold out immediately. As Akhmatova proudly noted, "From 1940 to 1961 *95,000* copies of my books were printed in the USSR and it was still *impossible* to buy a collection of my poetry."[7]

During the years of proscription, Akhmatova's social life had been limited to a small circle of longtime friends who were prepared to accept the risks of being associated with her. Once she was no longer stigmatized, her circle of acquaintances expanded vastly, and although she still professed to be indifferent to fame, her friend Natalia Ilyina noted that the situation was actually not that simple:

> Just as before, she paid "no attention" (her expression) to material goods, almost never lived in her new Leningrad apartment, wandered from one friend's apartment to another in Moscow, lived at Budka in Komarovo in summer, wore an old coat and worn-down shoes. But admiration and flattery, and timid admirers of both sexes, and flowers, and telephone calls, and having the whole day scheduled, and getting calls to appear or even just to show up—that had become necessary.[8]

If Akhmatova simply enjoyed the experience of recognition and admiration after so many years of self-effacement and public humiliation, it would hardly be surprising. But more than her own vanity or self-esteem was involved. In the dark days of the Terror, when it seemed that the aesthetic and ethical values of Russian literature were vanishing from the earth, she had regarded it as her duty as a poet to uphold that tradition, and she had fulfilled that duty at great personal cost, in circumstances that had seemed almost hopeless. Now, after decades of being officially scorned as a historical irrelevancy, out of touch with the brave new world of Soviet power, it turned out that the tradition she represented had endured, and a new generation was prepared to receive the heritage she had preserved so faithfully. Her ongoing revisions of *Poem Without a Hero*, the memoirs she wrote of her famous contemporaries—among them, Mandelstam, Blok, and Modigliani—were not merely the natural impulse of a woman in her seventies to look back on her youth: they were a conscious effort to transmit the life and experience of a lost world to those who came after.

As a poet-witness, it was inevitable that Akhmatova would come into contact with the writer who made it his life's work to understand the history of twentieth-century Russia, Alexander Solzhenitsyn. Like Akhmatova, Solzhenitsyn had regarded the early years of the Thaw warily, and though he had already written a number of works based on his prison experience, he regarded them as meant for publication at some distant future date, probably after his death. But following the swing toward increased repression that had led to Pasternak's disgrace and death, the reformist tendency again came to the forefront. At the Twenty-Second Party Congress, held in October 1961, Stalin was denounced in even more sweeping terms than in the initial attack of 1956. At the same congress, Alexander Tvardovsky, editor-in-chief of the liberal monthly *Novy mir* (*New world*) made it clear he was willing to consider publishing works that previously would not have passed the censorship. Solzhenitsyn, then an unknown provincial schoolteacher, decided to risk submitting a short novel he had written depicting a "typical" day in the life of a "typical" camp inmate. He gave the manuscript to an old friend from his prison days, Lev Kopelev, a specialist in German literature and culture, who in turn ensured that it reached Tvardovsky.

Kopelev was also a friend of Akhmatova, and while Tvardovsky was struggling to get permission to publish Solzhenitsyn's novella, Kopelev gave a copy of it to Akhmatova. She was deeply impressed by the work and told all her acquaintances, "Two hundred million people"—the entire population of the Soviet Union—"ought to read this."[9] Shortly before the novella, entitled *One Day in the Life of Ivan Denisovich*, was published in *Novy mir* for November 1962, Kopelev arranged for Akhmatova and Solzhenitsyn to meet. Studying the forty-three-year-old first novelist, Akhmatova wondered if he had the strength to hold up under the kind of concerted official attention to which she and, more recently, Pasternak had been subjected, and warned him, "Do you know that in a month you'll be the most famous man on earth?" "I know. But it won't last long." "Can you endure fame?" "I have very strong nerves. I endured Stalin's camps." "Pasternak couldn't endure fame. It's very difficult to endure fame, especially when it comes late."[10]

Despite the two writers' mutual admiration, the meeting did not go entirely smoothly. Solzhenitsyn, long accustomed to concealing his writings, could not bring himself to show his other completed prose works to Akhmatova, a mistake he later profoundly regretted.[11] Instead he showed her his poetry, which, as she justly and tactfully noted, was not his strength as a writer. In turn, she recited *Requiem* to him, and he told Kopelev after,

> A good poem, of course. Beautiful. Sonorous. But after all, a nation suffered, tens of millions, and it's a poem about an individual case, about one mother and son. . . . I said to her that the duty of a Russian poet is to write about the sufferings of Russia, to rise above personal grief and speak of the nation's grief. . . . She was silent, reflecting. Perhaps she didn't like that—she's accustomed to flattery, raptures. But she's a great poet. And a truly great theme. That has to be said.[12]

Certainly Akhmatova had not forgotten the "tens of millions," as the epilogue of *Requiem* shows. But Solzhenitsyn's remarks do point to a fundamental difference in the nature of the two writers. Solzhenitsyn's artistic ideal is the great nineteenth-century realist novel, the novel as it was understood by Tolstoy and Balzac and George Eliot, with its profound understanding of how social forces shape and misshape the lives of individuals. Akhmatova, by contrast, was fundamentally a lyric poet, whose most characteristic themes were love and loss. In appropriate circumstances, these themes could take on social and political meanings: when her beloved homeland was in danger, Akhmatova was a patriotic poet; when her son and other people dear to her were taken from her—

arrested, tortured, and sometimes killed–the poems that arose from those losses were acts of witness against state crimes. Unlike Solzhenitsyn, Akhmatova did not set out to become a witness as the result of a historian's resolve to establish the truth, or as an advocate seeking justice for the victims; she became a witness first for her son and then for all the other mothers who suffered as she did. To expect *Requiem* to "rise above personal grief" is a fundamental misunderstanding of its nature: it is through, not in spite of, the personal that a lyric poet understands the collective.

The differences in Akhmatova's and Solzhenitsyn's artistic approaches notwithstanding, their related subject matter naturally led Akhmatova to hope that if *One Day in the Life of Ivan Denisovich* could be legally published, so might *Requiem*. It soon became clear, however, that *One Day* was a high–water mark in Soviet liberalization and that the authorities were not going to allow any further literary works on controversial topics. Not only did Akhmatova's efforts to publish *Requiem* fail, but even the less obviously problematic *Poem Without a Hero* could not be published in its entirety, although excerpts from it had already appeared in print. In a notebook entry from December 1962, Akhmatova ironically wrote,

> Foreword to the poem *Triptych* [the alternate title for *Poem Without a Hero*]
> Forbidden: a) by the censor
> Rejected: b) by thirteen magaz⟨⟨ines⟩⟩
> Not accepted: c) by seven editors
> Upon mature reflection, the author herself renounced it.[13]

The other long poem of 1940, *The Way of All the Earth*, fared no better; when it was published in 1963, a third of it had been cut, including virtually all the final section.

In February 1964, the most gifted of Akhmatova's protégés, Josef Brodsky, was arrested on the charge of "parasitism"–that is, of not making an economic contribution to society. The twenty–three–year–old Brodsky eked out a living doing odd jobs so he could spend as much time as possible writing poetry. His poems, though widely admired by the liberal intelligentsia, had not been legally published, and he was not a member of the Union of Soviet Writers. Thus by Soviet standards he was not a poet and had no right to be spending his time in unprofitable writing when he could be pursuing a socially useful career instead. For people of Akhmatova's generation, seeing a poet arrested for writing unauthorized poetry had a sickening familiarity; but what happened next showed that there had, after all, been changes since Stalin's day. Brodsky's trial was not closed to the public, and a journalist named Frida Vigdorova–the same correspondent who had heard Akhmatova recite "Courage" in Tashkent in February 1942 and had forwarded the poem to *Pravda* for national publication–attended and boldly took notes on the proceedings. The notes, which were copied and circulated from hand to hand, revealed the utter mutual incomprehension between the poet and the Soviet legal system: for example, when the judge asked Brodsky who had recognized him as a poet, Brodsky replied, "No one. Who was it that recognized me as a member of the human race?" As in the Pasternak affair, publicity led to international embarrassment for the Soviet Union, and Brodsky's sentence of exile to a village in the Arkhangelsk region– itself a mild punishment by the standards of a generation before–was commuted to time served in September 1965.

Although Akhmatova was deeply concerned for Brodsky's well-being, she defiantly spoke of the trial as a distinction for him–"What a biography they're making for our Ginger"[14]–in the same way that after the Central Committee resolution in 1946 she had spoken of her own "martyr's fame." Anatoly Nayman recalled,

> *Requiem* began to circulate clandestinely at approximately the same time, in the same circles and in the same number of copies as Vigdorova's transcript of Brodsky's trial. Public opinion unconsciously made a link between these two things, though not one which could be named openly: the poet defends the right to be a poet and not to have any other occupation so that he or she should be able when necessary to speak on everyone's behalf. The transcript of the poet's trial sounded like poetry on the most profound themes of public concern; and *Requiem*, poetry on the most profound themes of public concern, sounded like a transcript of the repressions, a kind of martyrology, a record of acts of self-sacrifice and martyrdom.[15]

Such officially unauthorized circulation of a literary work was illegal, but Akhmatova was in no danger. At the age of seventy-five, she had become a monumental figure. Her life spanned so much history that every Soviet reader could see her in an acceptable light: for the dissidents, she was the poet who had upheld the moral authority of Russian literature by relying on the guidance of her inner voice rather than on official formulas, and she had written *Requiem*; for the Communists, she was the poet who had chosen not to emigrate after the Revolution, who had written patriotic poetry, and who had accepted the party's rebuke in 1946 with appropriate humility.

The fact that her literary biography could be presented in an officially acceptable, if checkered, form played a crucial role in Akhmatova's obtaining a privilege normally granted only to those enjoying the highest favor of the Soviet regime—the ability to visit the West. In 1964, Giancarlo Vigorelli, the chairman of the European Community of Writers (COMES), officially invited Akhmatova to come to Catania, Italy, so that she could receive the Etna-Taormina Poetry Prize at the COMES convention there. The invitation set off a battle between the hard-line and more moderate factions of Soviet literary officialdom. The moderates pointed to Akhmatova's at least partially legitimate place in Soviet literature, Vigorelli's known pro-Moscow sentiments, and the possible embarrassment of another Pasternak affair if Akhmatova was not allowed to receive the prize. In the end she was given permission to go as part of a Soviet delegation to COMES.

The ability to travel abroad—something that educated Russians had taken for granted before the Revolution—was one of the many aspects of Akhmatova's youth that she assumed had been lost forever, and the unexpected reemergence of such a possibility aroused in her both excitement and fear of what the consequences might be. As it turned out, her trip, although brief, was a great triumph. On December 4, 1964, fifty-two years after her previous visit to Italy, Akhmatova arrived in Rome. She stayed there for four days, driving down the oldest surviving Roman road, the Appian Way, and visiting Raphael's tomb in the Pantheon. Then the delegation traveled on to Sicily, where the Taormina Prize festivities were held on December 12. Akhmatova pronounced a brief address on Dante, giving citations in the original Italian but delivering her own remarks in Russian. As a result, many in the audience did not understand her speech, but, struck by her majestic presence and bearing, they applauded enthusiastically nevertheless. A German journalist who saw her wrote, "I suddenly understood why Russia can sometimes be ruled by tsarinas."[16]

The English moved to offer her their recognition as well, in the form of an honorary doctorate of letters from Oxford University. Akhmatova was granted her degree at a university ceremony during which she was described as "the Russian Sappho." The orator, in his summation of her achievements, stressed her patriotic poems and the collections of her poetry published in the post–Stalin era. He did not mention the official persecution she had suffered or the works she could not get published, including *Requiem*, which was circulating in the West accompanied by a disclaimer stating that it was printed contrary to the author's wishes. Akhmatova approved of this pro–Soviet version of her literary biography; she was not coming to England to stay, and she did not want any trouble when she went home.

During this trip she saw for the last time the "guest from the future," Sir Isaiah Berlin, now a celebrated professor at Oxford. She was not entirely impressed by his success, since she had understandably come to associate affluence with selling out, and she spoke of his life in England as a "gilded cage." But the two of them spoke of Russian literature and of all that had happened since their parting as freely as they had talked before. During the ten days she was in England, with a side trip to Paris added on, Akhmatova was able to see once again several of the survivors of her youth, including Boris Anrep and Salomeya Andronikova Halpern, and to meet a relative she had never seen–the posthumously born son of her brother Andrei Gorenko, who had committed suicide in 1920. And she took the occasion to write down the texts of several of her works, particularly *Poem Without a Hero*, which had been the subject of so much authorial tinkering that establishing a definitive reading for every single line was well–nigh impossible.

As moving as the two trips to the West were for Akhmatova, they were also exhausting. In October 1961, Akhmatova had had her third heart attack. Her doctor recommended against air travel, so both trips were made by rail. During both of them, she relied upon the assistance of a trusted companion–Irina Punina in Italy, Anna Kaminskaya in England. Akhmatova was still living with the two women (as well as with Irina's second husband). In 1961 the household had been evicted from the Krasnaya Konnitsa street apartment in Leningrad during supposedly temporary renovations and had wound up moving to Moscow, but had stayed together.

Officially registered as living with the Punins, in her last years Akhmatova kept up her wandering way of life. In the winter, she spent weeks or months as a guest among her Moscow friends. In the summer, she lived at her dacha, Budka, where, despite its minimal accommodations, she delighted in playing hostess. After her third heart attack, she had given up smoking, but in a congenial gathering she still enjoyed vodka.

Sadly, the group of friends and visitors who regularly surrounded Akhmatova lacked one important person—her son Lev. Ever since his Bezhetsk childhood, Lev had felt that Akhmatova did not care enough about him. While he was in the labor camp in the 1950s, he had allowed himself to be convinced that his famous mother could surely have obtained his release if she had really wanted to. When Akhmatova pointed out to him all she had done to try to help him, and how much pain she had borne as a result, he belittled her suffering. Conversation between the two became impossible. Akhmatova always blamed their estrangement not on Lev himself, but on his prolonged exposure in prison to the worst side of human nature, which she believed had made him harsh and cynical. In a diary entry dating from the time of Brodsky's release from exile in September 1965, one of his new poems inspired her to reflect: "Either I don't understand anything, or it's a work of genius, and in the moral sense it's what Dostoyevsky speaks of in [*Notes from the*] *House of the Dead*: not a hint of embitterment or arrogance, which F[yodor] M[ikhailovich] warned against. That's what ruined my son. He began to feel contempt and hatred for people and became no longer human himself. May God enlighten him! My poor Lyovushka."[17]

A month after Brodsky's release, in October 1965, a new collection of Akhmatova's works was published, appropriately entitled *The Flight of Time*. It was the most extensive publication of her works in the Soviet Union up to that time. Yet it did not fulfill Akhmatova's hope that she would be able to publish all three of the long poems of the year 1940—*Requiem, The Way of All the Earth*, and *Poem Without a Hero*—in their entirety. *The Way of All the Earth* made it into print with only small concessions to the censorship. But the lines of parts 2 and 3 of *Poem Without a Hero* that referred to the prison camps were cut, and *Requiem* continued not to exist officially. Only two of its poems, "The Sentence" and "Crucifixion," were published, with no indication that they belonged to a larger whole, and the title of "The Sentence" was removed, stripping it of its context. Thus

Akhmatova's feelings toward the new book were mixed: while it was an achievement that would have been unimaginable a decade earlier, nevertheless she had dreamed of seeing all her works published in her homeland in her own lifetime–a dream that would not come to pass.

On November 7, 1965, Akhmatova suffered her fourth heart attack and was taken to Botkin Hospital, one of the best-known medical institutions in Moscow. Her health was so precarious that she spent over three months there. On one occasion, Lev, who had heard that his mother was seriously ill, came to the hospital to see her. Akhmatova's friends, however, feared that the emotional excitement of such a reunion might overtax her strength and did not allow him into her hospital room. When she learned of this, Akhmatova was deeply upset. The sense that all her activities were being controlled by others in addition to the monotony of the hospital routine led her to compare her life as a patient to being in prison. She was delighted when, on February 19, 1966, she was discharged from the hospital into the care of the devoted Nina Olshevskaya–Ardova.

Because Olshevskaya, who had suffered a stroke a year and a half earlier, was herself in poor health, on March 3 the two women both entered a sanitorium in the little town of Domodedovo, not far from Moscow. Akhmatova's first night there was a difficult one, but the following day she was well enough to write in her notebook, "I'm completely absorbed by the Qumran news"–that is, deciphered fragments of the Dead Sea Scrolls that had recently been published.[18] She asked Anna Kaminskaya to bring her a New Testament, so that she could compare the two texts.

Kaminskaya told Lev Kopelev: "She woke up on the morning of March 5 in a very good mood. But she didn't go to breakfast, she felt weak. A nurse gave her an injection. She was joking with her–and died smiling."[19] It was thirteen years to the day since Stalin's death.

On March 7, a small Orthodox requiem for Akhmatova was held in Moscow. This observance was arranged by the cellist Maria Yudina. The Moscow branch of the Union of Soviet Writers, which normally organized memorial services for its members, offered no assistance. Akhmatova's body was then transported to Leningrad, where on March 10 her funeral service was held in the splendid Russian baroque edifice of the Sailors' Church of St. Nicholas. The indifference of officialdom did not prevent lovers of Russian poetry from coming to pay their respects, and the old women who were accustomed to being the only worshipers in the church were astonished and somewhat offended by the crowd that crammed the building and spilled out the doors. The chief mourners were Anna Kaminskaya and Lev Gumilyov. Josef Brodsky and Anatoly Nayman stood by the coffin. The age–old Orthodox requiem service was sung, fittingly reaching its climax in the hymn "Vechnaya pamyat" Eternal memory. After the church service, the funeral cortege made its way to the cemetery at Komarovo, the village where Akhmatova's tiny dacha was located. There, where the long–homeless Akhmatova had finally had a place of her own, she was buried.

There are people still alive who knew Akhmatova. Yet with the fall of the Soviet Union, the world in which she lived already seems far from us. Poets and poetry have perhaps less symbolic value now than they did then. But Akhmatova was confident that her poetry, although it reflected its own era, would outlast the vicissitudes of history. As she wrote,

> Tarnish darkens gold, steel scours away and breaks,
> Marble turns to dust. Death shadows all on earth.
> Of all things, the firmest-fixed is sorrow's ache,
> And the longest-lasting is the kingly word.

PART II

The Poems

Requiem

Not where the sky's dome enclosed a foreign space,
Nor where foreign wings sheltered and reassured,
But among my people I took up my place,
There, where by an ill fate, my own people were.

1961

Instead of a Foreword

In the terrible years of the Yezhov era, I spent seventeen months on prison lines in Leningrad. One day somebody "identified" me. Then a woman with blue lips who was standing behind me and who, of course, had never in her life heard my name before, awoke from the torpor normal to all of us and breathed a question in my ear (everyone spoke in whispers there):

"Can you describe *this*?"

And I said:

"I can."

Then something like a smile slipped across what once had been her face.

April 1, 1957

Leningrad

Dedication

A grief so great would lay a mountain low,
Would make the rush of mighty rivers cease,
But has no power to move the prison bolts
Or reach beyond them to the "convicts' holes"
And the mortal agony.
Some breathe fresh air and feel light breezes play,
Some love the lingering sunset's tranquil mood,
We don't know, for us it's all one place,
Our ears hear nothing but the keys' harsh scrape
And the tramp of soldiers' heavy boots.
Each day we'd rise as if for early Mass,
Troop through the feral city, get in line,
Stand, less alive than those who'd breathed their last,
The Neva fog grew thick, the day had passed,
And still we heard hope sing–but not nearby.
Someone's been sentenced . . . From the silent crowd
One cry breaks loose–a stricken woman groans
As if her beating heart had been torn out,
As if coarse hands had grabbed her, thrown her down–
She walks off somehow . . . staggering . . . alone . . .
Where now are my involuntary friends,
Companions of my two years spent in hell?
Amid the snowstorm's whirl what do they sense,
Or from the moon's white circle what portends?
I send them greetings and a last farewell.

Prologue

There was no one who smiled in those days
Except the dead, who'd found peace at last.
Like a tacked-on extra, a useless weight,
From its prisons dangled Leningrad.
Rank on rank the condemned marched along,
Crazed with pain, driven to their doom,
Their one farewell the short sharp song

The whistles of the cattle-trains blew.
The stars of death rose and stood above,
And Russia, guiltless, tormented, writhed,
Trampled under boots stained red with blood
And crushed by the Black Marias' tires.

I

Arrest at dawn. Like a funeral rite,
They bore you off, I followed in back.
In the dark high chamber children cried,
The flames of holy candles drowned in wax.
The icon's chill on your lips—can't forget!–
The deadly sweat encircling your brow . . .
Like the wives of those the Tsar put to death
I'll stand outside the Kremlin and howl.

Fall 1935
Moscow

II

Quiet, quiet the Don flows,
Yellow moon through the window goes.

The moon comes in, its cap askew,
And sees a shadow lost in gloom.

Here's a woman—she's sick, bereft,
Here's a woman with no one left.

Husband's dead, and son's in jail,
When you pray, tell God my tale.

III

No, it's not I, it's someone else who's suffering,
I couldn't take that, and the thing that happened,
Cover it over with black cloths
And take away the lanterns . . .

Night.

IV

If in your mocking youth long years ago
When friends and lovers showered you with praise,
Prodigal daughter of Tsarskoe Selo,
If you had seen then how you'd spend your days–
Standing in line at the Crosses Prison walls
With three hundred women ahead of you,
Clutching a package, and your hot tear falls
Upon the New Year's ice that it burns through.
A prison poplar stands with quivering boughs,
Not a sound–and yet how many they are,
How many innocents are dying in there now.

V

Seventeen months of futile pleas,
I cry for you to come,
I've knelt down at the hangman's feet
For you, my dread, my son.
Everything's broken, out of place,
I can't find my way through,
Is that a beast's or a human face,
And will they kill you soon.
Only the dusty flowers still last,
And a tinkling censer, and a path
That fades into thin air.
And a great star blazing on the heights
Unblinking looks me in the eye,
And death is in its glare.

VI

Weeks go lightly skimming by,
How it happened, I can't tell.
My sweet boy, into your cell
Peered the pale midsummer nights.
Once again they come and peer
With the hot eyes of a hawk,
It's of your high cross they talk,
And of death as it draws near.

1939

VII

The Sentence

The word fell, dropping like a stone
And striking my still–living breast.
It's no surprise, I should have known,
I'm ready for it, more or less.

Today there's so much I must do:
Must smash my memories to bits,
Must turn my heart to stone all through,
And must relearn how one should live.

Or else . . . A carefree festive hum,
Outside hot summer's rustling now.
How long I've known that this would come,
A brilliant day, an empty house.

Summer 1939

VIII

To Death

You're going to come, no matter what—why won't now do?
I want you now—I can't bear any more.
You're simple and yet magical—to welcome you
My lights are out, you'll find an open door.
Do what you please, take any shape that comes to mind,
Burst on me like a shell of poison gas,
Or creep up like a mugger, club me from behind,
Or let the fog of typhus do the task.
Or act what you dreamed up, that fairy tale of doom
So common that it makes us sick to hear,
Where a blue–capped uniform comes into my room
Led by a janitor who's pale with fear.
No matter now. The Yenisei runs swift and cold,
In polar dark the North Star gleams above.

And the final horror is dimming the blue glow
That once shone in the eyes of one I love.

August 19, 1939

IX

Already madness' outstretched wing
Half-hides my soul beneath its pall,
It gives me burning wine to drink,
I hear the dark path's siren call.

Admit it—fighting back's absurd,
My own will just a hollow joke,
I hear my broken, babbling words
As if some other person spoke.

I know that it will take my past,
What was mine—won't be any more
(However endlessly I ask,
However meekly I implore):

Not my son's eyes, their fearsome gaze
That suffering's turned stony-hard,
Not the first catastrophic day,
The meeting hour held under guard,

Not the beloved cool touch of hands,
The anxious shade of linden trees,
Not the faint sound from a far land—
The last words said to comfort me.

May 4, 1940

X

Crucifixion

Weep not for Me, Mother,
when I am in the tomb.

1

A choir of angels hailed that glorious hour on high,
Waves of fire swept the heavens, swelling like the sea.
"Father, why have You abandoned Me?" He cried,
Then, turning to His mother: "Do not weep for Me . . ."

2

Mary Magdalene beat her breast, tore her hair,
The beloved disciple froze as still as stone,
But where the Mother stood—no one would look there,
None dared to glance at her, so silent and alone.

Epilogue

1

I've learned how faces hollow down to bone,
How from beneath the eyelids terror peeks,
How cuneiforms cut by suffering show
Their harsh unyielding texts impressed on cheeks,
How curls that once were black or ashen-tipped
Can turn to palest silver overnight,
How a smile withers on submissive lips
And how a mirthless titter cracks with fright.
Not for myself alone, for all I pray,
All those who stood beside me without fail,
Alike in bitter cold and sweltering haze,
Beneath the brick-red blind walls of the jail.

2

Once more the hour of remembrance draws near,
I see you, I hear you, I feel you all here,

The one helped to the window—she barely could stand,
And the one who no longer will walk through our land,

And the one who stepped forward and tossed her fair hair—
"When I come here, it's like coming home," she declared.

I wanted to read off each name in its turn,
But the list has been seized, and there's nowhere to learn.

For them I have woven a mantle of words
Made up of the snatches that I've overheard.

Every day, every place, I'll remember them all,
I'll never forget, though new terrors befall,

And if torturers silence me, through whose one mouth
A nation of one hundred million cries out,

Let them all speak for me, mention me when they pray
Every year on the eve of my burial day.

And if ever in Russia I have such acclaim
That a monument's set up to honor my name,

My consent to a statue I only would grant
With a condition on where it should stand.

Not down by the southern sea where I was born–
My last tie to the seacoast has long since been torn–

Nor in the Tsar's park by the stump of that tree
Where an unconsoled ghost is still looking for me,

But here, where I stood while three hundred hours passed,
And the gates never budged, and the bolts remained fast.

Because in the blest ease of death I'm afraid
I'll forget the harsh rumble the prison vans made,

Forget how that door slammed, its harsh banging noise,
And the animal howl of an old woman's voice.

And as the snow melts from my statue each year,
From my bronze–lidded eyes may it trickle like tears,

And a single dove's cooing be heard from the jail
As far off on the river the quiet ships sail.

> March 1940
> Fontanka House

The Way of All the Earth

Sitting in the sleigh, setting out on
the way of all the earth . . .
—Testament of Vladimir Monomakh to his
children

1

Ducking right under bullets,
Through dense years I plow,
Januarys, Julys—
I'll still get there somehow.
None to see that I'm wounded
Or hear when I moan.
My city is Kitezh,
They're calling me home.
The birches' massed ranks
Drive me on from behind,
Through the frost a path streams,
Like a glass wall it shines.
A post long since burned
And a charred sentry shack.
"Here's my pass, comrade,

Let me go back."
He lowers his bayonet,
Lets me go by.
And then there sprang up
A magnificent sight!
An island of red clay
And sweet apple groves ...
O, Salve Regina!
The setting sun glows.
The little path trembles
In its steep climb.
I need someone's hand
To take hold of mine ...
But I don't hear the wheeze
Of the barrel organ now.
What the woman of Kitezh hears
Isn't that sound.

2

Trenches, everywhere trenches–
Can't find a clear path!
What's left of old Europe
Is only a scrap,
In its smoke–shrouded cities
Fire and death reign ...
The dark ridge of Crimea
Already shows plain.
Mourning women approach,
Follow me in a band.
Oh, the aquamarine cloak
Of that quiet land! ...
A medusa lies dead,
Over it I stand lost;
The Muse met me here once,
I pledged her my troth.
"You?"–she didn't believe me,
She laughed long and loud,
Drop after drop

Fragrant April spilled out.
And I approached
The high threshold of fame,
But then a cunning voice
Warned me away:
"You'll return many times,
This won't be the last,
But you'll strike against diamond
And it will stand fast.
Reviled and revered,
You'd best keep going straight,
Best go back to your father's,
His garden still waits."

3

The evening draws on
With its thickening gloom.
When I walk to the corner
Let Hoffmann come too.
He knows just how hollow
A stifled scream sounds,
And whose doppelganger
Is wandering around.
After all, it's no joke
That for twenty-five years
I've been seeing the same
Shadow figure appear.
"So just round the corner?
Go right—that's it now?
Thanks a lot!"—There's a ditch
And nearby a small house.
Who could know that the moon
Was in on it all.
Plunging down a rope ladder,
It's paying a call,
Through each empty room
Calmly making its way,
As at a round table

The fading night gazed
Into a shard
From a mirror long smashed,
In the dark slept a man
Whose throat had been slashed.

4

Sound at its purest,
How lofty its might,
As if separation
Brimmed full of delight.
Long–recognized buildings
Now face out from death–
But the real grief will come
From the meeting ahead,
Grief a hundred times keener
Than any I've known,
Through the crucified capital
Lies my way home.

5

A bird cherry tree flashed–
A dream slipping by.
And "Tsushima!" a voice
On the telephone cried.
It's coming, it's coming–
The time is at hand:
Korean and *Viking*
Set sail for Japan . . .
An old pain arises,
Winged like a bird . . .
In the distance the dark bulk
Of Fort Chabrol lurks,
Like a past era's tomb
Now reduced to a wreck,
Where a crippled old man
Became blind and deaf.
Boer sentries with rifles

Won't let him go past.
Their stern scowl confronts him:
"Get back, get back!"

6

The great winter is here,
My long wait is done.
Its pure white I take
Like the veil of a nun.
In the swift sleigh I sit,
My heart now is light . . .
To you, people of Kitezh,
I'll come before night.
The old way station's past,
Just one crossing to go . . .
Now the woman of Kitezh
Journeys alone,
Without brother, or friend,
Or the man I loved first,
Bearing only a pine branch
And one sunlit verse
Dropped by a beggar
And picked up by me . . .
In my last dwelling place
May I find peace.

Poem Without a Hero

A Triptych

1940–1962

DEUS CONSERVAT OMNIA
–Motto on the coat of arms on the Fontanka
House

Instead of a Foreword

Some are no more, and others far off.

The first time it came to me was in the House on the Fontanka on the night of December 27, 1940, after sending a small fragment ("You came to Russia out of nowhere") as a herald that autumn.

I didn't summon it. I wasn't even expecting it on that cold and dark day of my last Leningrad winter.

Its appearance was preceded by several trivial and insignificant facts, which I cannot bring myself to refer to as events.

That night I wrote two sections of the first part ("1913") and the "Dedication." At the beginning of January, almost to my own surprise, I wrote "Flip Side," and in Tashkent (in two bursts) I wrote the "Epilogue," which became the third part of the poem, and made some significant insertions to the first two parts.

I dedicate this poem to the memory of its first listeners—my friends and fellow-citizens who perished in Leningrad during the siege.

I hear their voices and remember them when I read the poem aloud, and for me this secret choir has become a lasting justification of the work.

April 8, 1943
Tashkent

Rumors have frequently reached me concerning false and absurd interpretations of "Poem Without a Hero." Someone has even advised me to make the poem more comprehensible.

I will refrain from this.

The poem does not contain any third, seventh, or twenty-ninth meanings.

I will neither change it nor explain it.

"What I have written, I have written."

November 1944
Leningrad

27 December 1940

Dedication

. . . .

. . . . and since my paper has run out,
I'm using your rough draft for writing.
And here a word not mine shows through,
like a snowflake on my hand alighting,
to melt trustlingly, without reproof.
And Antinous' dark downy lashes
rose suddenly–and there's green smoke
and a native breeze began to blow. . .
Is it the sea?
       No, just pine branches   10
on a grave, and closer, close at hand
in boiling foam comes. . .
          Marche funèbre . . .
              Chopin . . .

Night
The Fontanka House

Second Dedication

O.S.

Can it be you, Confusion–Psyche,
   Black–and–white fan waving lightly,
      You leaning towards me, bending down?
You want to tell me secretly
   That you've already crossed the Lethe
      And breathe a different springtime now.
Don't dictate–I've already sensed
   Upon the roof warm downpour pressed,   20
      In the ivy are little whispers.
Some small being made up its mind
   To live, turned green, fluffed up, and tried
      To put on a new cloak and glitter.
I sleep–
        only she above me hovers,
   The season that's called spring by others
      To me has loneliness as a name.
I sleep–in dreams I see our youth,
   That cup whose taste *he* never knew,
      And, waking now, for memory's sake   30
I'll give it to you, if you wish,
   Like a pure flame in a clay dish,
      Or like a snowdrop in a grave.

         May 25, 1945
         The House on the Fontanka

Third and Last
(*Le jour des rois*)

Once on an Epiphany Eve . . .
–Zhukovsky

Enough, I've frozen in fear too long,
    So now I'll summon Bach's Chaconne,
        And with it a man will come to me.
It's not for him to be my espoused,
    But what we together will bring about
        Will trouble the Twentieth Century.
I received him by mistake   40
    As one touched by a hidden fate
        And, with him, the worst of all drew near.
Along the Fontanka Canal he'll walk,
    Arriving late through night and fog,
        He'll drink my wine to greet the New Year.
And he'll remember Epiphany Eve,
    The maple, the wedding candles' beams,
        And the poem in its mortal flight.
But not the first lilacs of the spring,
    Nor love's sweet prayers, nor yet a ring–   50
        It's doom he'll come bearing me that night.

1956

Introduction

AS FROM A TOWER THAT COMMANDS THE VIEW,
FROM NINETEEN-FORTY I LOOK DOWN.
AS IF I BID FAREWELL ANEW
TO WHAT I LONG SINCE BADE FAREWELL,
AS IF I PAUSED TO CROSS MYSELF
AND ENTER DARK VAULTS UNDERGROUND.

August 25, 1941
Leningrad under siege

PART 1

The Year Nineteen Thirteen

A Petersburg Tale

Di rider finerai
Pria dell'aurora.

       —Don Giovanni

CHAPTER 1

The New Year's splendor lingers on,
Moist are the stems of New Year's roses.

       —Rosary

We're not to conjure with Tatyana.

       —Onegin

New Year's Eve. The House on the Fontanka. The author is visited, not by the one for whom she waited, but by shades from the year 1913 in the guise of maskers. The white hall of mirrors. A lyric digression, the "Guest from the Future." A masquerade. A poet. A specter.

> I've set the cherished candles alight
> To give enchantment to this night,
>   With you, the guest who didn't arrive,   60
>   I planned to honor Forty–one's birth.
> But . . .
>   God be with us, His power abound!
>   Within the crystal the flame has drowned,
>   "And the brimming wine like poison burns."
> There are splashes of cruel conversations
> As long–dead ravings reawaken
>   Although the hour has not struck yet.
> A rush of fear hits me at full force,
> Like a ghostly guard I stand by the door
>   To defend my final haven's rest.   70
> And the bell rings, insistent and shrill,

At its sound I feel a fever chill,
    I turn to stone, I freeze, I burn . . .
Then, as if something came back to mind,
    I turn slightly, looking half–behind,
        And the words I speak are quiet and firm:
"You've got it wrong–you just went past
    The Venice of the Doges . . . but your masks,
        Your cloaks, staffs, crowns and all the rest,
You'll have to leave in the entryway.   80
    I've decided to honor you today,
        You mischief–making New Year's guests!"
This one's Faust, over there's Don Juan,
    That's Dapertutto and Iokanaan,
        The most modest is the northern Glahn,
           Or perhaps the murderer Dorian,
              They hold their Dianas and chatter on,
                Mouthing the lesson they learned so well . . .
To receive them the walls spread out,
    Light flared up and the sirens howled,   90
        Like a cupola the ceiling swelled.
I don't care, let the scandalmongers gasp . . .
    What to me are Hamlet's stocking straps,
        What to me is Salome's whirlwind dance,
           What to me is the tread of the Iron Mask,
           I'm more iron than he is in my soul . . .
Whose turn is it now to be afraid,
    To flinch, fall back, and begin to pray
        Forgiveness for a sin of old?
Clearly
           I'm who they want, if not, who's meant?   100
    But not for them is my table set,
        Not by them is my path to be shared.
In coattails his own tail doesn't show . . .
    So lame and elegant . . . I do hope
        That's not the Prince of the realm below
           You chose to bring here–would you dare?
Be it a mask, a skull, or a face
    On it such spite and pain are traced

As only Goya could dare express.
Indulged by all, the mocking grinner–   110
   Next to him, the foulest sinner
      Would seem to be God's grace made flesh.
A good time–so have a good time now,
   But why exactly did it turn out
      That I'm the only one alive?
Tomorrow I'll wake up safe in bed,
   And there won't be any judge to dread
      And the blue sky laughing overhead
         Will greet me when I look outside.
But I'm afraid that among them all   120
   I'll see myself, wearing my lace shawl,
      Giving a smile, though I won't speak.
That woman I was long ago,
   Wearing a necklace of black stones,
      Till the Valley of Jehosaphat–no,
         That's someone I don't want to meet . . .
Won't the angel's trumpet soon be heard? . . .
   I'd forgot the lessons you conferred,
      False prophets juggling pretty words,
         But you hadn't forgotten me.   130
As in the past the future takes shape
   So in the future the past decays,
      A hideous fete of rotting leaves.

W *Steps of those who were and are no more*
H *Echo upon the parquet floor,*
I *Cigar smoke casts a bluish pall.*
T *And every single mirror reflects*
E *The man who hadn't shown up yet,*
    Who had no way to enter that hall.
H *He's neither better nor worse than others,*   140
A *But his hand's warm, and round him hovers*
L *Not chill Lethean air, but living breath.*
L *Guest from the Future!—Can it be*
    That truly he will come to me,
    Will reach the bridge and then turn left?

Something about maskers wakes my fears,
    Ever since my childhood, it appeared
        That some sort of superfluous shade
"Without face or name" had gotten in
    Hidden among them. . .But let's begin   150
        The proceedings for this New Year's Day.
I'd rather not have the whole world know
    About this midnight Hoffmanesque, so
        If I could ask a favor . . .
                    Wait,
You there, you're not among those listed
    With Cagliostros, magi, Lysiscas,
        Dressed as a milepost in striped array
Painted with crude and gaudy strokes–
    You're as old as the Mamre oak,
        You converse with the moon through centuries.   160
You pretend to groan, but no one's fooled,
    You use letters of iron to write your rules,
        Hammurabi, Lycurgus, Solon too
          Would have profited to hear you teach.
With what strange tastes this being's endowed,
    Not content to wait for gout and renown
        To rush to seat him on display
          In lavish thrones for his jubilee,
            He triumphs out on the flowering heath,
              Through the wilderness he takes his way.   170
And there's nothing he need repent,
    Not a single thing . . .
              In any event
    Poets and sins don't go together.
Where the Ark of the Covenant is,
    They must dance or vanish! . . .
                 And about this,
    It's been expressed in verses better.
We only dream we hear a cock's crow,
    The Neva smokes beyond the windows,
        A fathomless night–and on and on goes
          The Petersburg devils' holiday . . .   180

Not a single star in the pitch–black sky,
   There's no doubt disaster awaits nearby,
      But that doesn't blunt the shameless bite
         Of the masqueraders' repartee . . .
A cry:
     "Let's have the hero up front!"
No need to worry: he's sure to come,
   He'll replace that tall man, take the floor
And holy vengeance will fire his song . . .
   Why do you rush off in a throng,
     As if each saw the bride for whom he longed,   190
      While I'm left behind to stand forlorn,
Alone in the gloom, facing that black frame
   From which there looks out, still the same,
     That drama of the bitterest pain,
      That hour none ever rightly mourned?

It comes, not all at once, but slowly.
Like a musical phrase's flowing,
I hear a whisper: "Good-bye! All's done!
You will live, I will leave you behind,
Yet as a widow you will be mine,   200
My white dove, my sister, my sun!"
Two shadows fused on the landing there. . .
Then—flat planks, one by one, up the stair,
A shriek, "No, don't!" and far off somewhere
A pure voice:
        "I am ready for death."

The torches go out, the ceiling is lowered. The white hall (of mirrors) again becomes the author's room. Words out of the gloom:

There is no death, as everyone knows.
   Why repeat that, it's already old.
     But what there is—that I'd like explained.
Who's knocking?
        I've let them all indoors.
   Is it the guest in the mirror? Or   210

The shape that flashed past the windowpane?
Is it the new moon playing a joke?
  Or between the cupboard and the stove
    Is someone standing, as in times past?
His eyes are open, his forehead pale...
  What that would mean is—gravestones are frail,
    That would mean granite's softer than wax...
No, nonsense, nonsense! If it's that way
  I'll soon become completely gray
    Or turn into someone else instead.   220
Why do you gesture, beckoning me?
  For just a single moment's peace
  I'd give up my peace after death.

Across the Landing
Interlude

Somewhere around here ("But that doesn't blunt the shameless bite of the masquer-
aders' repartee") lines like this were wandering, but I didn't let them into the main
text:

"That story's being told all over,
  You're a mere child, Signor Casanova..."
    "St. Isaac's at six, be sure to go..."
"Somehow we'll make it through the fog,
  From here we're heading for the *Dog*,
    Where are you going next?"
                  "God knows!"
Sancho Panzas and Don Quixotes,   230
  And, alas, Lots, upright and lonely–
    All are tasting the deadly draft.
Rising from foam, Aphrodites shimmer,
  In the mirror Helens glimmer,
    The hour of madness approaches fast.
And from the Fontanka meeting place,
  Where love's langour moans in the grotto's shade,
    Returning through the spectral gate,
      Someone with a shaggy red–haired face

And a goat–legged female satyr pass.   240
The tallest one, the most dressed to please,
    Although she neither hears nor sees,
        Nor swears an oath, nor prays, nor breathes,
           Is the head of Madame de Lamballe.
And you, so meek, such a pretty girl,
    In a goat–heel–tapping dance you twirl,
        Then sweetly, languidly, you purr,
           "Que me veut mon Prince Carnaval?"

And simultaneously in the depths of the hall, of the stage, of Hell or on the summit of Goethe's Brocken She herself appears (or perhaps—her shade):

Like cloven feet stamp her prancing boots,
    Like jingling bells chime her earring hoops,   250
        Amid blond curls wicked horns peep through,
           She's drunk with the dance, accursed, possessed–
As if from black–figure pottery
    She leapt into life and ran towards the sea
        In full ceremonial undress.
You, in the helmet and cloak, behind her,
    Who came unmasked, your face unobscured,
        Like a fairy–tale youth, your heart is pure,
           What is it that chokes your soul with grief?
In your every word pain opens up,   260
    So black a sorrow runs through your love,
        And why does that little stream of blood
           Drip down the petal of your cheek?

CHAPTER 2

Or do you see the one who before you knelt,
Who sought out white death to escape your
spell?

The Heroine's bedroom. A wax candle is burning. Over the bed hang three portraits of
the mistress of the house in her roles. On the right she is the Goat-legged Girl; in the
middle, Confusion-Psyche; on the left, the portrait is in shadow. To some it seems to be
Columbine, to others Donna Anna (from "The Steps of the Commendatore"). Outside
the mansard window blackamoor boys are having a snowball fight. A blizzard. New
Year's Eve. Confusion-Psyche comes to life, steps down out of the portrait, and imag-
ines a voice that reads:

> The fur coat's flung open, all satin–lined!
>   Don't think, my Dove, it's to be unkind
>   That my hand has lifted this goblet high:
>   It's myself, not you, I'm punishing now.
> Still the time of reckoning draws close,
>   Do you see, beyond the swirling snow,
>   The blackamoor boys of Meyerhold   270
>   Are playing games and horsing around?
> And all round us is old Peter City
>   That skinned people's hides off without pity
>   (As at the time the people said),–
> In flour carts, in horses' manes and harness,
>   In tea roses crudely daubed with varnish,
>   In shadows cast by ravens overhead.
> But the prima, smiling in feigned delight,
>   Across the Marinsky stage takes flight–
>   Our swan, an inscrutable dazzling sight–   280
>   A latecoming snob can't resist a crack.
> As though otherworldly music played
>   (Somewhere briefly glimmered some kind of shade),
>   Didn't a looming sense of the coming day
>   Send a chill down the audience's back?
> And again the voice that won such renown
>   Like thunder among the hills resounds–

It pours forth in glory without end!
It shakes one's heart to the very core,
 And across the trackless wastes it soars,   290
  Over the land that fed it, it ascends.
Against bluish–white snow, twigs are etched. . .
 Peter's corridor of colleges stretched
  Like an endless line, resonant and straight.
(Anything can happen there, it seems,
 But it will stubbornly haunt the dreams
  Of anyone who walks there today.)
The end's approaching absurdly fast,
 From behind the screens peers Petrushka's mask,
  Round the bonfires waiting coachmen dance, 300
   On a yellow flag flap black eagle's wings. . .
It's all in place, ready for the bell:
 From the Summer Gardens comes the smell
  Of Act Five . . . The ghost of Tsushima's hell
   Is there too. A drunken sailor sings . . .
Boldly and gaily the sleigh runners chime,
 And a goathair lap robe trails behind.
  Shades, begone!–He stands alone indeed.
The wall shows his profile, firm and clear.
 Say, my lady, is your chevalier   310
  Gabriel or Mephistopheles?
The Demon himself with Tamara's smile,
 But such a sorcerer's power to beguile
  Lurks in that terrible dusky visage.
Flesh that has almost turned to spirit,
 An ear with an antique curl falling near it,
  No one knows what kind of being this is.
In the crowded hall where the gypsies sang
 Did he send a black rose in champagne
  Or was that just a dream after all?   320
With a gaze and a heart both cold and numb
 Did he see the Commendatore come
  To meet him in that accursed hall?
And in his own words he narrates
 How the two of you were in a new space,

How outside of time you arose–
And in what polar crystals' gleaming,
  And in what amber–golden beaming
    There, where the Lethe–Neva flows.
From out of the portrait down you came,   330
  Upon the wall the empty frame
    Will be waiting for you until dawn.
So you're to dance now–unescorted!
  And the role of the fatal chorus
    I myself have agreed to take on.

Spots are glowing scarlet on your cheeks,
Into the canvas you'd best retreat;
After all, this is the sort of night
When one has to pay up what one owes . . .
And to me this stupefying doze   340
Seems even harder than death to fight!

You came to Russia out of nowhere,
  O my wonder with flaxen hair,
    The Columbine of the nineteen-teens!
Why show such a troubled and keen-eyed gaze,
  You Petersburg doll, acclaimed on stage–
    You're one of my doubles, another me.
That's one more title you must append
  To the others. O poets' beloved friend,
    The fame you once had is now my own.   350
To an amazing musical meter
  Leningrad's wind swoops and sweeps here,
    In the shade of a precious cedar
      I behold dancing courtiers' bones. . .
Down the wedding candles wax slowly drips,
  The white-veiled shoulders wait to be kissed,
    The church thunders: "Dove, come to the groom!"
Parma violets in April piled high,
  And the Maltese Chapel rendezvous lies
    Deep in your heart like a threat of doom.   360
Is it a glimpse of the Age of Gold
  Or a crime of antiquity untold

From the dread time when chaos held sway?
Answer this at least: is it really true
   That once there lived such a one as you?
      Across squares with wooden pavement laid
         Did your dazzling feet really make their way?
Circus wagons pale beside your home,
   Around the altar of Venus go
      Cupids with features pitted and gouged.   370
Your birds weren't caged, you let them fly free,
   You made your bedroom a garden retreat,
      The people living on your street
         Back home in Pskov wouldn't know you now.
Behind the walls a hidden stair winds,
   Upon the walls saints in sky blue shine,
      These goods aren't quite stolen, but it's close . . .
Like Botticelli's "Spring," flower-bedecked,
   You received lovers in your bed,
      And anguish filled the dragoon Pierrot–   380
Most superstitious of all you enticed,
   With his smile of evening sacrifice,
      You're to him what a magnet is to steel.
With an ashen face, tears dimming his view,
   He sees the roses offered to you,
      Sees the foe whose fame he keenly feels.
Where your husband is, I didn't see, couldn't guess,
   I, the hoarfrost against the window pressed. . .
      There, that's the chime of the fortress bells. . .
Have no fear–I don't mark crosses on doors,   390
   I'm waiting for you, come boldly forth,
     It's long been known what your stars foretell.

CHAPTER 3

And under the Galernaya arch . . .
—A. Akhmatova

In Petersburg we'll all gather again,
As if it were there we buried the sun.
—O. Mandelstam

That was the final year . . .
—M. Lozinsky

Petersburg in 1913. A lyrical digression: last reminiscence about Tsarskoe Selo. The wind, either recalling or prophesying, mutters:

To heat the holidays bonfires burned,
    And carriages on bridges overturned,
        And the black–draped city was borne away
To drift on toward an unknown goal,
    Following or fighting the Neva's flow–
        But always moving away from its graves.
The Galernaya arch sank into gloom,
    In the Summer Garden a weathervane's tune   400
        Rang delicately, and a silver moon
            Hung frozen over the Silver Age.
Because along every road approaching,
    Because upon every door encroaching,
        Slowly, steadily, a shadow fell.
The wind tore fluttering posters down,
    Smoke squatting on rooftops whirled around,
        And lilacs had a funereal smell.
And, cursed by the wife the tsar hadn't wanted,
    Dostoyevskian and demon–haunted,   410
        The city plunged into its foggy night.
Out from the murk an old Peterite peeked,
    Some sidewalk idler–and solemn drums beat
        As if a firing squad stood nearby . . .

And through the cold and choking atmosphere
    Of prodigal prewar days, one could hear

A rumble, a distant warning sound,
But then it was still only faintly heard,
And, having no great power to disturb,
It sank in the Neva snows and drowned. 420
Just as night's fearsome mirror reflects
A man whom blind fury has possessed
Who denies what he knows himself to be,
So along the legendary quay
Approached, not what the calendars say,
But the real Twentieth Century.

Now homeward—take me at full speed
Past the Cameron Gallery
To the mysterious icy park
Where the waterfalls make no noise, 430
Where the Nine will greet me and rejoice
With the same joy that once filled your heart.
Past the park and past the island shore
Won't we see each other as before
Through earlier unclouded eyes,
Won't you speak to me again, repeat
The word that causes death's defeat
And solves the riddle of my life?

Fourth and Final Chapter

Love passed, and then the mortal features
Showed themselves clearly and drew near.
—Vs. K.

A corner of the Field of Mars. A house built in the early 19th century by the brothers Adamini. It will take a direct hit during an air raid in 1942. A bonfire is blazing up. The tolling bell of Our Savior on the Blood can be heard. On the field, through the blizzard, appears a ghostly Winter Palace ball. In the space between these sounds, Silence itself speaks:

Who froze at the darkened windows there,
On whose heart lay "a lock of blond hair," 440

Who watched the black before his eyes?
"Help, please someone, now, while there's still hope!
   You've never been so bitterly cold
     And alien as now, o night!"
The wind has the bite of Baltic salt,
   On the Field of Mars there's a blizzards' ball,
     Unseen hooves keep up their echoing beat . . .
An anxious dread too deep to express
   Fills one who has so little time left,
     Who in his prayers asks only for death,   450
       Who will leave behind no memory.
Beneath the windows he paces and stamps,
   Midnight is past, a streetcorner lamp
     Sheds a merciless and sickly glow–
And his vigil ends. The pretty masker
   Coming back from "The Road from Damascus"
     Has come home at last–and not alone.
She's with someone "without face or name,"
   Their parting, glimpsed through bonfire flames,
     Tells him everything he sought to know.   460
Buildings crash in ruin, the ashes smoke,
   And he answers through his sobs, half–choked,
     "My white dove, my sister, my sun,
You will live, I will leave you behind,
   Yet as a widow you will be mine,
     And now . . .
            Time for farewell, all is done!"
On the landing a lingering scent is sweet,
   And a young dragoon bearing poetry
     And senseless death will ring the bell,
If the courage he calls up doesn't fail   470
   He will use his final breath's travail
     To honor you.
           Look where he fell:
Not in the mud by some Polish creek,
   Not upon the blue Carpathian peaks,
     He is at your door!
         There on the floor.

167

Mercy, oh show mercy, Lord!

(How many ways the poet could meet death—
The foolish boy, he didn't suspect
And so he chose this one—he couldn't bear   480
The first assaults, he never realized
What sort of door would soon be opened wide,
What sort of road would stretch out, and to where . . .)

I, your olden conscience, here affirm:
    I tracked down the tale that had been burned,
        I went to the deceased's house
        And there I laid it down
        On a window shelf–
               and then I tiptoed off. . .

Afterword

ALL'S AS IT SHOULD BE: THE POEM RESTS NOW,
AS USUAL, WITH NO MORE TO SAY.   490
BUT WHAT IF A THEME SUDDENLY BURSTS OUT,
KNOCKS WITH ITS FISTS ON A WINDOWPANE—
AND TO THAT SUMMONS THERE REPLIES
A DISTANT SOUND FRAUGHT WITH ALARM—
GURGLING, GROANING, AND SHRIEKING CRIES
AND A VISION OF CROSSED ARMS? . . .

PART 2

Flip Side

Intermezzo

> . . . I take the waters of Lethe,
> Doctor's orders—I'm not allowed to be depressed.
>   —Pushkin

> In my beginning is my end.
>   —T. S. Eliot

Place: the House on the Fontanka. Time: January 5, 1941. In the window, the specter of a snow-covered maple tree. The hellish harlequinade from the year 1913 has just passed, after rousing the great silent epoch from its wordlessness, leaving behind it the debris common to every holiday or funeral procession—smoke from torches, flowers on the floor, sacred souvenirs lost forever . . . The wind is howling in the stovepipe, and in this howl one can make out very deeply and cleverly hidden fragments of Requiem. As for what appears in the mirrors, it's better not to think about it.

> . . . a jasmine bush that bloomed
> Where once Dante walked and the air is mute.
>   —N. K.

1

My editor was dissatisfied,
Swore he was busy, and sick besides,
His phone number went under cover,
He grumbled, "Three themes are mixed up here!   500
The reader gets lost—it's still not clear,
When all is done, who are the lovers,

2

"Who did what with whom, and when, and why,
Who got killed, and who remained alive,
Who the author or the hero is,
And why anyone nowadays

169

Needs this stuff about all these shades
And a poet—what's the point of this?"

3

"Three of them are in it," I averred,
"There's one dressed like a milepost, first,   510
As a demon the second appeared—
Their poems gave them a guarantee
Of survival through the centuries,
But the third lived only twenty years

4

"And I felt sorry for him." Just then
Words began to fall in again,
A music box pealed and echoes rung,
And above the broken flask the glow
Of a mysterious poison rose,
Flamed up in a crooked, angry tongue.   520

5

And I kept on writing in my dream
A libretto for someone, it seemed,
While the unceasing music poured.
Yes, a dream, but in it some truth stirs—
The "soft embalmer," the long-sought blue bird,
The parapets of Castle Elsinore.

6

Let me just say that I didn't rejoice
When I heard the distant roaring noise
Set up by that hellish mocking crew.
I hoped that, like a smoky pall,   530
Pine branches would drift past the white hall
And be swept off into the gloom.

7

He's still putting on his old show,
That motley clownish Cagliostro–
The most elegant Satan of all,
Who won't join my funeral lament,
Who doesn't recognize the word "repent,"
And won't listen to conscience's call.

8

No trace of a Roman carnival night–
The Chant of the Angels, thrust aside,   540
Trembles at churches that bar entry.
No one comes to knock at my door,
Mirror dreams of mirror and nothing more,
Over silence silence stands sentry.

9

[And I bear my *Seventh* in my arms,
It lies scarcely breathing, mute and scarred,
Its mouth agape with corners downturned
Like a tragic mask of ancient days,
But its face is blackened, smeared with paint,
And its mouth is crammed full of dry earth.]   550

10

[They tortured: "Spill it, tell us what you know!"
But not a single word or cry or moan
Gave her enemy anything to use.
Years add up to decades–and each brings
Torments, prison, deaths–for me to sing
Amid such horrors–that I cannot do.]

11

[Ask any of the women of my age–
Any of those arrested, exiled, caged–

And she'll try to make you understand
How terror left us half–demented,   560
How we raised children to be sentenced
To firing squads or concentration camps.]

12

[Having tightly sealed our bluish lips,
Bereaved Hecubas who've lost their wits
And Cassandras from Chukhloma as well,
In a silent chorus we'll proclaim
(We, united by the brand of shame):
"We are here, on the far side of hell."]

13

Shall I plunge into a state hymn and drown?
Don't give, don't give, don't give me the crown   570
That on a dead man's brow was borne.
I sing no longer to Shakespeare's lyre,
Now comes Sophocles' hour to inspire–
Fate steps forward, knocking at the door.

14

But here's what that theme was like for me–
A flower that fell to the floor unseen
And was crushed when a coffin went past.
Friends, "remember" and "call to mind"
Are as different as Luga's countryside
Is from the city of satin masks.   580

15

I opened a trunk and dug things out–
The devil made me do it–well, but how
Does that mean I'm the one most to blame?
I'm simple at heart, I don't try to shock,
You know my books: *Wayside Herb*, *White Flock*. . .
To defend myself–what can I say?

16

But know this: if plagiarism's the charge . . .
Well, am I the guiltiest one at large?
Though I for one don't care any more.
It all turned out badly, yes, I know,   590
I'll freely let my confusion show . . .
But this chest contains drawers within drawers.

17

I admit, too, that there are some things
I inscribed in sympathetic inks . . .
I've learned how to do mirror writing.
On every road was a barricade–
It's a miracle I found this way,
And forsaking it is not inviting.

18

So let the envoy from an age long gone,
From a dream El Greco brooded on,   600
Explain to me, not using any speech
But only a smile like the summer sun,
That for him all the sins most to be shunned
Were almost lawful compared to me.

19

And then let the man from the coming age,
The one yet unknown, not hesitate
To look around with audacious eyes,
And to me, a shade vanished into gloom
He'll offer heaped–up lilacs in bloom
In that fair hour when this storm's gone by.   610

20

But the hundred–year–old enchantress
Suddenly woke, head full of fancies.
I didn't invite it, I was just there.
Her lace kerchief languidly falls,

From behind the lines her coy looks call
In a Bryullov pose, her shoulders bare.

21

I drank her in every drop and was cursed
With a raging demonic thirst,
I didn't know what to do, couldn't bear it,
I had to get away from this raver,   620
I threatened her with the Star Chamber
And forced her back home to her garret–

22

To the darkness under Manfred's pines
And to where, face turned to see the sky,
Shelley's body lay upon the shore,
And the ethereal sphere was riven
As all earth's skylarks soared to heaven,
And George Gordon held a torch.

23

But her reply was firm and stately:
"No, I am not that English lady,   630
And I'm certainly not Clara Gazoul.
I don't claim any forefathers' glories,
Save from the sun and mythical stories
And July itself brought me to you.

24

"As for your ambiguous fame,
For twenty years left to lie unclaimed,
Yet I shall not have it served like this.
In triumph we two shall celebrate,
And your evil midnight will be repaid
With the splendor of my royal kiss."   640
          January 5, 1941
          The House on the Fontanka
          in Tashkent
          and after

PART 3

Epilogue

May this place be empty . . .

                                        –?

And the mute empty spaces of the squares
Where people were executed at dawn.
                                        –Annensky

I love you, Peter's great creation.
                                        –Pushkin

To my city

The white night of June 24, 1942. The city in ruins. A panoramic view from the harbor to Smolny. Here and there old fires are burning themselves out. In the Sheremetev garden, lindens are blooming and a nightingale is singing. A third-floor window (with a crippled maple in front of it) is shattered, and behind it is a gaping black hole. The rumble of heavy artillery is coming from the Kronstadt area. But in general things are quiet. The voice of the author, seven thousand kilometers away, speaks:

> Under the roof of the Fontanka House
> Where the evening langour wanders round
> Bearing a lamp and keys on a ring,
> I hallooed and distant echoes answered,
> And my inappropriate laughter
> Troubled the unbroken sleep of things
> In the place where each day, at dusk and dawn,
> Witness to everything that goes on,
> The old maple gazes into my room.
> As it sees our parting in advance,   650
> It extends to me a gnarled black hand
> As if giving help, remaining true.
> But the earth beneath me stirred and moaned,
> And into my not–yet–abandoned home
> Glared the star that heralds death and fear
> Ready to march on the appointed day . . .

It's in Tobruk somewhere–still far away,
It's right around the block–it's almost here.
(You, not the first nor the last there'll be,
Dark listener to bright fantasy,   660
What revenge on me are you engaged in?
You're just sipping it, you won't drink up
This grief to the bottom of the cup–
The bitter news of our separation.
Don't lay your arm upon my shoulder,
Let the world never grow any older,
Let the hands of the watch you gave me freeze.
Ill fate and sorrow will not pass us by
And the cuckoo will no longer cry
Amid our leafless fire–blackened trees . . .)   670
Guard towers and barbed wire carve out a space
Deep within a measureless cold waste,
And there–but when, I don't know and won't guess–
Made an unperson, every trace wiped out,
Horrific facts changed to word of mouth,
My double's being taken to "confess."
Then, duly escorted by his keepers,
Two envoys of the noseless Reaper,
My double's being taken away.
And even as far distant as I am–   680
Truly an amazing happenstance!–
I hear what my own voice has to say:
    No IOUs–I paid hard cash
        For all you've done,
    A full ten years, no less, I've passed
        Beneath the gun,
    I didn't dare look right or left
        A single inch,
    And after me at every step
        The slanders hissed.   690

Where I faced doom but didn't perish,
You, city of granite, hellish, cherished,
Have fallen silent, turned deathly white.

My parting from you is only feigned,
Part of each other we still remain,
Upon your buildings my shadow lies,
Upon your waters my image falls,
My steps echo through the Hermitage halls,
Where my love and I once made our way,
And across old Volkovo Field,   700
Where my tears don't have to be concealed
Amid the quiet of common graves.
Everything written in the first part
About love, betrayal, and the heart,
Free poetry has shaken off in flight,
And my city stands "as good as new . . ."
A heavy burden lies upon you,
The gravestones placed on your sleepless eyes.
I fancied that you followed as I fled,
You who stayed behind to meet your death   710
With gleaming waters and spires of gold.
How you awaited bearers of good news—
They didn't come . . . Now all that's left to you
Is your white nights, still dancing as of old.
And the blest word—home—has become unknown,
All of us who have nowhere of our own
Peer through others' windows from outside.
Some are in New York, some in Tashkent,
And the bitter air of banishment
To the exile is like poisoned wine.   720
And all of you could marvel, if you wished,
When in the belly of a flying fish
I eluded the malice of foes,
And over war-ravaged forests I soared
Like she who, impelled by demonic force,
Into the air above Brocken rose.
Already I could see ahead
Where the icy Kama River stretched.
"Quo vadis?" I heard someone ask,
But before I could have made a sound,   730
Across the mad Urals I was bound,

177

Their tunnels and bridges roaring past.
And open before me lay the road
Along which so many were forced to go,
And my son, too, suffered that cruel command.
The track of that funereal column
Unfolded through the crystalline, solemn
Silence of the Siberian land.
Seized by terror and overmastered
By dread of those who'd turned to ashes,   740
Knowing the length of retribution's reach
And acknowledging its hour had arrived,
Wringing her hands, with dry downcast eyes
Russia went before me to the east.

Finished in Tashkent
August 18, 1942

PART III

Critical Essays

Bearing the Burden of Witness:
Requiem

§ § §

Requiem was born of an event that was personally shattering and at the same time horrifically common: the unjust arrest and threatened death of a loved one. It is thus a work with both a private and a public dimension, a lyric and an epic poem. As befits a lyric poem, it is a first-person work, arising from an individual's experiences and perceptions. Yet there is always a recognition, stated or unstated, that while the narrator's sufferings are individual, they are anything but unique: as befits an epic poet, she speaks of the experience of a nation.

Finding the proper balance between the lyric and the epic was crucial to the creation of *Requiem*. The individually numbered poems of *Requiem*, in which the personal element dominates, were originally composed as separate lyrics. The composition in March 1940 of the "Dedication" and the "Epilogue," in which the public element dominates, allowed Akhmatova to conceive of the work on the broader scale appropriate to the epic. Once a framework was established by the "Dedication" and the "Epilogue," the individually numbered poems were arranged within it symmetrically. Thus if the midpoint of *Requiem* is taken as running between poems 5 and 6, it will be noted that these two poems are both direct addresses from the narrator-mother to a son who is in prison and facing death, and that such a direct mother–to–son address occurs nowhere else in *Requiem*. Further, poems 2, 3, and 4, in which the emotionally dissociated narrator alternates between viewing herself as "I" and "not I," have a counterpart in poems 7, 8, and 9, in which the narrator contemplates extreme forms of escape from her own consciousness–the reduction of her personality to that of an automaton (poem 7), death (poem 8), and madness (poem 9). In fact, both "No, it's not I . . ." (poem 3) and "Already madness' outstretched wing . . ." (poem 9) were written after March 1940, and both were duly inserted into the work in such a way that the already existing axis of symmetry was maintained.[1]

The relationship between the personal and social aspects of *Requiem* is also a key theme of its four–line verse epigraph and the "Instead of a Foreword," both of which were added years later, during the Thaw, as if to clarify the poem's significance for a widened circle of potential readers whose understanding could not be as readily assumed. The verse epigraph is spoken by an "I," but it is an "I" who, although she could have been somewhere else, nevertheless has chosen to be "among my people," sharing their sufferings. In "Instead of a Foreword," as Akhmatova stands in a prison line, a walking dead woman–torpid, blue–lipped, her voice shrunk to a whisper–asks the poet, "Can you describe *this*?" The question is not only a challenge, but a plea: you yourself have experienced what has happened to us; do not let our sufferings be unrecorded and forgotten. When Akhmatova answers the the woman, "something like a smile slipped across what once had been her face." The questioner has been so crushed that a full restoration of her individual humanity, her face, is not possible. Unlike the poet, she no longer has words that can convey her personal agony. But it is still possible for the poet to describe the forces that crushed women like her interlocutor and to evoke at least a "something like," a shadowy glimpse of the lives that were destroyed.

The suffering that is implicit in "Instead of a Foreword" is powerfully explicit in the "Dedication." The anguish of the prisoners' relatives is an elemental force, mightier than Nature itself (lines 1–2); it is so all-consuming that they can see or hear nothing unrelated to it (lines 6–8). Their lives are turned upside down, so that the spirit of communal harmony (*sobornost'*) that is the ideal characteristic of Russian Orthodox worship (the "early Mass" of line 11) is replaced by a forced unity of common grief; for them, the city has ceased to be a center of culture and become a savage place (line 12); and the women themselves, though alive, are even more lifeless than the dead (line 13). The announcement of a sentence has an effect so terrible as to suggest a brutal murder (line 18) or a rape, with the woman thrown backward to the ground, then staggering off (lines 19–20).

One hesitates at first to speak of the formal qualities of such a poem; it seems inappropriate, like discussing a film on the Holocaust as an example of cinematography. But one reason *Requiem* affects the reader so powerfully is that Akhmatova is able to express intense and almost overwhelming emotion within a precisely designed artistic structure, giving her words the force that confinement within a narrow channel gives to flood waters. This careful design is apparent from the very first line of the "Dedication," which reads in Russian, "Pered etim gorem gnutsya gory"– a striking alliteration that I have tried to suggest by the translation, "A grief so great would lay a mountain low." The words set in quote marks in line 4 are a citation, readily recognized by any educated Russian, from Pushkin's poem "Deep within Siberian mines. . . ." Pushkin's poem is a message of hope to the imprisoned Decembrists, telling them that just as his free voice can reach them even within the "convict holes," so one day freedom itself will break their chains. By contrast, the voices of Akhmatova and the bereaved women for whom she speaks are powerless, incapable of reaching those "inside" or of freeing them. This sense of hopelessness is reflected in the slow and heavy movement of the poem. The "Dedication" is written in five–line stanzas—a form not quite as rare in Russian as in English, but still so uncommon that the reader, whose expectations have been formed by four–line stanzas, unconsciously perceives five lines as prolonged or drawn out. The pace is further slowed by the poem's use of repetition: "*Dlya kogo-to* veter veet svezhy / *Dlya kogo-to* nezhitsya zakat" ("*Some* breathe fresh air and feel light breezes play, / *Some* love the lingering sunset's tranquil mood"); "*Slovno* s bol'yu zhizn' iz serdtsa vynut, / *Slovno* grubo navznich' oprokinut" ("*As if* her beating heart had been torn out, / *As if* coarse hands had grabbed her, thrown her down"); "*Chto* im chuditsya v sibirskoy v'yuge? / *Chto* mereshchitsya im v lunnom kruge?" ("Amid the snowstorm's whirl *what* do they sense, / Or from the moon's white circle *what* portends?"). Time itself seems to lose meaning and blur into an endless round of suffering; line 22 reveals that the previous stanzas are describing events of two years earlier, but the verbs in those stanzas switch freely and almost imperceptibly from past to present tense and back again.

The final stanza of the "Dedication" sounds the theme of witnessing. Akhmatova realizes that the women with whom she stood in line were "involuntary friends," each too preoccupied with her own personal grief to offer any real support to another. The description of the stricken woman walking away alone and unregarded (line 20) is echoed in Nadezhda Mandelstam's memoirs:

> . . . I shall never forget the woman whose son had been arrested by chance, instead of a person of the same name who lived next door and happened to be out when the secret police came to pick him up. Though it meant moving mountains, the woman had managed to get through to some official and prove that her son had been arrested by mistake. An order had gone out for his release, but she was now told that her son was dead, having been killed in some quite improbable accident.
>
> On hearing this in the Prosecutor's Office, the woman screamed and sobbed. The Prosecutor himself came out of his cubby–hole and shouted at her . . . to make her understand that he could not be expected to do his work properly unless he had peace and quiet . . .
>
> Other people from the line gathered around the Prosecutor and the howling woman, but she got no sympathy from them. "What's the use of crying?" asked one long–suffering woman who was also trying to find out about her son. "That won't bring him back to life, and she's only holding us up." The disturber of the peace was removed and order was restored.[2]

But while someone like this "one long–suffering woman" has had her focus pitilessly narrowed by pain, Akhmatova's view is broadened by her ordeal. While those who are safe and well are able to ignore the tragedies around them (there is a bitter irony in that "Some breathe fresh air and feel light breezes play . . ."), Akhmatova's own suffering makes her recognize her affinity with others who are suffering. Without expressing any fear of what might happen to her, she is concerned about the fate of others like her, including the possibility (suggested in lines 23–24) that they might end up following their male relatives into Siberian camps. One might say that, paradoxically, it is precisely Akhmatova's consciousness that she is just another woman in the line that makes her more than just another woman in the line, that gives her the unique power of being able to speak not just for herself, but for them all.

This consciousness of oneself as merely part of the crowd–"herded with the herd" in Mandelstam's phrase–reaches its high point in the next poem, "Prologue." Of all the poems in *Requiem*, this is the least personal in nature, eschewing any use, explicit or implicit, of the word "I." (Perhaps this difference in tone accounts for its not being originally included in *Requiem*; according to Chukovskaya, it was added only in 1960.)[5] The central figure of this lyric is Russia, which in the original Russian is referred to not by the official and imperial term "Rossiya," but by the time–hallowed and emotionally evocative "Rus." The poem draws on one of the oldest Russian political myths: the image of the country as neatly divided into *we* and *they*. *We* are the ruled, the ones below, while *they* are the rulers, the ones on top; *they* are evil, responsible for all the hardships of *our* life, while *we* are good but powerless to stop *them*; *they*, despite all *their* power, are a mere handful, while *we* are the real Russian nation. Like many myths, this one has some truth in it, but it is also a convenient simplification, since it disregards the troublesome question of the degree to which ordinary people were indifferent to or complicit in the government's crimes (what might be called the "willing executioners" problem). For Akhmatova, Russia in the late 1930s is a nation of victims, of prisoners and those mourning for them, a tortured nation in which "no one smiled . . . except the dead, who'd found peace at last." This was how the Terror was experienced by the Russian intelligentsia; an ordinary factory worker might have described the same time period quite differently. But to regard Akhmatova's poem as an oversimplification on the grounds that not every Russian lived in imminent fear of arrest, that the Terror's direct impact on the USSR's population of some 170 million was limited to "only" a few million deaths or permanently mutilated lives, is an act of moral blindness. Not many years before Akhmatova was born, thinking Russians regarded the suffering of the innocent as a moral factor of such weight that Dostoyevsky had Ivan Karamazov ask whether one could accept universal happiness if it came at the cost of the unredeemed torment of a single child. By a standard anywhere close to Dostoyevsky's, no matter what the material achievements of the Soviet regime were, the Terror would nevertheless have to be regarded as the defining event of the "Yezhov era."

The first numbered poem, as noted earlier, grew out of the arrest in 1935 of Punin and Lev Gumilyov. Its first words, which I have translated as "Arrest at dawn," would literally read as "They took you away at dawn"; in Stalin's Russia, "they came for him" or "they took him" was a common euphemism for "he was arrested." The image of taking naturally suggested a funeral procession, in which the body is borne away. Yet clearly this is not a Soviet funeral: the word *gornitsa* ("high chamber") in the third line is an archaism; candles are burning before the household icons (*u bozhnitsy*); and an "icon's chill" comes from the dead man's lips. The all-too-contemporary image of an arrest has fused with Russia's Orthodox past. Line 7 gives the precise historical bearings: "the wives of those the Tsar put to death" would literally translate as "the wives of the *streltsy*." During the seventeenth century, the *streltsy* ("shooters" or, more freely, "musketeers") were an elite military regiment that took on some of the attributes of a palace guard, intervening violently in the succession dispute of 1682. The young Tsar Peter—not yet known as Peter the Great—learned to fear and hate them, and when they staged an abortive revolt in 1698, the tsar turned on them with a ferocity that left a permanent mark in Russia's historical consciousness. After savage tortures, sometimes presided over by Peter himself or those closest to him, hundreds of *streltsy* were publicly executed. Some were literally hung from the Kremlin battlements. Pushkin, in his poem "Stanzas" (1826) spoke of this event as the terrible beginning of what ultimately became a glorious reign; Akhmatova's poem "Stanzas" (1940) borrows Pushkin's title and develops its imagery—the enlightened later Peter, by founding the new capital of Petersburg, rightly repudiates the Kremlin, the scene not only of his own early brutalities, but of the crimes of Ivan the Terrible and old Muscovy's power-hungry rulers. Yet it was to this haunted place that, in 1918, the Bolsheviks returned the seat of government. And it was to the Kremlin that, in 1935, Akhmatova went to petition the new tsar to spare her husband and son. The image of the Kremlin as the enduring seat of unjust power allows the motif of the helpless suffering of ordinary individuals to expand from the contemporary images which dominate the "Dedication" and "Prologue" to encompass centuries of Russian history.

While the first of the numbered poems expands the motif of arrest and its resultant suffering across time, the second expands it across space. From Leningrad and Moscow, the scene shifts to the Don River, the "quiet Don" of Cossack songs (as well as of Mikhail Sholokhov's novel of Cossack life). The opening lines of the poem have a decidedly folkloric cast, with nature personified in the form of a "yellow moon" wearing a jauntily tilted cap, Cossack-style. The seemingly naive quality of the verse is reinforced by its simple couplets in trochaic tetrameter. (In Russian poetry, the trochee–a two-syllable pattern of an accented syllable followed by an unaccented one–is regarded as "folkish," in contrast to the more literary iamb, which has the reverse pattern; one of the best-known lines of trochaic tetrameter in English is "Mary had a little lamb.") The peaceful traditional picture of the first four lines is unexpectedly shattered by the blunt tragedy of "Here's a woman . . ." The jarring effect of the sudden transition suggests the influence of Pushkin's narrative poem *Poltava*, in which a celebrated descriptive passage, "Quiet is the Ukrainian night . . ." abruptly segues into a scene in the prison cell of Kochubey, an unjustly arrested Cossack who has been tortured and is awaiting execution.[4] Like Pushkin, Akhmatova is able to depict even the most intense suffering in a few precisely chosen words: the tragedy that has overtaken this unknown woman in the dark is summarized in a brilliantly laconic parallel construction, *Muzh v mogile, syn v tyur'me* (literally, "Husband in grave, son in jail") whose implicit equating of the two fates, prison and death, sounds one of *Requiem*'s recurring themes. And the reader barely has a chance to begin to take in the destruction of this woman's family before getting hit with a second shock in the final line, when the anonymous woman turns without warning into a first-person narrator who directly addresses the reader.

This bifurcation of the suffering woman, who is both "I" and "she," continues in the next two poems. The third poem, "No, it's not I . . ." is the first appearance of a motif which reappears in poems 8 and 9, the attempt to escape a reality that is too painful to bear–in this case by the narrator's dissociating herself from "the thing that happened," denying that she was the one it happened to, refusing to face it, demanding that it be hidden away. In the fourth poem, "If in your mocking youth . . ." the split in the narrator's consciousness becomes even more pronounced: the poem is addressed by the narrator (an implied "I") to herself ("you") and reflects on how unimaginable the sufferings of her present life would appear to her own prerevolutionary self (an implied "she"). Poems 3 and 4 are also linked by their broken-off quality. In poem 3, the only one written in free verse, each successive line becomes shorter, as if the poem were succumbing to the fall, not only of darkness, but of silence. Poem 4 consists of eleven lines, two quatrains followed by what appear to be three lines of an unfinished quatrain, so that its concluding lines "Not a sound—and yet how many they are, / How many innocents are dying in there now" are followed by an absence, an empty space where one expects the sound of the last line to be.

In poems 5 and 6, the narrator has a clear and fixed identity, as the mother of an imprisoned son; it is the surrounding reality that has become fractured and unstable. Time shifts between the precision of "seventeen months" and the vagueness of "weeks . . . lightly skimming by." In a world without mercy, human and beast become indistinguishable (*homo homini lupus*, the Latin proverb has it—"man is a wolf to man"). The one certain feature in this broken universe is death, which in poem 5 is evoked by metaphors: the blooming flowers covered by the dust of mortality, the censer of a church procession (like the funeral of "Arrest at dawn . . ."), the path to nowhere that suggests an abrupt end to "the journey of our life" (in the words of Akhmatova's beloved Dante). In poem 5 a "great star blazing on the heights" has "death . . . in its glare"—an expanded and more disturbing version of the "stars of death" image of "Prologue." Similarly, in poem 6, the white nights of the far northern summer that peer into the prisoner's cell are reminiscent of the yellow moon that enters the hut of poem 2; but while the moon is merely an inappropriate intrusion into the woman's solitary gloom, the white nights are a clearly predatory and threatening gaze. Not only the human beasts, but the natural world and the cosmos itself have become a hostile force.

In the "Dedication," the narrator–observer watches the agony of a woman who hears the cruel sentence passed upon her husband or son; in poem 7, "The Sentence," she experiences it herself. However, unlike the bereaved mother described by Nadezhda Mandelstam, this narrator understands thoroughly well what prison–line etiquette requires of her: although the news is as crushing as a heavy stone falling on her chest, she makes herself speak as if it were just an everyday piece of bad luck, dismissing her own suffering in offhand, colloquial language: "It's no surprise, I should have known, / I'm ready for it, more or less" (*Nichego, ved' ia byla gotova, / Spravlius' s etim kak-nibud'*). This bizarrely level, matter-of-fact tone continues into the second stanza, in which the narrator contemplates what needs to be done to maintain such forced equilibrium: she must destroy everything that makes her a unique and irreplaceable individual–her memories, her feelings, her hopes and dreams–after which she can "relearn how to live." What kind of existence this "relearned" life might be is something better not contemplated; surely it was such a life that Nikolai Punin was warning against when "he said to his friends who had sunk into apathy, 'Don't lose despair!' "[5] As it turns out, however, the narrator is in no such danger, for although she has emotionally shielded herself against every form of direct attack, a single unexpectedly benign moment is enough to pierce her brittle defenses. The simple light and warmth of the summer sun–in contrast to the darkness (night, moon, stars) and cold which run through most of the poems of *Requiem*–suggests the possibility of a gentler world, and by that very suggestion serves as a terrible yardstick, a stabbing reminder of how far any such hope is from becoming realized in the narrator's life.

"The Sentence" has a surface resemblance to poem 4, "If in your mocking youth . . . ," in that both are monologues addressed by the narrator to herself. On closer examination, however, there is a significant difference between the two lyrics. In the earlier poem, the narrator sees her personality as divided between two irreconcilable selves, one past and one present. In "The Sentence," the narrator exhorts herself to split her life apart, to become a different person than she is; but such a fracture does not actually occur, and as a result, the pain she hoped to be able to escape continues unabated.

This intense pain gives rise to poem 8, "To Death." "Prologue" has already spoken of the dead as being the only ones at peace. Now the narrator asks to be granted that peace herself. Akhmatova's image of the death she anticipates is no mere abstraction, no "half in love with easeful death." Death is welcome even though it presents itself in concrete and ugly forms: poison gas, a skull fractured by a robber, typhus. Such images were not randomly chosen but, in the context of 1939, reflected real dangers. In August 1939, when this poem was written, it was clear that a major European war was approaching; and for those who, like Akhmatova, were old enough to remember the gas warfare of the First World War, it was natural to assume that any impending conflict could include gas attacks against the civilian population. Russia in the 1930s was also going through a series of vast social upheavals that had uprooted millions of people, and though no Soviet statistician would have dared admit it, no doubt one of the obvious results was an upsurge in both violent crime and infectious disease.⁶ Yet none of these vivid, tangible threats appear to the narrator to be as likely a cause of death as the very thing that has driven her to want death in the first place–the shadow of what Solzhenitsyn called "the destructive labor camps." This form of slow death is assumed to be so familiar to the reader that the poem does not need to spell it out in full: the first scene, that of arrest, is sufficient. And even that one scene is reduced to its easily recognized essentials: the appearance of a faceless "uniform" (in the Russian original, this figure is referred to simply as a "blue hat," alluding to the color of the security organs' hatband and epaulets), the sight of whose insignia inspires automatic terror, not only in the person about to be arrested, but also in a mere bystander such as the janitor. So strong, however, is the narrator's desire for the peace of death that even this seemingly all–consuming terror does not make her flinch– "No matter now." Her imagination, her fear, her horror are all focused on a different picture: not her own potential sufferings, but the hunger, cold, and exhausting labor being endured on the wild stretches of the Yenisei River or in the Far North by "one I love."

The search for a way to deal with unbearable pain continues in poem 9. Just as complete insensitivity appeared to be a refuge in poem 7 and death in poem 8, so in poem 9 dementia seems to promise relief. This promise gives rise to the initial image of the poem, "Already madness' outstretched wing . . ." The wing, as in the epigraph of *Requiem*, is a protecting shelter, a metaphor presumably derived from the Bible, where it is regularly used to describe God's protection (Deut. 32:11; Ruth 2:12; Psalms 57:1, 61:4, 91:4; and Luke 13:34). Yet this poem sounds a different emotional note from its predecessors in that the proffered relief that is welcomed on one level is simultaneously repudiated on a deeper level. Madness is alluring, but its allure is recognized as dangerous; it is overwhelmingly powerful, yet the narrator tries to resist it. Madness would take away her pain, but pain is an integral part of her memories of her son. To lose one would be to lose the other, and the loss of her memories is too high a price to pay for relief.

This perception of madness as at once attractive and repulsive produces a paradox: at the same moment that the narrator declares herself already lost, unable to recognize her own voice as she speaks "broken, babbling words," she nevertheless demonstrates the tenacity of her sanity by listing all the things she would *not* be able to remember, or to list, if she truly were insane. In contrast to the highly charged imagery of the first stanza, the last stanza conveys a striking precision of description that could never be achieved by a disordered mind. This quiet, level tone hints at the possibility of a different way of responding to the pain: not by trying to dissociate from one's own experience (as in poems 2, 3, and 4), nor by trying to wipe out one's consciousness (as in poems 7 and 8), but by taking the very thing that is the source of the pain—one's love for a person who is being tormented—and turning that love, that loyalty, into a source of power that makes one capable of doing what at first seemed beyond human strength: standing by the victim, supporting him, and, when that is no longer possible, remembering him. When the suffering woman overcomes the first and most natural impulse of fleeing from pain and is able to perform the great spiritual feat of choosing to stand and endure, she can no longer be crushed like the blue–lipped woman of "Instead of a Foreword." She has gained the stature necessary for the role of witness.

It is this type of witnessing and enduring that is at the heart of poem 10, "Crucifixion." Here Akhmatova invokes the figure of Mary, mother of Jesus, as she stands at the foot of the cross, as the supreme example of the anguish and courage of the mother/witness. The identification of Mary with the mothers whose sons died in the Terror is strengthened by the epigraph, a slight misquotation of the Russian Orthodox service for Easter Saturday. The correct text would read, "Weep not for Me, Mother, when you see Me in the grave." But the families of those who died in the Gulag would never know where their sons were buried, never be able to lament at the grave as Mary had done; and Akhmatova accordingly deletes that image from the epigraph.

Throughout "Crucifixion," it is the human drama, not the theological one, that is at center stage. Glorious and terrible manifestations of divine power do not answer Jesus' question, "Father, why have You abandoned Me?" for what the dying Son seeks is not signs and wonders, but the simple comfort of human communion. And so he turns to his mother and addresses her, comforting her—"Do not weep for me"—just as in poem 9 the narrator clings to her memory of her son's words of comfort. Jesus' direct address to Mary is an acknowledgment that she has actively assumed the role of supporter and witness. By contrast, although Mary Magdalene and John the beloved are both present, spiritually they are bystanders. Their grief echoes the grief of the narrator in the earlier poems: Mary Magdalene's violent shriek of grief calls to mind the "howl" outside the Kremlin walls of poem 1, while John's freezing "as still as stone" evokes the narrator's resolve in poem 7 to "make my heart stone." Like the narrator in the earlier poems, both Mary Magdalene and John flee the confrontation with ultimate pain: they do not dare to look at the suffering mother. Yet what they cannot even bear to look upon, she can endure.

The witness achieves not freedom from pain, but clarity of purpose and stability within pain, like the calm at the eye of a hurricane. It is this quiet strength that underlies the first part of "Epilogue," in which pain is both distant and near. What these lines describe, with sober photographic precision, is not suffering itself but its aftereffects, the physical marks left by the ordeal: the fearfully lowered eyes, the faces lined with care, the prematurely gray hair. The pain is past, and yet it is not past, for the ways it has changed the women are irreversible.

Once the poet–witness is no longer overmastered and blinded by her own agony, she is able to respond to the suffering of the women who surround her. The steadfastness with which she holds on to her memories of her son is extended to "all those who stood beside me," and through this faithfulness the "involuntary friends" of the "Dedication," each concerned primarily with her own loved one, become a true community.

This sense of mutual responsibility is expressed in Russian Orthodox terms: the "hour of remembrance" (*pominal'nyi chas*) in the second half of the "Epilogue" suggests the practice of prayer for the sick or for the souls of the dead (*pominanie*), a suggestion reinforced by the fourth couplet's image of a list bearing the name of each sufferer, which would allow them to be individually mentioned during a religious service. When this list is confiscated, making such individual remembrance impossible, the poet responds by weaving "a mantle [*pokrov*] of words." *Pokrov*, which may be translated as both "veil" and "protection," is also the name of a major Russian Orthodox festival commemorating an appearance of the Virgin Mary at the church of Blachernes in Constantinople in the tenth century: after praying before the altar, the Virgin took off her shining veil and extended it over all the people present in the church, thus offering her protection, not merely to the two saints who were able to see her, but to the entire congregation. Similarly, the poet's "mantle of words" safeguards the memory of the whole community of grieving women. And just as she speaks for and commemorates all the stricken, if she herself is struck down, all of them are called upon to speak for and commemorate her.

The role of the poet–witness is to ensure that the suffering women are not forgotten, to continue always to grieve on their behalf. Time and change go on in the world around her, threatening to efface the memory of the victims, but she refuses to change: for her, time is stopped, fixed in one place perpetually, so that the memory of the Terror never grows any less keen to her. The possibility of a mental escape from the agony of the present into the past has been destroyed: both the narrator's childhood by the sea and her youthful rendezvous "in the Tsar's park" seem emotionally distant and inaccessible, and the former beloved has vanished into the realm of shades, as an "unconsoled ghost." The only time that seems real to her is the present, which stretches out in an endless ordeal: "And the gates never budged, and the bolts remained fast." Yet if no change, no lessening of pain, could be hoped for during her lifetime, there was still the possibility of the "blest ease" of liberation through death. Now, in a supreme act of self–sacrifice, the poet chooses to continue her witness by not allowing herself that last avenue of escape, by willing herself to remember and to suffer even beyond the grave. Transformed into a fixed and unchanging statue (the Russian word is *pamyatnik*, from *pamyat'*, memory) she will perpetually represent the memory of the victims, and each spring, the time of rebirth and renewal, her "tears" will once again be shed for her never–lightened sorrow.

There is no bronze statue where Akhmatova waited. But she was enough of a classicist to know Horace's ode on his own poetry, "Exegi monumentum aere perennius"–I have built a monument more lasting than bronze. *Requiem*, the monument she built, will stand throughout the ages, watching over the dead with grief and faithfulness and love.

Forward Into the Past:
The Way of All the Earth

§ § §

The themes of time and memory underlie all three of Akhmatova's long poems of the year 1940, *Requiem*, *The Way of All the Earth*, and *Poem Without a Hero*. In *Requiem*, the approach to these themes is simple and direct: to preserve the memory of one particular time, one particular experience. But this simplicity contains a paradox: *Requiem* preserves memory by forever freezing time in one place. It saves one time and one memory at the cost of disallowing all others. It is natural she should have such a constricted view of time in the immediate aftermath of a devastating personal loss such as that Akhmatova experienced when her son was arrested. But as the first shock wore off, such an uprooted life, a life in which everything that had occurred before the bereavement was regarded as devoid of meaning, became impossible for Akhmatova to maintain. Her consciousness of being rooted in an age–old Russian culture was a fundamental part of her worldview, of who she was as a poet. Confronted with personal and historical catastrophe in the present, she needed to seek out their roots in the past.

In its early stages, this need expressed itself not as a conscious program, but as a force that unconsciously began to express itself in her poetry. During World War II, when she was a refugee in Tashkent, Akhmatova gave the following account of the creation of *The Way of All the Earth*:

From a letter to *** (instead of a foreword)

In the first half of March 1940, lines that were not connected to anything else began to appear on the margins of my rough drafts . . .

At that time, I found the meaning of these lines obscure and, if you wish, even strange; for quite a long time they gave no promise of turning into a complete whole and appeared to be ordinary fugitive lines, until their hour struck and they fell into the forge from which they emerged in the form you see them here.

In the fall of that year, I wrote another three works which were not lyric poems; at first I wanted to combine them with *The Woman of Kitezh* [the alternate title of *The Way of All the Earth*] . . . but one of them, *Poem Without a Hero*, broke free . . . [and] would not tolerate any companions; two others, "Dostoyevsky's Russia" and "My fifteen–year–old hands," suffered a different fate: apparently they have been lost in besieged Leningrad, and what of them I restored from memory here in Tashkent is hopelessly fragmentary.

In fact, neither "Dostoyevsky's Russia" nor "My fifteen–year–old hands" were lost as completely as this letter suggests. "My youthful hands" (the revised first line of "My fifteen–year–old hands") is indeed fragmentary, but enough of it has survived to indicate that its theme was the world of Akhmatova's youth, evoked through typical scenes and details of the time and the destruction of that world:

> That house has left no trace, no splinter,
> That tree–lined walk has been chopped down,
> Long since the hats and shoes worn then
> Were laid to rest in a museum.
> Who knows how empty the sky is
> After the tower has collapsed,
> Who knows how silent the home is
> After the son has not come back.

After the war, the reestablished text of "Dostoyevsky's Russia" became the first of a cycle of poems entitled *Northern Elegies*. This work was originally conceived of as biographical, sequentially addressing Akhmatova's experiences at various stages of her life; and although the final version of the work did not maintain this strictly chronological order, the biographical intent is still discernible.[1] Thus Akhmatova's childhood and early fame were the inspiration for the fifth elegy ("For me there was no rose–colored childhood..."') and a poem written in 1921 reflecting the early years of her marriage to Gumilyov ("It was terrifying living in that house...") became the sixth elegy. The seventh and final elegy was intended to depict her official persecution, in the form of a speech of the accused to her judges; it was never finished. "Dostoyevsky's Russia," which in the *Northern Elegies* was renamed "Prehistory," serves to set the stage for what follows. "Prehistory," like "My youthful hands," summons the spirit of a lost era–in this case, late nineteenth–century Russia–through a series of characteristic tableaux. These tableaux are drawn from the literary works of the period–from Leo Tolstoy, Ivan Turgenev, Nikolai Nekrasov, Mikhail Saltykov-Shchedrin, and above all from Fyodor Dostoyevsky, whose sufferings (including near-execution on the Semyonovsky Square in 1849 and subsequent imprisonment in Siberia) give him a prophetic insight into the underlying instability of his own time and the catastrophes that will soon befall:

> The fevered country shakes, and the Omsk convict
> Saw all, and placed a cross as on a grave.
> Now he mixes everything together
> And, brooding over elemental chaos,
> He hovers like a spirit. Midnight strikes.
> His pen squeaks, and from the piled–up pages
> Comes the smell of Semyonovsky Square.
>
> So that's when we dreamed up the bright idea
> Of being born, and having picked our time–
> A perfect one for seeing spectacles
> Without a peer–we bid nonbeing good-by.

Thus, despite whatever changes or omissions the restored texts may have from the lost 1940 versions, it is safe to say that "My fifteen–year–old hands" and "Dostoyevsky's Russia" both sought to reestablish the link between the past and the present of 1940. "Somewhere close to the age of fifty the whole beginning of life returns," Akhmatova would later write;[2] she had turned fifty in June 1939.

This wish to reconstruct the past, to bring the past back to life, also underlies *The Way of All the Earth,* as shown by the epigraph that gives the poem its title. The epigraph is a conflation of two quotes from different sources that are linked by parallel circumstances. The source that Akhmatova identifies is the Testament of Vladimir Monomakh, a medieval prince who ruled Kiev from 1113 until his death in 1125. The Testament opens with the words, "Sitting in the sleigh, I ponder in my heart and praise God." In Old Russian, the phrase "sitting in the sleigh" evokes the image of a funeral cortege; the Testament, then, is the work of a man who anticipates his death and who looks back upon his life to see what lessons he has learned so that he may pass them on to his sons. The source of the second part of the epigraph is the Old Testament, which recounts the final advice that the dying King David gave to his heir: "When the time of David's death drew near, he gave this last charge to his son Solomon: 'I am going the way of all the earth. Be strong and show yourself a man. Fulfil your duty to the Lord your God'" (I Kings 2:1–3). Thus both sources of the epigraph suggest the possibility that although men die the past does not, that its experience remains valid for those yet living.

This search for historical continuity is expressed in the poem's form: in contrast to the blank verse of "My youthful hands" and "Dostoyevsky's Russia" and the complex, highly literary stanza structure of *Poem Without a Hero*, *The Way of All the Earth* is written in a metrical scheme strongly suggesting a literary imitation of the centuries-old folk song tradition.[3]

Russian folk tradition is also the source of the central image of *The Way of All the Earth*, the legend of the city of Kitezh. While this tale goes back to medieval Russian chronicles, the treatment of it to which Akhmatova is most clearly indebted is Nikolai Rimsky-Korsakov's opera *The Legend of the Invisible City of Kitezh and Lady Fevronia* (1907), which combines the Kitezh legend with elements from the *Lives of Saints Peter and Fevronia of Murom*. In the opera, Fevronia is a beautiful and wise maiden who lives a simple, pious life in a forest on the Volga. One day when Prince Vsevolod is out hunting, he comes upon her hut and is moved to love by her beauty and innocence. He tells her that he is the son and heir of the ruler of the cities of Little Kitezh and Great Kitezh and proposes marriage to her. She is initially reluctant to leave her quiet life but realizes that he is her fate and accepts. Just as the wedding procession is making its way through Little Kitezh, the brutal Tatar army descends upon the city (an event reflecting the devastation of the state of Kievan Rus' by the invading Tatars in 1240–41). All the people who have gathered to celebrate are slaughtered; only Prince Vsevolod manages to fight his way through. Fevronia is seized, but her life is spared because her beauty arouses the khan's lust. The Tatars also spare a drunken good-for-nothing, Grishka, on condition that he show them the hidden pathway to Great Kitezh. Meanwhile, in Great Kitezh, Prince Vsevolod raises an army to fight the Tatars, while the noncombatants gather to pray to Christ and the Virgin that the city be spared from desecration by the infidels. Prince Vsevolod's army is overwhelmed by the Tatar horde, and he falls on the battlefield. But in response to the prayers of the city's assembled people, the city of Great Kitezh, its church bells ringing, vanishes from the sight of the Tatars, as it simultaneously descends into Lake Svetly Yar and ascends into heaven. The Tatars, cheated of their prey, console themselves by encamping on the now-empty site and sharing out the plunder. In the general drunkenness that follows, Fevronia and Grishka are able to make their escape. The two of them take refuge in the forest, living on what food they can find or beg from peasants; Grishka, who has been driven half-mad by guilt, reviles both Fevronia and his fate, but Fevronia bears everything patiently. Finally she is so exhausted she can go no further. Grishka abandons her, and she collapses to the ground. She is awakened by her bridegroom, Prince Vsevolod, who appears in a shining aureole. He leads her into the heavenly city of Great Kitezh, where they will be united in joy and light forever.

The first lines of *The Way of All the Earth* immediately evoke Fevronia's fate. The narrator-heroine wanders alone, wounded and suffering, through a war-torn landscape, driven onward by a harsh Russian winter, seeking her way back to her home in Kitezh. Then a contemporary detail jarringly intrudes: she approaches a Soviet sentry (addressed as "comrade") and shows him her pass. In response, he lets her through, and she enters a landscape that is exactly the opposite of the one she just left: peaceful, fruitful (the apple grove), beautiful, with the possibility of "someone's hand / To take hold of mine." But she realizes that this idyll is nevertheless the wrong place, not the place to which she was summoned:

> But I don't hear the wheeze
> Of the barrel organ now.
> What the woman of Kitezh hears
> Isn't that sound.

198

Citing other mentions of a barrel organ in Akhmatova's poetry, Kees Verheul suggests that "the barrel organ formed one of the associative symbols of everyday life of the early twentieth century."[4] Thus its absence would imply that the place the narrator–heroine has reached is not the place that the woman of Kitezh must find–her past. Alternatively, in her notebook entries on *Poem Without a Hero*, Akhmatova several times mentions "Fate in the form of an organ grinder" who shows prominent figures of 1913 their future.[5] In this case, the absence of the barrel organ implies that the place the narrator–heroine has reached is not her fated one. The two interpretations are compatible because when her period of wandering is completed, Fevronia will find her destined future in a miraculously preserved past.

In the second and third sections of *The Way of All the Earth*, the analogy between Fevronia and the narrator–heroine breaks down; for while the heroine does indeed return to her past, it is a past that has become distorted, infected by the chaos and agony of the present. The "old Europe" of the past has become a scene of devastation. The narrator turns from it to the island of Crimea, where Akhmatova spent the summers of her girlhood and where she became aware of her poetic vocation (a theme echoed in her long poem of 1914, *At the Edge of the Sea*). But everything about this return to the past is wrong. The heroine finds not the promise of youth, but the panoply of death: the mourners who escort her, the dead medusa washed up from the sea. The Muse to whom she offered her youthful fidelity now treats her with incredulous scorn. Instead of the admiration that Akhmatova's early poems received, the only fame that is offered the narrator–heroine is the "ambiguous fame" spoken of in *Poem Without a Hero*, the Soviet-era fame of the "reviled and revered" poet–a fame so costly that the heroine is warned that it would be better to forego it (and poetry) altogether, to return to the safety of the paternal home.

Instead, the narrator–heroine continues her journey into her past. In the third section of *Way*, she tries to return to the early years of her first marriage; but here terror and bloodshed block her way back. The last time in her life that Akhmatova had a home of her own was when she and Gumilyov were married, and the image of the eerie, abandoned house is associated in her poetry with his death. In a poem written days after his execution, "Terror that picks through objects in the dark...," she describes herself as being alone at night in a house where a moonbeam falls on an ax and ominous noises come from behind the walls. She imagines her own execution, which is seen as preferable to waiting in fear and breathing in the bedsheets' smell of decay. The sixth poem of the *Northern Elegies*, "It was terrifying living in that house," describes the narrator's constant gnawing sense that behind the facade of the happy home, behind the youthful successes of the two poets and their love of their infant son, something terrible was lying in wait. The poem concludes with the lines, "Now you are where all is known, so answer me: / What was it living in that house besides us?" In the context of these two poems, the imagery of *Way of All the Earth*'s third section becomes comprehensible: she calls upon E. T. A. Hoffmann, the literary master of the uncanny and supernatural, to help her understand the ominous shadow she has glimpsed for twenty-five years–since 1915, when, no doubt, it was the thing "living in that house besides us." As in "Terror that picks through objects in the dark . . ." and another lyric alluding to Gumilyov's death, poem 2 of *Requiem* ("Quiet, quiet the Don flows . . ."), the moonlight reveals a place that was once a home but now is horribly emptied, its inhabitants struck down by violence: "In the dark slept a man / Whose throat had been slashed."

The fourth section of *Way* returns the narrator to Akhmatova's own present as the author of *Requiem*. "Sound at its purest"–poetry–is associated with separation, just as Akhmatova's poetic energies, renewed after years of virtual silence, were being used to commemorate those whom she had lost. The familiar and beloved city of Petersburg/Leningrad has now become the haunt of death, the "feral city" of *Requiem*'s "Prologue," the "crucified capital." (To the credit of the often–obtuse Soviet censorship, someone apparently had the sense to recognize the subversive implications of this line, for in the version of *Way* published in the Soviet Union, the words "Through the crucified capital" were replaced by "On through new losses.")

It is through the crucified capital, through the historical ordeal of her generation, that the narrator–heroine must pass to reach her journey's destined end. Thus in the fifth section of *Way*, when she again returns to the era of her adolescence, the era of the second section of *Way*, she sees it with a new consciousness born of her knowledge of the subsequent course of events. The bird cherry is a symbol of spring, of beginnings, in an era that was the beginning of Akhmatova's adult life as well as the beginning of the twentieth century. But the seeds that are germinating in this spring are those of "old Europe's" catastrophic collapse. The Russian warships *Koreets* (*Korean*) and *Varyag* (*Viking*) were among the vessels sunk at the Battle of Tsushima (1905), a Russian naval disaster that further undermined tsarism's already declining prestige and underscored the rise of Japan as a new, non-European world power. The Boer War of 1899–1902 was fought between the British and the Boers (descendants of Dutch settlers) for control of South Africa; while the superior military resources of the British Empire ultimately enabled the English to prevail, the Boers put up an unexpectedly strong resistance that damaged both Britain's self-confidence and its international image. A Fort Chabrol played a role in this war; but the name was also satirically ascribed to a house on Chabrol Street in Paris which served as headquarters for the conservative Catholic and military circles opposed to reopening the case of Alfred Dreyfus, a Jewish army officer unjustly convicted of treason in 1894. The case became a touchstone issue in a culture war between the French right and left, a war that at times was not merely figurative: "Fort" Chabrol acquired its nickname in 1899 because of its armed resistance when the police came to arrest a particularly vitriolic anti-Semitic agitator. The poem alludes to each of these events because they are all part of the same larger phenomenon, the decay of the old European order that would soon be shattered by World War I. Just as the narrator–heroine cannot reach her own past despite all her efforts, so the past, symbolized as an enfeebled old man, is hemmed in and unable to advance, to go into the future (the narrator's present).

If the heroine, in the present, cannot reach the past and the past cannot reach her, how is the "woman of Kitezh" to return to her lost home? Here again Fevronia's story offers guidance, for Fevronia is able to enter Kitezh only after enduring every hardship, until she reaches death. As Valentin Tomberg notes, Fevronia's "suffering is undeserved from the point of view of her own individual destiny; she did not cause it herself . . . [Rather, it] is experienced as something that is a preparation for future glory. Suffering is not interpreted merely as a payment of debts, but also, and above all, as a divine choice."[6] It is just such a choice that is made by the narrator–heroine of *The Way of All the Earth*. In the poem's first section, the heroine is driven on by winter, the season of death; in the last section, she accepts the winter in a spirit of self-renunciation. (The translation's image of her as taking the nun's veil is correct but inadequate; in the Russian original, she takes the *schema*, the strictest of all monastic vows.) Like Vladimir Monomakh, she "sits in the sleigh" that will take her on her last earthly journey. She has already forfeited all the human ties that sustained her during her mortal life and goes "Without brother or friend / Or the man I loved first." Instead, she bears with her the tokens of immortality: a pine branch, whose green in winter makes it a symbol of lasting life; and a poem, which, though treated as if it were of little value (even a beggar makes no effort to hold on to it) nevertheless is "sunlit" (*solnechny*), preserving in winter the radiance and warmth of the sun, giver of life. And the poem ends with a prayer for the rest of her own soul: "In my last dwelling place / May I find peace."

With its daring combination of motifs from the traditional, religion-based culture of Old Russia and images reflecting the twentieth-century historical experience of instability and disintegration, *The Way of All the Earth* stands at the beginning of a new creative path for Akhmatova. Henceforth, rather than regarding the past and present as irrevocably severed, she would strive to bring them together, to make each of them shed light upon the other. The result would be the great work that dominated the last quarter century of her life, *Poem Without a Hero*.

Rediscovering a Lost Generation:
Poem Without a Hero

Akhmatova regarded *Poem Without a Hero* as the "summit of my creative path."[1] Certainly it consumed her to an extent without parallel among any of her other works. The first draft of the *Poem*'s first part, "The Year 1913," was written in 1940; the date of its completion is usually given as 1962. Yet even then Akhmatova did not necessarily regard it as finished: a jotting in her notebook dated September 8, 1962, that proudly notes, "It appears that today I finished *Poem Without a Hero*" is followed by a single word added later: "No."[2]

A comparison of the earliest surviving version of the *Poem*, written down in Tashkent in 1942, with the version of 1962 shows that what happened during those twenty years was a process of development and elaboration of an existing structure. The *Poem* of 1942 already had the basic three-part structure which led Akhmatova occasionally to refer to it by the alternate title *Triptych*; by 1962 this structure had been orna-mented with new dedications, epigraphs, prose sections, and supple-mentary materials such as footnotes and not-quite-discarded stanzas. Almost all the lines from 1942 remained in the 1962 *Poem* either un-changed or with minor changes. But the total number of lines had dou-bled, as images which originally were barely suggested in a line or two expanded to fill whole stanzas.

Akhmatova was well aware that some of the readers of the ever-longer and more intricate creation thought that by adding afterthought upon afterthought she was spoiling the original. But from her perspective, she had no choice. To her, the *Poem* was not something that came into being as she made it and that she could choose to make differently; it was a preexisting work that presented itself to her. She consistently spoke of *Poem Without a Hero* as a living being (an image facilitated by Russian grammar: in Russian the word *poema*, –a long narrative poem, –is of feminine gender, so the proper pronoun for referring to *Poem Without a Hero* would be "she," not "it"). This being had a will of its own, one not subject to explanation or contradiction; it revealed itself to the poet, bit by bit, when and where it chose to do so. To use Akhmatova's terminology, the *Poem* would "go away" for a period of time and then "come back" unpredictably. In short, Akhmatova never let go of the *Poem* because, in her understanding, the problem was not a matter of her letting go of it, but of its letting go of her. But why didn't the *Poem* let go? Why did it always "come back?"

The notebooks that Akhmatova kept during the last years of her life, from 1958 to 1966, give some insight into this inability to gain release from the *Poem*. What immediately strikes a reader of Akhmatova's entries regarding the *Poem* is how little resemblance they have to what one imagines as the "writer's workshop." A scholar seeking to trace the line-by-line evolution of the *Poem* would gain relatively little information. Instead, the notebooks contain numerous passages such as this:

> The horror is that *"everyone"* was at that masquerade. No one sent their regrets. Osip Mandelstam, who hadn't yet writtten a single love poem, but who was already well-known. . . . The mysterious villager Klyuyev, and [of course, he wasn't factually there] the great Stravinsky who made the whole 20th century resound to him, and the demonic Doctor Dapertutto, and Blok, who had already been plunged for the past five years into hopeless weariness (the tragic tenor of the epoch), and Velimir I, who came as if to the "Dog," and Salomeya, the immortal shade, who even now could confirm that all this [was *so*] is the truth (although I dreamed it, and not she), and Vyacheslav Ivanov–Faust, and Andrey Bely, whose dancing footsteps came running up, carrying the manuscript of "Petersburg" under his arm, and Tamara Karsavina like a fairy tale, and . . . in the depths of the hall, the stage, hell (I don't know which) something makes the times resound like thunder–either a mountain

echo or the voice of Chaliapin. Sometimes there soared past either a Tsarskoe Selo swan or Anna Pavlova. And already the pre–Brik Mayakovsky was probably smoking a cigarette over by the fireplace. I don't see myself, but I've probably hidden myself somewhere, if I'm not that Nefertiti of Modigliani's drawing. That's how he depicted me many times in 1911, in an Egyptian headdress. Fire consumed the sheets, but a dream brought one of them back to me.[3]

Some (though far from all) of the images in this passage appear in "The Year 1913," but this is clearly not a summary of that section of the *Poem*. Instead, although work on the *Poem* was far advanced by the time this was written, what such a passage most resembles is an embryonic stage of the *Poem*, something that might have been written before a single line of verse was actually set down.

The creation of a work of art is, crudely speaking, a progression from chaos to order. It starts with a stage of fruitful but chaotic inspiration, in which images, observations, and reflections arise in a jumble. The artist then must sort through this jumble and establish a structure within which the initial creative impulse can be expressed in an ordered and aesthetically appropriate form. An artistic work is fully completed only when all the parts of the original chaotic inspiration have found their rightful place within the organized whole. *Poem Without a Hero*, however, resisted such completion. No matter how many images, how many details, Akhmatova incorporated into it, some crucial part of the *Poem's* generating impulse always remained outside, unable to be transformed from chaos to order.

Akhmatova tried to deal with this problem by considering radically different forms of structure. She did not confine work on the *Poem* to verse: she wrote an article entitled "Prose About the *Poem*" and inserted explanatory prose paragraphs before each section of the *Poem*. She refused to categorize its genre and seized upon a phrase from Peter Viereck's *The Tree Witch*: "This book may be read as a poem or verse play." Most startlingly, there were moments when Akhmatova ceased to think of the *Poem* as a work of literature at all. Twice she attempted to turn it into a ballet—or, in her characteristic description, "it [the *Poem*] twice went off into a ballet libretto"—before it decisively resumed its verse form.

Thus it appears that the reason Akhmatova never stopped working on the *Poem* was that she was never able to feel she had achieved the basic task of the artist: to find a form suitable for organizing the images and emotions that provide the artist's original impetus and making that raw material into a work of art. Since in the case of the *Poem* this impetus was Akhmatova's memories of the world of her youth, finding a form which could organize the *Poem* was a task equivalent to putting her youthful experience in the context of her entire subsequent life, understanding what that experience meant, and passing judgment upon it.

Thinking of Akhmatova's work on the *Poem* as an attempt to come to terms with overwhelming memories helps to explain the apparently obsessive hold the *Poem* had over Akhmatova. Her friend Nadezhda Mandelstam wrote about this hold:

> Akhmatova complains about the way in which *Poem Without a Hero* totally swallowed her up from the beginning and never let go of her. She threw herself into her housework—scouring saucepans, washing clothes, sweeping, cleaning up, and all the other things she normally neglected—in a desperate attempt to gain some respite and struggle free of this current carrying her off into the unknown. She remained in the grip of the poem for a number of years.[4]

When the poem came, there was literally nowhere she could go to escape it: in 1965, she jotted in her notebook, "In one of the rejected 'Fore-⟨⟨words⟩⟩' the author declares that from 1946–56, when lyric poetry didn't come, the *Poem* pursued her even in her sleep."[5]

Try as she might, Akhmatova could not gain the release of putting her youthful experience into a unified, meaningful perspective because history had ensured that no such perspective could exist. The world of Akhmatova's youth had not faded away into a natural death. It had been violently broken apart and replaced by a new order that did its best to disavow and destroy the old. Witnesses to the past were dead or scattered, its physical traces obliterated or given new interpretations. Such a fracture in a culture also produces a fractured perspective in those who live through it, so that even one who had seen the older world could not feel entirely convinced of the reality of her memories:

> Answer this at least: is it really true
> That once there lived such a one as you?

> Across squares with wooden pavement laid
> Did your dazzling feet really make their way?

Here only one small fragment of the world of the remembered past–the fact that in prerevolutionary Petersburg the pavements were made of wood, not asphalt or concrete–can be confidently affirmed as having had a genuine existence. Everything else, although memory confirms it to be true, nevertheless on some emotional level feels impossible and thus untrue.

To be both real and not real is, of course, the property of the other-worldly, and the confrontation of incompatible time periods within the *Poem* is regularly described in terms of supernatural imagery. The wind becomes a living force and speaks, "either remembering or prophesying" (implying that the past cannot be distinguished from the future); spectral masqueraders from the Silver Age suddenly make their appearance in the author's apartment in 1940; a "guest from the future" appears in the mirror.

In her deployment of supernatural imagery, Akhmatova draws upon Russian folk tradition. In this tradition, the New Year was regarded as the time when the boundary between this world and the other world was most permeable. In particular, young women practiced various forms of fortune-telling or divination (*gadanie*) to learn the identity of their future suitors. In one well-known ritual, the woman was to place two lit candles between two mirrors that faced each other; it was believed that an image of the lover would become visible in the deep recesses of the mirrors' mutual reflections. A variant of this was a spell to bring back an absent lover: if, in addition to the candles, a table with two places was set before a mirror, at midnight the man would return to dine with his beloved. It is this ritual that is suggested by the first lines of "The Year 1913." How-ever, the spell apparently has an unexpected effect: instead of summon-ing the beloved, it calls up the masqueraders from 1913. In the Tashkent version, this is its sole effect; in the later versions, it also calls up the "guest from the future" who appears in the mirrors, just as the future lover should do. When the time finally does come for this guest to make a flesh-and-blood appearance, however, he turns out not to be a lover after all:

It's not for him to be my espoused,
But what we together will bring about
Will trouble the Twentieth Century . . .
But not the first lilacs of the spring,
Nor love's sweet prayers, nor yet a ring–
It's doom he'll come bearing me that night.

These lines enable us to recognize the "guest from the future" and ad-dressee of the Third Dedication as Isaiah Berlin, whose meeting with Akhmatova in 1945 she regarded as a cause of the cold war ("will trouble the Twentieth Century"), as well as of the 1946 resolution against her.

It is also significant that the "guest from the future" appears not just in any mirror, but in the so-called White Hall of Mirrors in the Fontanka House, which was just across the landing from Akhmatova's apartment. This location links him to a long chain of Petersburg history. An entry in Akhmatova's notebook reads,

More about the "Poem"
. . . besides the things (cf. the 1st frag(ment)), the Fontanka House itself got involved in it: the old trees from when it was still Swedish, the White Hall (of Mirrors)–across the landing, where Parasha herself sang for Tsar Paul I, the grotto destroyed in the year . . . , some sort of spectral gate and the golden cuneiform of the streetlamps on the Fontanka . . .[6]

"Parasha" is Parasha Zhemchugova (1768–1803), a serf who became a renowned singer in the domestic theater of her owner, Count Pyotr Borisovich Sheremetev. As a boy, Count Sheremetev had been a play-fellow of the future emperor Paul I, and in later years, despite Paul's increasing paranoia, he never lost his trust in Sheremetev. In honor of this royal friendship, Parasha gave a private performance for the mon-arch, and the pearl ring with which he rewarded her provided the sur-name by which she became known ("zhemchuga" in Russian means pearl). Sheremetev fell in love with the celebrated performer and openly treated her as if she were his wife, but given the great difference in their social ranks, he hesitated to marry her. When Parasha was diagnosed with tuberculosis and the doctors warned Sheremetev that her days were numbered, he made her his legal wife, and she died soon after the birth of the couple's only child, a son.

Despite Akhmatova's confident assertion, Parasha Zhemchugova could not have sung in the White Hall of Mirrors, since it had not yet been built at the time.[7] One can offer two reasons for Akhmatova's allowing herself to believe her revised version of history. One is that she wished to strengthen the link between her own residence and a site associated with Parasha, with whom Akhmatova strongly identified as a woman who was a gifted artist, whose social position was marginal, and who, like Akhmatova, was officially forbidden to practice her art (her doctors feared that singing would hasten the progress of her disease). Further, Akhmatova wrote of the White Hall as the place "where Paul I used to hide behind the mirrors and eavesdrop on what the Sheremetevs' ball guests were saying about him."[8] Such a position—seeing without being seen, hearing without being heard—suggests the relationship of the narrator of "The Year 1913" to both the maskers and the "guest from the future": she can relive the past and hence see the maskers, but they cannot see her present (their future); she can foresee the "guest from the future," but he cannot make his way to her. This combination of awareness and inaccessibility is reminiscent of Wislawa Szymborska's lines: "We read letters of the dead and are like helpless gods, / yet gods after all, for we know what happened after."

It was just such "letters of the dead" which gave the initial impetus to *Poem Without a Hero.* In a subsequently rejected prose foreword to the *Poem* entitled "From a letter to NN," Akhmatova wrote, "In the fall of 1940, while sorting through my old papers (subsequently destroyed during the Siege), I came across some letters and poems which I had had for a long time but hadn't read before ('I opened a trunk and dug things out— / The devil made me do it'). They were related to the tragic event of 1913 recounted in *Poem Without a Hero.*" The "tragic event" was the suicide of Vsevolod Knyazev, a rejected lover of Akhmatova's friend Olga Sudeikina. When Sudeikina had emigrated in 1924, she left Akhmatova her small amount of furniture, including an eighteenth–century carved Italian wedding chest which contained her personal papers. Among these papers were Knyazev's letters to her and a small, posthumously published collection of his poems.

It is not surprising that Akhmatova had not thought about Knyazev for so long. There was, in fact, nothing particularly memorable about him: a handsome young man of about twenty (he was born in 1891), a cornet in a hussar regiment stationed in Riga, an aspiring though not especially promising poet. In 1912 he fell passionately in love with Olga Sudeikina and began to write love poetry in which he depicted himself as Pierrot pursuing Columbine. Sudeikina accepted and enjoyed Knyazev's attentions, but she was too accustomed to being admired by men to be content for long with a single lover. Perhaps because of his youth, Knyazev had failed to realize this, and when he saw her offer her favors to others, he became jealous and demanding. This did not endear him to her, and finally she told him that it was over—a declaration which, of course, only inflamed his feelings further. In January 1913, he tried to win her back by writing her two love poems whose intent was unmistakable, but Sudeikina remained unmoved. Knyazev returned to his regiment in Riga and there, on March 29, 1913, he shot himself.[9]

As Ya. Vilenkin, a literary scholar who was a friend of Akhmatova's in her later years, has pointed out, such dramas were part of the spirit of the times:

> At the beginning of the nineteen-tens the suicide of young people, especially in literary-artistic circles and the bohemian society of Moscow and Petersburg, became a widespread phenomenon. Thus in Moscow in 1910 there was a great deal of excitement and noisy discussion in the newspapers of the "triple suicide," as it was then called, "on romantic grounds" of the young society beauty O. V. Glebova, the talented engineer N. M. Zhuravlyov and N. L. Tarasov, a millionaire patron of the arts, who had belonged to the inner circle of the Moscow Art Theater. In 1911, the young Petersburg poet Viktor Hofman committed suicide ("He shot himself in a cab," said Akhmatova, who had become acquainted with him not long before). The disturbing motif of voluntarily ending one's life... was echoed in literature (L. Andreyev) and on stage (F. Bedekind's "Spring's Awakening" at the Komissarzhevskaya Theater, S. Yushkevich's "Miserere" at the Moscow Art Theater).[10]

Beyond this generalized phenomenon, Akhmatova had personally been loved by more than one man who took her refusal as a reason to put an end to his life. As we have seen, during his difficult courtship of Akhmatova, the young Nikolai Gumilyov had attempted suicide more than once. Akhmatova told Chukovskaya that one of the Kuzmin-Karavayev brothers (Gumilyov's cousins, whom she had met at Slepnyovo) had tried to kill himself on her account.[11] There is some evidence that Akhmatova believed she was the cause of the suicide of the cadet Mikhail Lindeberg, who shot himself in his barracks in Vladikavkaz on December 23, 1911.[12]

The similarity of Sudeikina's and Akhmatova's experience allows Akhmatova to speak of Olga as her "double," an alternate or shadow self. What separates Akhmatova from this alternate self is time: for while the poet found herself in the Soviet era, she could only think of Sudeikina as belonging to the prerevolutionary period. Indeed, for Akhmatova, Sudeikina was a symbol, an embodiment of that era: "The heroine of the *Poem*," she jotted in a notebook, "is not at all a portrait of O. A. Sudeikina. Rather, it's a portrait of the epoch—artistic Petersburg of the 1910s, and since O. A. was a woman of her time down to her fingertips, she probably is closer than anyone else to Columbine."[13]

The reference to "artistic Petersburg" is significant, for Olga, the "Petersburg doll" and actress (line 346) is repeatedly characterized in terms of the roles she played and the way others saw her. For Knyazev, she is Columbine to his Pierrot. When the narrator addresses her in the "Second Dedication" and at the opening of chapter 2 of "The Year 1913," she appears as the portrait her husband, Sergei Sudeikin, painted of her in the role of Confusion, the title character of a one-act vaudeville by Yuri Belyayev (a combination of heroines from two Belyayev plays produced the "Confusion-Psyche" of the "Second Dedication").[14] And Sudeikina is also the "Goat-legged Girl," or female satyr, an image derived from her performance in the lead female role in the Romanov–Sats ballet *The Fauns* (1912), which contemporaries described as "a bacchanale after the manner of [Michel] Fokine" and "extremely provocative." A review in the newspaper *Day (Den')* wrote of "the half-naked Olga Glebova-Sudeikina's frenzied dances, her unself-conscious twists and leaps, reflecting the movement of a nonhuman being."[15] In this aspect, she represents an unbridled, predatory female sexuality that attracts the "foolish boy," the "fairy-tale youth" whose "heart is pure," as the flame of a candle attracts a moth.

This conflation of a person with the role she is playing is not limited to the heroine. The guests from the year 1913 arrive as masqueraders, that is, as role-players, and the roles they are playing are derived from works of art. In the Tashkent version of the *Poem*, the guests named are Don Juan and Faust; later redactions add Dapertutto (a character from one of E. T. A. Hoffman's stories whose name Meyerhold took as his pseudonym), Iokanaan (the name given to John the Baptist in Oscar Wilde's play *Salomé*, which later formed the basis for Richard Strauss's opera), Glahn (from Knut Hamsen's novel *Pan*), and Dorian (from Oscar Wilde's novel *The Picture of Dorian Gray*). The one guest who is not a literary character is the Milepost, who represents not a work of art, but Art itself. In a note dated December 1959, Akhmatova noted that through all the drafts of *Poem Without a Hero*, the symbolic meaning of this figure had never changed: he "was always . . . the Poet in general, the Poet with a capital P (something like Mayakovsky)."[16] For Shelley, poets were "the unacknowledged legislators of the world," but the Milepost takes this further: he is a lawgiver to lawgivers, someone who could give lessons to such celebrated legislators as Hammurabi, Lycurgus, and Solon. It is the Milepost's power to write in "letters of iron" that makes Akhmatova associate him with Mayakovsky, of whom she wrote in the lyric "Mayakovsky in 1913" that "What you tore down—was overthrown indeed, / In each word you spoke, a judgment struck." And, like the unconventional Futurists, the Milepost is bound by no human custom or opinion: without waiting for the acknowledgment of others, he celebrates a triumph for himself in the unpopulated wilderness. He sees himself as a prophet in the one religion he acknowledges, the religion of art, which he serves as King David served God, "dancing before the Ark of the Covenant" (II Samuel 6:14).

Thus in the world of artistic Petersburg in 1913, as Akhmatova depicts it, life has become art, and art has become a justification for everything. There is no question that the resulting performance is a brilliant one; but it is also a self-enclosed one, indifferent to the ugly and unscripted realities of pain and death:

> We only dream we hear a cock's crow,
> The Neva smokes beyond the windows,
> A fathomless night—and on and on goes
> The Petersburg devils' holiday . . .
> Not a single star in the pitch-black sky,
> There's no doubt disaster awaits nearby,
> But that doesn't blunt the shameless bite
> Of the masqueraders' repartee.

Not only is the midnight masquerade a "devils' holiday," but Mephistopheles himself, the "lame and elegant. . . Prince of the realm below," puts in an appearance. In a commentary on the *Poem* dated 1961, Akhmatova wrote,

> Most of all, people will ask who is "the Prince of the realm below" (they already have asked about the Milepost . . .), that is, to put it bluntly, the devil. He is also in "Flip Side": "The most elegant Satan." I don't much like to talk about this, but for those who know the whole history of 1913—it's no secret. I will only say that he must have been born under a lucky star, he was one of those people for whom everything is possible. I won't recount now what was possible for him, but if I did so, it would make the contemporary reader's hair stand on end.[17]

This figure, like that of Olga / Columbine or Knyazev / Pierrot, is not a literal copy but a stylized representation of one of Akhmatova's contemporaries. But, as Akhmatova says, it is possible for those familiar with Russian artistic circles of 1913 to identify the real-life prototype: Mikhail Kuzmin, a well-known writer of poetry, prose, and criticism whose article "On Beautiful Clarity" (1910) had in some regards anticipated the Acmeist program and who wrote the introduction to Akhmatova's first book, *Evening*. Kuzmin's cultivated elegance of appearance and manner was striking even by the self-dramatizing standards of Silver Age Petersburg. A biographer sums up his reputation as "the legendary possessor of three hundred and sixty-five vests . . . of exotic perfumes, careful manicures, the slightly rouged cheeks" which led contemporaries to refer to him as "the Prince of Aesthetes" and "the St. Petersburg Oscar Wilde."[18] As the latter comparison suggests, Kuzmin was openly homosexual and was particularly attracted to younger men. In fact, prior to Knyazev's infatuation with Sudeikina, he and Kuzmin were lovers, and it was Kuzmin who introduced Knyazev to avant-garde Petersburg literary society.

Akhmatova's reference to this Mephistophelean figure as "the mocking grinner" (*nasmeshnik*) clearly echoes the description of Kuzmin she gave Chukovskaya: "Kuzmin was a very nasty, malevolent and rancorous person. . . . He loved no one, was indifferent to everyone, except his latest boy. There was a real cult of gossip at his salon. This salon had the most pernicious influence on young people: they took it as the height of intellect and art, but in reality it was the perversion of intellect, because everything was considered a game, everything was mocked or jeered at."[19]

But significantly, the feminine form of this word (*nasmeshnitsa*) is precisely how Akhmatova describes herself in poem IV of *Requiem*, when she looks back on her own youth. Thus Akhmatova could have said to the "most elegant Satan" what she tells Columbine: "It's myself, not you, I'm punishing now." This association would explain why the lines on Kuzmin / Satan are immediately followed by the narrator's guilty fear that she will have to face her own younger self–"someone I don't want to meet."

This demonism is not limited merely to the artist–masqueraders: it is part of Petersburg itself:

> To heat the holidays bonfires burned,
> And carriages on bridges overturned,
> And the black–draped city was borne away,
> To drift on toward an unknown goal,
> Following or fighting the Neva's flow–
> But always moving away from its graves.

These lines echo the masqueraders' refusal to acknowledge the proximity of death (the city moves away from, not towards, its graves). In addition, as Akhmatova herself pointed out,[20] this passage reflects the influence of Nikolai Gogol's short story "Nevsky Prospekt" (the name of the main street in St. Petersburg):

Oh, do not trust that Nevsky Prospekt! I always wrap myself more closely in my cloak when I pass along it and try not to look at the objects which meet me. Everything is a cheat, everything is a dream, everything is other than it seems ... You imagine those ladies ... but ladies are least of all to be trusted ... However attractively a fair lady's cloak may flutter in the distance, nothing would induce me to follow her and try to get a closer view. Keep your distance, for God's sake, keep your distance from the street lamp! and pass it by quickly, as quickly as you can! It is a happy escape if you get off with nothing worse than some of its stinking oil on your foppish coat. But even apart from the street lamp, everything breathes deception. It deceives at all hours, the Nevsky Prospekt does, but most of all when night falls in masses of shadow on it, throwing into relief the white and dun–colored walls of the houses, when all the town is transformed into noise and brilliance, when myriads of carriages roll over bridges, postilions shout and jolt up and down on their horses, and when the devil himself lights the street lamps to show everything in false colors.[21]

Gogol's image of the seemingly innocent but deceptive Petersburg beauties finds an echo in Akhmatova's Columbine, the "Petersburg doll," the actress not only in her professional but in her personal life, who has so thoroughly disguised her provincial origins that her former neighbors in Pskov would no longer recognize her, whose home has been turned into a stage set, a "circus wagon," a "garden retreat." But for both Gogol and Akhmatova, the deceptive woman does not exist in a social vacuum; she is the natural inhabitant of a city of false illumination rather than natural light, a city where collapse is always nearby, where streetlamps spill their oil on passersby and carriages are tripped up by the steep bridge ramps.

This myth of Petersburg as the deceptive and unreal city is not limited to Gogol but runs through prerevolutionary Russian literature. Like many myths, it has a basis in historical fact. Petersburg, unlike Moscow, was a planned city, founded by Peter the Great on a site chosen for its strategic possibilities as a naval and commercial port. But the site also had a problem which Peter resolutely ignored: it was not well designed for human habitation. The low marshy ground made construction a slow and difficult operation; when this demanding work was combined with the unhealthful effects of the cold, damp, foggy climate, it resulted in a mortality among the conscripted laborers so high as to give rise to a saying that the city was built on bones. Once the city was completed, another problem became evident: it was subject to flooding. Under certain conditions, the Neva River backed up, and its waters, deprived of any outlet, would surge destructively through the city. One of the deadliest floods, in 1824, served as the inspiration for Pushkin's long narrative poem *The Bronze Horseman*, which takes its title from a famous equestrian statue of Peter the Great in the center of the city. The poem, a founding document of the Petersburg myth in Russian literature, is a meditation on both the grandeur of Peter's achievement and the human cost of that achievement. Its ambivalent stance toward the city it depicts anticipates the ambivalence of *Poem Without a Hero* toward the time it depicts. In Akhmatova's words, the *Poem* is "the apotheosis of the nineteen–tens in all their magnificence and their flaws."[22] Thus it is not surprising to find

215

echoes of *The Bronze Horseman* in the *Poem*: the subtitle of Pushkin's work, "A Petersburg Tale," is also the subtitle of "The Year 1913," and the epigraph to part 3, "I love you, Peter's great creation," is from Pushkin's poem.

The idea expressed in *The Bronze Horseman*–that Peter had founded his capital at a place where a city, humanly speaking, should not be–gave rise to the sense that the city in fact could not be there, that it was an unreality, a mirage. The narrator of Dostoevsky's novel *The Adolescent* put this sense into words: "Hundreds of times, as I've walked through the Petersburg morning fog, this strange and clinging thought has cropped up: 'What if, when the fog lifts and disperses somewhere high up over the earth, this rotten, slimy city is lifted up with it and vanishes like vapor until only the former Finnish marsh remains and, I suppose in the middle of it as a decoration, that bronze horseman on his panted, exhausted horse?'"[23]

The feeling that Petersburg was only a facade, that it could easily vanish, was echoed in a persistent legend claiming that the city was destined to disappear. For just as Peter had repudiated Moscow, the capital of Old Russia, in favor of his new European capital, so he had repudiated his first wife, the pious, conservative Tsaritsa Avdotia, to marry his lowborn Livonian mistress. To the popular imagination, this parallel was so neat as to be irresistible, and so the scorned Avdotia, in the convent which Peter had forced her to enter, was imagined as laying a curse not on the "other woman," but on the "other capital," Petersburg. Her implacable words, "May this place be empty," were remembered with each new urban disaster and would supply one of the epigraphs for the epilogue of *Poem Without a Hero*, which evokes the bombed and starving city of 1942. But while 1942 is an advanced stage in the working out of the curse, its potential already hangs over the city in 1913:

> And, cursed by the wife the tsar hadn't wanted,
> Dostoyevskian and demon–haunted,
> The city plunged into its foggy night.
> Out from the murk an old Peterite peeked,
> Some sidewalk idler–and solemn drums beat
> As if a firing squad stood nearby ...
>
> And through the cold and choking atmosphere
> Of prodigal prewar days, one could hear
> A rumble, a distant warning sound,

> But then it was still only faintly heard,
> And, having no great power to disturb,
> It sank in the Neva snows and drowned.

As the poem developed, these related motifs of the replacement of real life and feeling by a mask (albeit a beautiful one), of demonism, and of the doom awaiting Petersburg and the Petersburg period of Russian culture and history (which ended with the transfer of the capital back to Moscow in 1918) all converged to create the third figure of the *Poem's* triangle, the successful suitor of Olga / Columbine. In the version of 1942, the few lines describing the suitor already make it clear that he is no ordinary man: "Say, my lady, is your chevalier / Gabriel or Mephistopheles?"—an angel of light or a fallen angel. In later versions, this picture is substantially enlarged:

> Say, my lady, is your chevalier
> Gabriel or Mephistopheles?
> The Demon himself with Tamara's smile,
> But such a sorcerer's power to beguile
> Lurks in that terrible dusky visage.
> Flesh that has almost turned to spirit,
> An ear with an antique curl falling near it,
> No one knows what kind of being this is.
> In the crowded hall where the gypsies sang
> Did he send a black rose in champagne
> Or was that just a dream after all?
> With a gaze and a heart both cold and numb
> Did he see the Commendatore come
> To meet him in that accursed hall?

In keeping with the *Poem's* fondness for "mirror writing," Akhmatova identifies the figure of Alexander Blok not directly, but through a series of allusions which the reader is expected to be able to recognize. Blok's image as a poet was the Romantic one of the fallen angel, still bearing some traces of a former ideal of heavenly purity while being drawn irresistibly to debauchery and blasphemy. This image is evoked by a reference to Mikhail Lermontov's ultraromantic poem *The Demon*, which tells of the love of a demon for a beautiful and chaste maiden, Tamara: she flees to a convent to escape him but is gradually worn down by his

217

persistent entreaties and prayers and finally yields to him. She dies from his kiss, and he attempts to claim her soul, but an angel drives him off and bears her soul to heaven. Lines 318–20 ("In the crowded hall where the gypsies sang . . .") are a paraphrase of the first two stanzas of Blok's poem "In a Restaurant" (1910), and the next three lines refer to his "The Steps of the Commendatore" (1912). This poem is a deeply personal re-telling of the Don Juan legend, transferred from sixteenth-century Se-ville to then-contemporary Petersburg. As the poem opens, Don Juan has already seduced Doña Anna, the "Maiden of Light" (*Deva Sveta*), who lies motionless on her bed in a state which might be either sleep or death. Alone in the predawn darkness of the silent house, Don Juan throws a challenge to life and fate, which he sees as empty and pointless. In re-sponse, as the dawn breaks, the Commendatore appears to destroy Don Juan, an act which will restore Doña Anna. The loss or ruin of an ideal of feminine purity, the profound world-weariness and sense of life's mean-inglessness, and the anticipation of a doom perceived as a just retribu-tion are all recurring themes in Blok's poetry; thus Akhmatova identifies Don Juan, as he is depicted in "The Steps of the Commendatore," with Blok himself.

There is in fact no historical evidence of an affair between Sudeikina and Blok. This brings us to a crucial point in understanding *Poem Without a Hero*: although it is a work about history, it does not aim to be simply a versified narrative of fact. It is an attempt to convey the meaning, the essence, of a particular time and place, and facts that do not contribute to this overall vision are freely revised. Thus Sudeikina / Columbine, as the personified feminine ideal of her times, must inevitably attract and be attracted to Blok, "the tragic tenor of the epoch." Similarly, Akhmatova "sharpens" the plot line, altering the facts of Knyazev's life and death in a way that underscores the role of unrequited love in the cornet's suicide, first by making him witness the infidelity of the woman he loves, and second, by having him respond to what he has just seen by committing suicide that very night upon the doorstep of his beloved.

Akhmatova also changes the cornet's regiment from the hussars to the dragoons, a change which seems unnecessary at first glance, but which may have been made precisely to avoid sticking too close to the facts of Knyazev's biography and thus making it appear that the poem was only about a specific individual case. For Akhmatova, Knyazev, as the first to die, represented a whole generation of doomed poets–Blok, Gumilyov, Khlebnikov, Yesenin, Mayakovsky, Klyuyev, Mandelstam:

> How many ways the poet could meet death–
> The foolish boy, he didn't suspect
> And so he chose this one–he couldn't bear
> The first assaults, he never realized
> What sort of door would soon be opened wide,
> What sort of road would stretch out, and to where . . .

Here we can feel the psychological and moral distance between the Akhmatova of 1913 and the Akhmatova of 1940. While for the young Akhmatova death as a result of unrequited love was the acting out of a romantic convention, for the Akhmatova of 1940 it was something very different. Time had taught her there was no aesthetic form of death; death was only horrible. For the author of *Requiem*, death was the enemy. Art could not save the victims, but it was the task of the artist to keep their memory from dying with them. The core values of the later Akhmatova–artistic responsibility and faithfulness to the dead–are incomprehensible to the masqueraders from 1913: they flee and leave her alone to face the memory of Knyazev's death:

> Why do you rush off in a throng,
> As if each saw the bride for whom he longed,
> While I'm left behind to stand forlorn,
> Alone in the gloom, facing that black frame
> From which there looks out, still the same,
> That drama of the bitterest pain,
> That hour none ever rightly mourned?

All of them had allowed Knyazev's death to be forgotten, the very site of his grave lost, and this failure haunted Akhmatova. In a note dated December 17, 1959, she wrote: "A picture snatched from the darkness of the past by the searchlight of memory–Olga and I in the Smolensk Cemetery after Blok's funeral looking for Vsevolod's grave–'It's somewhere by the wall,' Olga said, but we couldn't find it. For some reason I remembered that moment *forever.*"[24]

The lost, nameless grave again suggests the fate of Mandelstam, and in the "First Dedication" the link between the two is made explicit. This dedication is indisputably addressed to Vsevolod Knyazev, as shown by the fact that variant editions of the *Poem* include the words "To the memory of Vs. K." or simply "Vs. K." But the date of the dedication, December 27, 1940, was the second anniversary of Mandelstam's death, according to the death certificate issued to his widow. Nadezhda Mandelstam confirms that this date was not a coincidence and offers an explanation of why in some variants of the *Poem* the date appears at the end and in others at the beginning: Akhmatova, she says, "complained that nobody paid any attention to the date at the foot of the 'First Dedication' and for this reason she had transferred it to the top and thereby given it the greatest possible prominence."[25] Further, the words that Akhmatova ascribes to Knyazev just before his suicide—"I am ready for death" (*Ya k smerti gotov*)—were the same ones Akhmatova remembered Mandelstam saying to her shortly before his arrest in 1934. By thus associating the minor poet Knyazev with a much more important figure, Akhmatova makes Knyazev's status as a forgotten victim all the more unforgivable; it is a crime evoking the parallel, though greater, crime of consigning his "double" Mandelstam to oblivion.

Thus just as Olga/Columbine and Blok/the rival are symbolic figures, so is Knyazev/Pierrot: the "foolish boy," the "pure-hearted youth from a fairy tale," is the archetypical innocent victim, doomed by Petersburg history and by the sins of his generation—a generation which tried to remove him from its consciousness, to wipe out every trace of the reproach that his fate represents. And as the last survivor of that generation, Akhmatova takes its guilt upon herself and attempts to make restitution by reversing that oblivion, by restoring the memory of the dead:

> I, your olden conscience, here affirm:
> I tracked down the tale that had been burned,
> I went to the deceased's house
> And there I laid it down
> On a window shelf—
>
> and then I tiptoed off . . .

While the theme of commemorating the dead links *Poem Without a Hero* with *Requiem*, the word *conscience* never appears in *Requiem*, nor does it need to. In *Requiem*, Akhmatova appears as the representative of a "guiltless Russia" that suffers cruel and incomprehensible torments. But in *Poem Without a Hero* she appears as the representative of a guilty generation, a generation that allowed its artistic brilliance to mask a moral failure. It was Akhmatova's inexorable sense of her own part in this collective guilt, and her consequent need to understand what had happened and why, that over and over again brought her back to the *Poem*.

Such an outlook, suggestive of Dostoyevsky's belief that "everyone is responsible to all for all," was, of course, a profoundly un-Soviet one. Akhmatova's ironic realization of the incomprehensibility of *Poem Without a Hero* to a "typical" Soviet reader underlies the second part of the poem, which in Russian is titled "Reshka," literally "tails," in the sense of "heads or tails." This section is thus the "flip side" of "The Year 1913," being both as inseparably connected to it as are the two sides of one coin and as irreconcilably different as tails is from heads.

"Flip Side" begins on the morning after, literally and figuratively, as the demonic brilliance of the ghostly visitors from the year 1913 gives way to the obtuseness of a Soviet bureaucrat-editor. Akhmatova displays a grim flash of humor in her depiction of this figure's bewilderment at a work that does not fit the Socialist Realist pigeonhole: he tries to avoid dealing with it by claiming he is "busy and sick" (one excuse wasn't enough!) and ensuring that he can't be reached by phone. When his evasions fail, his uncomprehending response to "The Year 1913" echoes standard Soviet literary criticism: it's much too complex, and why does "anyone nowadays"–"anyone" presumably meaning the heroic factory workers and collective farm milkmaids–"need this stuff"?

With surprising forbearance, the narrator tries to explain the poem in a manner simple enough for the editor to understand. Since he has at least recognized that the story line includes "a poet," she starts with that:

> "Three of them are in it," I averred,
> "There's one dressed like a milepost, first,
> As a demon the second appeared–
> Their poems gave them a guarantee
> Of survival through the centuries,
> But the third lived only twenty years
> And I felt sorry for him ..."

However, in true speak-of-the-devil fashion, no sooner does she start to talk about the poem than the poem reasserts itself. Its return is signaled by the "music box" of line 517 and the "unceasing music" of line 523: as Akhmatova's prose writings on the *Poem* show, she strongly associated it with music. The "libretto" of line 522 alludes to her failed attempts to turn the *Poem* into a ballet, an association strengthened by a rejected variant in which the libretto is not "for someone" but "for Artur"–suggesting her earlier work with Artur Lourie in creating a ballet based on a poem (Blok's "The Snow Mask"). The "tongue" of line 520 has the same metonymic use in Russian as in English, so that it refers not only to the organ of speech but to language itself ("the mother tongue"); and as a tongue of fire it suggests not only speech but inspired speech, as at Pentecost.

But this poetic speech that has been released from a repressive confinement (the broken flask) is disturbing, "poisonous," and "angry": it brings back memories that the narrator is not necessarily willing to confront. The words "soft embalmer" (line 525) are in English in the original, and a note by Akhmatova indicates their source, Keats's sonnet "To Sleep." In this poem, sleep is called upon to provide an escape from a restless conscience that strives to unearth a hidden shame, "for darkness burrowing like a mole"–exactly the role that conscience plays in "The Year 1913." This image of something better left unrevealed is echoed in a passage of Maurice Maeterlinck's *The Blue Bird*, in which night is accompanied both by Sleep and by his sister whom "it is better not to name."[26] And it is on the parapets of Castle Elsinore that Hamlet learns his father was murdered and thus becomes aware of a moral duty (retribution) he finds all but beyond his strength to carry out. These images point to the narrator's desire not to assume responsibility for the past, to forget the ghosts of 1913 (the "hellish mocking crew"). The "pine branches" of line 531, which are green in winter, symbolize the still-living remembrance of the dead, as they do in the "First Dedication"; thus the narrator hopes, in vain, that they will be swallowed up in the dark and lost, rather than entering the White Hall–the part of the Fontanka House associated with Parasha Zhemchugova and with Akhmatova herself. But though the narrator wishes that the burden of memory and conscience would pass her by, when instead it is placed squarely before her, she consents to take it upon herself. To fail to do so, she realizes, would make her no better than the "motley clownish Cagliostro" (another guise of the Satanic figure of Kuzmin, who was the author of a biography of Cagliostro) from whom she so pointedly dissociates herself.

The narrator's hesitation at the prospect of assuming the role of witness is entirely understandable, since what she expects to suffer as a result is not merely her own remorse for the past, as in "The Year 1913," but also state-sponsored attacks intended to silence her, by violence if need be. It is not merely the demonic "Roman carnival" of 1913 that vanished in the wake of the Revolution; so too did the sacred speech of the liturgy ("the Chant of the Angels"), which has been driven from the forcibly closed churches. In such a terror-filled atmosphere, poetic inspiration falters (as it did for Akhmatova for years). In contrast to "The Year 1913," in which "words out of the gloom" are associated with someone knocking (line 209), now there is no one knocking and no words; the mirror which previously revealed the "guest from the future" now reflects only another mirror; the "unceasing music" of the *Poem* is replaced by silence, and one must keep silent even (or especially) about the fact of being silenced.

The four stanzas in brackets (lines 545–68) were never included in any Soviet edition of Akhmatova's works, even as late as the Akhmatova centennial of 1989. In their place was a series of dots with a note by Akhmatova: "The omitted stanzas are an imitation of Pushkin. Cf. "On *Eugene Onegin*": 'I humbly admit that there are also two omitted stanzas in [Byron's] *Don Juan*,' Pushkin wrote."[27] This note is an example of Akhmatova's use of "sympathetic ink," intelligible only to the reader with a key: in her published research on *Eugene Onegin*, Akhmatova established that Pushkin left a visible gap in the sixth canto (between stanzas 37 and 39) because the stanza that should have filled the gap was too politically unacceptable to risk even submitting it to a publisher. The initiated reader would assume that the stanzas which were omitted here were "an imitation of Pushkin" in this sense. The missing text was preserved by Lidia Chukovskaya and appears also in Akhmatova's notebooks.[28]

Several candidates have been put forth for "my Seventh" (line 545): Shostakovich's Seventh Symphony, Akhmatova's seventh book, and the seventh and final poem of Akhmatova's "Northern Elegies." Aside from the fact that the Seventh Symphony is mentioned in an early version of the "Epilogue," no evidence can be offered to support its claim. It was widely performed in the Soviet Union, and this stanza is a wrenching description of a suppressed or silenced work of art. At first glance, Akhmatova's seventh book would fit this description, since it had been printed but not yet released to bookstores at the time of the Zhdanov resolution in 1946; the entire edition, except for a few copies which employees of the publisher held on to, was destroyed. As Susan Amert points out, however, its claim is weakened by the fact that in the collection of Akhmatova's poems *The Flight of Time* (1965), Akhmatova was able to restore the title of "Seventh Book" to the section containing the poems from this destroyed work, thus, in effect, reversing its suppression.[29] The strongest candidate, and the one that Chukovskaya supports in her gloss on the omitted stanzas, is the seventh Northern Elegy. This poem, written in 1958 and apparently never finished, was referred to by Akhmatova as "The Last Speech of the Accused." It opens with the lines

> And I have been silent, silent for thirty years.
> The silence of arctic ice
> Surrounds me through innumerable nights,
> It comes to put out my candle.
> A silence like the dead, but theirs makes sense
> And isn't as terrible . . .
>
> My silence can be heard in every place,
> It fills up this hall of judgment,
> Confronted with its shout, the buzz of hostile talk
> Would fade, and like a miracle
> It leaves its stamp engraved on everything.

Silence is here associated not only with weakness (state repression of the power of speech), but also, as in stanza 10 of "Flip Side," with strength (refusal to acknowledge an unjust power).

Silence may also be the result of inability to describe a horrific ordeal, not simply because of fear but because of the inability to find words capable of conveying the nature of the experience. It is this silence of incommunicability that marks the women of stanzas 11 and 12, who want to speak of their lives but know they cannot make a listener understand them. The introductory prose text to "Flip Side" notes that "one can make out very deeply and cleverly hidden fragments of Requiem": here, evidently, is where they are hiding. The women of line 563, with their "bluish lips," are sisters of the blue-lipped woman in the "Instead of a Foreword" who whispered to Akhmatova, "Can you describe *this*?" It is the poet's duty to "describe this" when no one else can, and thus the narrator becomes the witness not only of the past (as in "The Year 1913"), but also of the present.

Just as in stanza 7 the narrator accepted her duty to commemorate the dead by repudiating a poet who in her eyes had failed to do so (Kuzmin), so in stanza 13 she accepts the dangerous role of truth–teller in a repressive regime by repudiating a poet who had once aspired to the role of official spokesman for that regime (Mayakovsky). The recognition Mayakovsky had craved, however, came in full measure only after his suicide, when Stalin proclaimed him "the best and most talented" of Soviet poets; thus his "crown" is worn on "a dead man's brow." Once again, the reluctance of the narrator's consent to her difficult calling is brought out: to understand her own path, she looks not to Shakespeare, who allows for the possibility of alternate outcomes, but to Sophocles, for whom fate cannot be escaped but only accepted.

Each of the two tasks–remembering the past and witnessing to the present–presents its own artistic challenge. Although the narrator still knows the facts of the past, the living emotions associated with them have faded: she compares them to a withered flower fallen from a funeral cortege. Before the past can provide the impetus for a work of art, the narrator herself needs to experience an emotional reconnection with it–a process that occurs when she opens Olga's trunk. Recalling the genesis of *Poem Without a Hero*, Akhmatova wrote, "The *Poem* is a peculiar revolt of things. Olga's things, among which I had lived for a long time, suddenly demanded their place under the poetic sun. They came to life for a moment, as it were."[30] In the aftershock of that moment, the narrator is able to feel again what she felt years ago, when she was the author of *White Flock* (published in 1917) and *Wayside Herb* (published in 1921). Invoking this earlier persona is at the same time a response to the second challenge, that of finding a way to bear witness, to convey a message without its being choked off by the censorship. Her response, reflecting her years of Pushkin scholarship, is to conceal the message and then draw attention to its concealment, so that the reader capable of opening the hidden "drawers within drawers" will look in them. The narrator's ironic professions never to have gone beyond her past self, to have nothing new to say (and even to be guilty of plagiarism), to have failed completely and beyond any excuses–all of this is to be understood in an exactly opposite sense, as a proclamation that she does have a timely, original, and vital message.

There was, of course, a real danger that the obfuscation would succeed too well, that no one would be able to understand the *Poem*'s meaning. Akhmatova was so concerned about the problem of maintaining sufficient but not self-defeating concealment that she envisioned the *Poem* being published along with two sets of commentaries, one ascribed to the author and one to an editor; while the author's notes would all be misleading, the editor's notes would all be true.[31] This fear of overconcealment is also reflected in an omitted stanza, in which the "encoding" of the *Poem* is described as a "forbidden (*zapreshchenny*) device." Presumably this danger is also the reason the envoy from a past age of European civilization, an age when circumstances did not require such artistic subterfuge, finds her "more forbidden" (*zapretnei*) than a mortal sin. Nevertheless, she has no doubt that just as she could read Pushkin's hidden messages, so her destined reader, the "man from the coming age" (line 605), would be able to break her cryptogram.

Then, just as the future seems open to the narrator, suddenly a figure out of the past appears. Who is this "hundred–year–old enchantress"? The reference to a "Bryullov pose" apparently points to Sudeikina. Bryullov, a Russian painter of the 1830s, accepted court patronage and did a number of portraits of society ladies. Poems by both Knyazev and Kuzmin compare a beautiful woman to a Bryullov portrait, and a specialist on Kuzmin has noted that "this comparison in Kuzmin's own works is a code for Sudeikina herself."[32] But could it indeed be valid to see Olga, that quintessential woman of the 1910s, in terms of 1830s portraiture? Or, in more general terms, could an artistic form from the age of Romanticism be adequate to convey the experience of Sudeikina's–and Akhmatova's–generation?

The full relevance of the question to the *Poem* becomes clear when one remembers that the Russian genre of the *poema* itself came into being during the age of Romanticism. Akhmatova regarded Pushkin's self-described "novel in verse" *Eugene Onegin* as the first Russian *poema*.[33] *Onegin* was begun in the early 1820s, a period when Pushkin was enthusiastically reading the works of Byron in the original, and the first chapters of *Onegin* clearly reflect the influence of Byron's long narrative poem *Don Juan*. The narrator thus fears that the *poema* that possesses her and that she cannot escape is the offspring of nineteenth–century Romanticism, which would make it an inappropriate artistic form for the creation of a work that she was resolved would address "the real Twentieth Century." Accordingly, she tries to drive the *poema* out by forcing her (as already noted, in Russian the word is feminine gender) back to her supposed origins in English Romantic history.

But the *Poem* stands its/her ground, telling the narrator that such qualms are based on a misunderstanding: it/she is not "that English lady," but a new and contemporary work, one without immediate literary ancestors–a reflection of Akhmatova's belief that every successful *poema* in Russian literature was essentially unlike its predecessors. And, implicitly bringing "Flip Side" full circle back to its initial image of an uncomprehending and hostile reader, the *Poem* promises Akhmatova that such a fate will not always befall her work:

> In triumph we two I shall celebrate,
> And your evil midnight will be repaid
> With the splendor of my royal kiss.

The initial versions of the first two parts of *Poem Without a Hero* were written within days of each other, and these two parts are obviously organically linked. By contrast, the "Epilogue" was written a year and a half later and reflects an event still in the future when "The Year 1913" and "Flip Side" were written–the German invasion. This evokes a question: given the fact that Akhmatova worked on the *Poem* for many years after the "Epilogue" was written, during which time it acquired a whole array of prefatory material (three dedications, an "Instead of a Foreword," and an "Introduction"), why is there one, and only one, "Epilogue"? If the "Epilogue" was added after the composition of the first two parts in response to World War II, couldn't further sections have been added in response to subsequent events that affected Akhmatova's fate–say, de-Stalinization?

The answer to this question is provided by the dedication to the "Epilogue"–"To my city." *Poem Without a Hero* is, as its subtitle tells us, "a Petersburg tale." The tragedy of 1913 has not one living witness, but two–the poet and the city. As we have already seen, Akhmatova spoke of the Fontanka House itself as "getting involved in" the *Poem*. Its involvement is that of a representative of the city's history, a living presence continuing across generations–"witness to everything that goes on," as the maple tree in its courtyard is described. Akhmatova was aware of the maxim of both Roman and Jewish law that a fact is established upon the testimony of two or more witnesses.[34] The testimony of the poet and that of the city are mutually reinforcing; they are a community of witness to the unforgotten past. The crucial event that inspired the "Epilogue"–an event that affected the *Poem* as no subsequent event in Akhmatova's life would–was the separation of the two witnesses when the poet was forced to flee the threatened city.

The original dedication of the "Epilogue" in 1942 was "To my city and my beloved [*Gorodu i drugu*]." The grammatically and phonetically parallel dedication reflects two parallel relationships: just as the poet is physically separated but spiritually united with her city, so Akhmatova is physically separated but spiritually united with Garshin. Like the city, the beloved serves as both inspiration and listener, thus assisting the poet in fulfilling her destiny:

> You, awe–inspiring, the last there will be,
> Bright listener to dark fantasies,
> Forgiveness, honor, intoxication!
> Like a flame that lights my way you burn,
> Like a banner before me you stand firm,
> And you kiss me sweetly as temptation.

After the breakup with Garshin, the dedication "to my beloved" was removed, and the lines quoted above were revised to indicate that he would prove to be just one more of the lovers who had ultimately disappointed Akhmatova:

> You, not the first nor the last there'll be,
> Dark listener to bright fantasy,
> What revenge on me are you engaged in?
> You're just sipping it, you won't drink up
> This grief to the bottom of the cup–
> The bitter news of our separation.

Thus in the final version of the "Epilogue," the Akhmatova/Garshin relationship is not a parallel to but a contrast with the poet/city relationship: the brevity and inconstancy of the former serves as a bitter irony underscoring the enduring nature of the latter.

The digression that follows (starting with the line "Guard towers and barbed wire carve out a space . . .") points to a different form of possible separation of poet and city: not through war, but through arrest. The "double" who is being taken to a prison camp interrogation is not merely another person with whom Akhmatova identifies (in the sense that Sudeikina is her "double" in "The Year 1913") but is genuinely herself, in an alternate but all–too–plausible reality.

Yet in the end, not only the nightmare that did not come true (arrest) but the one that did (the siege) proves capable of destroying the link between poet and city:

> My parting from you is only feigned,
> Part of each other we still remain,
> Upon your buildings my shadow lies,
> Upon your waters my image falls . . .

The relationship between the two belongs not to time, but to eternity. And as the two mortal beings, poet and city, confront death, each steps out of the realm of chance and into that of fate. The poet's exile from her city is not merely her personal misfortune, but a part of the destiny of her generation, which is scattered to the four corners of the earth: "Some are in New York, some in Tashkent." And the desolation of the stricken city, its population dying or fleeing, is the fulfillment of the curse of Tsaritsa Avdotia, which serves as one of the epigraphs of this section. "May this place be empty. . . ."

In physically leaving the city, the poet goes not from a known place to an unknown one, but from a part of a whole to a greater whole. In the earliest ending of the "Epilogue," this greater whole is the realm of art itself, the art created in and imbued with the spirit of Petersburg/Leningrad. Akhmatova herself was a living representative of this tradition, and as she fled the city, she bore with her a manuscript of a work created there even as the enemy guns were firing, Shostakovich's Seventh ("Leningrad") Symphony:

> And all of you could marvel, if you wished,
> When in the belly of a flying fish
> I eluded the malice of foes,
> And over Lake Ladoga I soared

> Like she who, impelled by demonic force,
> Into the air above Brocken rose.
> And in my wake, lit by mysterious flame,
> A being that took "Seventh" as its name
> Dashed to a festival without peer.
> Disguised as musical notation,
> The Leningrader's renowned creation
> Returned to its ethereal native sphere.

This ending, however, was discarded in favor of another in which the greater whole to which both poet and city belong is not art, but Russia. In her flight from the front, the poet joins millions of her compatriots, as those who cannot fight seek safety and those who can fight seek a place to regroup before taking the offensive. Like the poet, Russia is going to the east.

And the course of the poet's flight underscores a tragic similarity between her youthful community of Petersburg in 1913 and her wartime community of all Russia. For Akhmatova, the Petersburg of 1913 had committed the crime of willfully forgetting its dead, "always moving away from its graves." It ceased to have the sense of mutual responsibility that holds a community together, and in a historical retribution, its physical existence as a community came to an end–its members were decimated, the survivors scattered, "some in New York, some in Tashkent." But Russia, too, has dead whom no one mentions, graves that remain unmarked and unhonored–the graves of those who died in the Gulag. These officially forgotten dead haunt the path Akhmatova travels; for in going east, following the Kama River and crossing the Ural Mountains, she retraces the route along which generations of prisoners had been marched or transported into Siberia.

But there is also a crucial difference between the Petersburg of 1913 and the Russia of 1941. Artistic Petersburg has become so corrupted, so demonic, that it no longer acknowledges the concept of guilt. It cannot repent, and thus cannot be saved. By contrast, Akhmatova's Russia acknowledges the national guilt toward the dead and accepts the ordeal of wartime in a spirit of penance:

> Seized by terror and overmastered
> By dread of those who'd turned to ashes,

Knowing the length of retribution's reach
And acknowledging its hour had arrived,
Wringing her hands, with dry downcast eyes
Russia went before me to the east.

As grim as this final image is, it contains an implicit hope. By using the vocabulary of guilt and retribution, Akhmatova evokes the Old Testament understanding of history: when the nation falls into sin, God allows it to suffer defeat; when disaster leads to national self-examination and repentance, God saves the nation from its enemies. Thus, in Akhmatova's view, Russia's acceptance of what is recognized as expiatory suffering offers the promise of ultimate salvation.

Sadly, the poet's vision of Russia's path was not fulfilled. The high hopes for national regeneration that World War II evoked in many Russian intellectuals (among them Pasternak, as shown by the final pages of *Doctor Zhivago*) were crushed by the intense repression of the late Stalin years. Only years later, and then in painfully slow and piecemeal fashion, would Russian society openly acknowledge the memory of the millions of innocent victims.

But what Russian society could not do in the public realm, the realm of external power, Russian literature could do in the realm of the mind and spirit. Just as Akhmatova believed that Russia would accept its guilt toward the forgotten dead, so the poet herself, as the last representative of her generation, accepts that generation's guilt and repents for its wrongs and her part in them. The writing of the *Poem*, as "Flip Side" makes clear, is itself an act of expiatory suffering, involving both inner pain and external danger. The result is a form of salvation, not only for the poet, but for her generation. Their culture had been destroyed, and the new regime had done its best to distort or suppress their experience and their memories. The poet, through her willingness to confront even her most painful memories, is able to save them from oblivion, to bring back a true image of "the nineteen-tens in all their magnificence and their flaws." And to ensure that this memory is preserved among the living, she incorporates it into a work of art, giving it a place in a tradition that she saw stretching far beyond any one generation, the continuous and unbroken inheritance of Russian and world culture.

PART IV

Commentary

Commentary on *Poem Without a Hero*

§ § §

The first problem confronting a translator of *Poema bez geroya* is to choose which text of the work to follow. Since the work was never published in full in Russia during Akhmatova's lifetime, she repeatedly made manuscript copies of it to give to friends. The result is a text with a large number of variants, not only because of the deliberate revisions that Akhmatova made in the *Poem* over time, but also because repeated hand copying of a text, like any other form of handicraft, inevitably gives rise to individual variations.

The earliest known redactions are three very similar manuscript copies made by Akhmatova in Tashkent during 1942 and 1943. One of these, reproduced in *Tale without a Hero and Twenty-Two Poems by Anna Akhmatova* (Dutch Studies in Russian Literature 3 [The Hague: Mouton, 1973]), was used for the translation given in appendix I. During the late 1940s and early 1950s, when Akhmatova lived in constant fear, she made it a practice to destroy her manuscripts, lest they be seized in a search of her apartment and used against her or her son. Not surprisingly, no redactions of *Poem* from this period survive, even though she was continuing to work on it. In the post–Stalin years, when Akhmatova felt relatively safe and her circle of literary friends expanded, she made a number of manuscript copies of the *Poem*. Some of these were recopied by their recipients or others and, circulating privately, became the sources for the earliest editions of the *Poem* to appear in the West. Thus one cannot speak of a definitive edition of *Poem*, although some redactions may have stronger claims for consideration than others. For the specialist interested in this problem, Carlo Riccio has dedicated an entire book to it (*Materiali per un'edizione critica di "Poema bez geroja" di Anna Achmatova*, Testi e documente 4 [Macerata: Giardini, 1996]), in which he describes the provenance of some twenty redactions and systematically compares, line by line, variations occurring in them.

Out of all these redactions, I have particularly relied on two. One is the text of *Poema bez geroya* given in the first Western edition of Akhmatova's complete works, edited by Gleb Struve and Boris Filipoff (Anna Akhmatova, *Sochineniya*, 3 vols. [Munich, 1967–83]); the other appears in the first edition of Akhmatova's collected works to be published in Russia after her death, which was edited by Victor Zhirmunsky (Anna Akhmatova, *Stikhotvoreniya i poemy*, Biblioteka poeta, Bolshaya seriya, 2d ed. [Leningrad, 1979]). Struve and Filipoff based their text upon a manuscript that was authenticated by Akhmatova during her visit to Oxford in June1965, making it one of the latest-dated copies of the *Poem* to have been personally verified by the author. Zhirmunsky, unlike Struve and Filipoff, labored under the difficulty of the Soviet censorship, but as a compensating advantage he knew the Russian literary world from inside and was a longtime friend of Akhmatova who had access to her personal papers and archives. The two editions agree in most regards; where they differ, I have relied on Riccio in choosing which appears to have greater authority (e.g., whether a clear majority of redactions favor one reading rather than another). Any difference between the two editions is indicated below. My commentary also notes the more important textual variants that do not appear in either the Struve–Filipoff or Zhirmunsky editions, but it does not strive to match Riccio's exhaustive approach.

Deus conservat omnia (Latin): God preserves all things. Some manuscripts of the *Poem* include a translation of this motto, and there are variations in the wording of the ascription, which sometimes uses the phrase "the building where I lived when I was writing this poem" instead of "Fontanka House."

Some variants of the *Poem* contained the following additional prose section preceding the "Instead of a Foreword":

From a Letter to NN

... and you, knowing the circumstances of my life at that time, will be able to judge of this better than others.

In the fall of 1940, while sorting through my old papers (subsequently destroyed during the Siege), I came across some letters and poems which I had had for a long time but hadn't read before ("I opened a trunk and dug things out– / The devil made me do it"). They were related to the tragic event of 1913 recounted in *Poem Without a Hero*.

Then I wrote the verse fragment "You came to Russia out of nowhere" (the second female portrait of my contemporaries–the first was entitled "A Contemporary"). You may even remember how I read you both these poems in the Fontanka House in the presence of the old Sheremetev maple ("Witness to everything that goes on"). During the sleepless night of 26–27 December this verse fragment unexpectedly began to grow and to turn into the first draft of *Poem Without a Hero*. The history of the poem's further growth is more or less presented in the mutterings entitled "Instead of a Foreword." (I wrote this fragment during my evening of reading at the Union of Writers in March 1941.)

You can't imagine what wild, absurd and ridiculous rumors this Petersburg tale has given rise to. Strange as it may be, the ones who have passed the harshest judgment on it are my contemporaries, and their indictment of it was formulated perhaps most precisely by X. when he said that I'm settling some sort of old accounts with the epoch (the 1910s) and with people who either are no more or are not able to answer me. To those who don't know about these accounts, the poem will be incomprehensible and uninteresting . . . Others, especially women, regard *Poem Without a Hero* as a betrayal of some sort of former ideal and, what's even worse, as an exposé of my poems of long ago, which they "love so much."

Thus for the first time in my life, instead of a stream of syrupy compliments which sometimes turn a poet into an idiot, I experienced the genuine indignation of readers, and this, naturally, inspired me.

For fifteen years this poem, like attacks of some incurable illness, has unexpectedly seized me anew, and I cannot break free of it, as I add to and correct the apparently already completed work.

> I drank her in every drop, and was cursed
> With a raging demonic thirst
> I didn't know what to do, couldn't bear it,
> I had to get away from this raver.

And it's no surprise that Z, as you know, said to me, "Well, you're done for! It'll never let you go."

But . . . I see that my letter is longer than it should be, and I still have to . . .

May 27, 1955
Moscow

Instead of a Foreword

"Some are no more, and others far off": This line, from Pushkin's *Eugene Onegin*, is traditionally read as an allusion to the fate of Pushkin's friends, the Decembrists, who were victims of persecution by the repressive regime of Tsar Nicholas I (as described in chapter 3 above). This epigraph thus suggests not only the changes brought about by time in general, but also the specifically political hardships that were to be endured by Akhmatova's generation.

"What I have written, I have written": Akhmatova's original is in Church Slavonic, not Russian, emphasizing its New Testament source (John 19:22). In the Gospel account, Pilate is responsible for the inscription on Christ's cross: "Jesus of Nazareth, the King of the Jews." The Jewish leaders come to him to complain, since they see the reference to a convicted felon as their king as mocking them, and urge Pilate to change the inscription to "He said, 'I am the King of the Jews.'" Pilate, whose relations with the Jewish leaders were not good and who presumably enjoyed annoying them when it was not too politically costly to do so, refused to make the change, saying, "What I have written, I have written." The passage is an example of Johannine irony: although Pilate's motives for refusing to change what he had written may well have been unworthy ones, nevertheless what he has written is (for the Evangelist) an inspired truth.

1st dedication

In some editions of the poem, the date appears at the end rather than the beginning of this dedication, and some include the words "To Vs[evolod] K[nyazev]" or "To the memory of Vs. K." For a discussion of the significance of this date, see the essay on *Poem Without a Hero*, above.

Line 7, "Antinous": Akhmatova noted, "Antinous–(handsome youth of ant⟨iquity⟩)."[1] He was the homosexual lover and constant companion of the Roman emperor Hadrian until his death in 130 AD: "During a royal progress through Egypt, Antinous, then in his twentieth year, was mysteriously drowned in the Nile. It is generally thought that he committed suicide after believing a soothsayer's prediction that the death of his imperial lover was imminent. The act was one either of preemptive grief, or a prophylactic placation of the gods. . . . His statues show a prominent lock of hair over the forehead and sculpted eyelashes."[2] As noted above, the young Knyazev had a homosexual affair with the older poet Mikhail Kuzmin, who referred to Knyazev as Antinous in his love poems to him. However, the reference to "eyelashes" also suggests Mandelstam, whose long, fluffy eyelashes were remarked upon by many contemporaries, including Akhmatova.[3]

Line 8, "green smoke"–in Kuzmin's poem "A Trout Breaks Through the Ice," for which the Kuzmin–Knyazev affair and Knyazev's death form the subtext, the color green is repeatedly associated with Knyazev, who had green eyes. "A Trout Breaks Through the Ice" was published in 1929. On August 7, 1940, Akhmatova asked Chukovskaya to get her a copy of it, saying, "I only saw the book briefly, but it seemed to me to be a good book, and I'd like to read it through properly."[4] Thus at the time that *Poem Without a Hero* was conceived, this work would have been fresh in Akhmatova's memory.

2nd dedication

Variants give the dedicatee as "O. A. Glebova–Sudeikina" and "O. A. G.–S."

Line 13, "Confusion–Psyche": "Confusion" and "Psyche" are the names of heroines in plays by Yu. Belyayev. In "Confusion," a work described by its author as a "Christmas farce," the title character is an allegorical figure who appears in the apartment of a respectable civil servant and "brings into the everyday world the element of the unforeseen and fantastic." The stage directions describe Confusion's costume as "a light–colored ball dress, splendid, a bit short, in the style of pictures of the time [the play takes place in 1840], over her dress she wears a dark green velvet coat edged with ermine; a large ermine muff; a laughing face with loose curls straying around its temples looks out from under the brim of a large velvet hat; on her feet are fur–trimmed velvet boots–her whole figure looks like a merry Christmas tree covered with snow."⁵ Sergei Sudeikin's portrait of his wife in the role of Confusion shows her in just such a costume.

Line 17, "crossed the Lethe": this line implies that Akhmatova had learned of Olga's death in Paris on the night of January 19–20, 1945. Note, however, that Olga also "breathes a different spring"–an image suggesting not death, but life and rebirth, albeit not a rebirth to the same life that Akhmatova is experiencing in the spring of 1945, the date of the dedication.

3rd dedication

Le jour des rois (French, "the day of the kings")–some variants of the *Poem* contain the explanatory note, "Epiphany Eve, January 5." It was on January 5, 1946, that Isaiah Berlin, the addressee of the third dedication, said farewell to Akhmatova before leaving the Soviet Union. In some editions the phrase "Le jour des rois" does not appear at the beginning of the third dedication but at its end, along with the date "1956" or "January 5, 1956."

"Once on an Epiphany Eve": The epigraph is from Vasily Zhukovsky's poem "Svetlana," which opens with the lines, "Once on an Epiphany Eve / The girls were telling fortunes." The poem's heroine, saddened by the prolonged absence of her lover, performs the same conjuring ritual with a mirror, candles, and two place settings as that performed by the narrator in chapter 1 of *Poem Without a Hero.* When the spell brings her lover to her, she proposes that they be wed immediately. He lifts her into his sleigh, and they drive off to the church, where there awaits not a wedding party, but a funeral. She realizes that the dead man is her fiance, and that by giving herself to him she has doomed herself. She is terrified . . . and then the dawning light and the cock's crow awaken her, and she finds that it was all just a nightmare. But whereas for Zhukovsky there is a clear border between the nightmare and the prosaic, safe reality, for Akhmatova there is no such border.

The Year 1913, Chapter 1

"Di rider finerai / Pria dell'aurora" (Italian)–"You will stop laughing before the dawn." These lines, from Mozart's opera *Don Giovanni,* occur in a scene in which Don Giovanni has escaped his pursuers by slipping into a graveyard, where he laughingly boasts about his exploits to Leporello. In response, these words are intoned by the statue of the Commendatore. In the Struve–Filipoff edition, this epigraph appears on the *Poem's* title page.

"We're not to conjure with Tatyana"–This line, from Pushkin's *Eugene Onegin* (chapter 5, stanza 10) tells of how Tatyana, who is deeply in love with Onegin, is tempted to try to divine the identity of her future husband in a manner similar to that of Zhukovsky's Svetlana but becomes too frightened to complete the ritual. Instead she goes to bed and has a nightmare that turns out to be prophetic: the jaded, worldly–wise Onegin kills the naive young poet Lensky.

Some editions contain a third epigraph: "In my hot youth–when George the Third was king" from Byron's *Don Juan.* The case for omitting this epigraph from the final version of the text is made in Riccio, *Materiali per un'edizione critica,* 61.

Akhmatova's notebooks[7] contain an additional prose section:

> The old clock which stopped exactly 27 years before (Dec. 31, 1913) after having struck 13 times by mistake, started up again without any outside intervention, struck a quarter to midnight (in the manner of an orator who coughs before beginning his speech) and started to tick again so that it could appropriately greet the New Year (which, in its opinion, was presumably 1914).
>
> Wedding candles, spiralled, green with age (as at an *auto da fé*), in glass candlesticks, start burning on their own, with a suspiciously bright flame; in the dark corners of the room there's something that's not really good, not to mention that the music box (as if it couldn't bear the long silence) began either to sing or to rave about something completely pointless. The foam atop the glasses stands still.
>
> In this instant the author either heard or foresaw everything that would follow:

> > I've set the cherished candles alight
> > To give enchantment to this night,
> > With you, the guest who didn't arrive,
> > I planned to honor Forty-one's birth.
> > (Written June 10, 1963. Komarovo)

Line 64, "And the brimming wine, like poison, burns": The line is from Akhmatova's poem "New Year's Ballad" (1923), which seems to anticipate the plot of "The Year 1913." In a gathering of six people, including the hostess, who greet the New Year, the host proposes to drink "to our native soil, in which we all lie" (implying that, as in "The Year 1913," the guests are the shades of the dead); a second reveler offers a toast "to her songs, in which we all live" (the poet brings the lost past back to life); a third offers a toast "to the one who is not yet with us" (the guest from the future).

Line 75, "I turn slightly, looking half-behind": In the original Russian, this line ("Povernuvshis' vpoloborota") echoes Mandelstam's poem "Akhmatova," which starts with the line, "Half-turned, oh sorrow" ("V poloborota, o pechal'"). Since Mandelstam's poem was written in 1914, it suggests the narrator's reversion to her youthful self or at least the recovery of her youthful memories.

Line 85: Akhmatova noted, "Dr. D⟨apertutto⟩–pseudonym ⟨of⟩ Meyerhol⟨d⟩." Meyerhold used this pseudonym in his experimental theatrical productions as a means of distinguishing them from the more conventional work which he did as a stage director of the Imperial Theater. She also noted, "Iokanaan–John the Baptist." John the Baptist is referred to as Iokanaan in Oscar Wilde's drama *Salomé*, which in turn became the source of an opera by Richard Strauss and a ballet by Fokine. The latter was staged in Paris with Ida Rubinstein dancing the title role.

Line 86: Glahn is a character from Knut Hamsun's novel *Pan* (published 1898, Russian translation 1901) who kills himself for love. In an article on Akhmatova's prose, her friend Emma Gershtein mentions Hamsun among the authors whose works were valued by the young Akhmatova and adds, "*Victoria* . . . appealed to her less than *Pan*, which is not surprising. The motifs of this romance are close to Akhmatova's early love lyrics, to the small dramatic novellas about love as a struggle, about contests between strong characters who resemble Lt. Glahn, the hero of *Pan*."[8]

Line 87: The reference is to Oscar Wilde's novel "The Picture of Dorian Gray," in which the title character preserves his youthful beauty while the ravages of time and his dissolute life are reflected in his portrait, which becomes ever more hideous. In 1915, Meyerhold made a film based on this story.

Line 93: Compare this with Ophelia's description of Hamlet's madness in act II, scene I:

> Lord Hamlet,—with his doublet all unbrac'd;
> No hat upon his head; his stockings foul'd,
> Ungarter'd, and down-gyved to his ankle.

Line 100: In the original this reads, "No ko mne, tak k komu zhe?" where Akhmatova noted, "The three 'k's express the author's confusion." I have tried to preserve this "stuttering" effect with the repeated 't's in "I'm who they want, if not, who's meant?"

Lines 107–12: This stanza had an earlier variant:

> Like an icy lake, his gaze is still,
> When I meet his eyes, I feel a chill
> As if I saw my last hour on earth.
> Indulged by all, the mocking grinner–
> Next to him, the foulest sinner
> Would gleam like a gem of peerless worth.[9]

Riccio[10] gives another Kuzmin-related stanza:

> And with his Byzantine tricks and airs
> Harlequin the killer is with them there,
> *Maitre* and friend is what he's called now–
> (As if from a portrait his eyes gaze,
> On a harpsichord he lightly plays
> And comfort and ease are all around.)

Line 124, "of black stones": literally, "of black agates" (Russian *agatov*); Akhmatova's notebook contains the variant "garnets" (Russian *granatov*).[11]

Line 125: Akhmatova noted, "The Valley of Jehoshaphat–(site of the Last Judg⟨ment⟩)."

Lines 134–45: The "guest from the future" ("future" as seen from the perspective of New Year's Eve 1940) is Isaiah Berlin. Blue cigar smoke as well as the Bach Chaconne of the third dedication are details which are also associated with Berlin in Akhmatova's cycle of poems, *Sweetbriar in*

Blossom. To arrive at Akhmatova's apartment from Berlin's starting point, a bookstore on Nevsky Prospect, one would indeed have to go to the bridge (the Anichkov bridge) and then turn left.

Line 149, "Without face or name": This image will occur again in the description of the heroine's successful suitor (in line 458 in the "Fourth and Final Chapter") and so presumably refers to Blok, although at this point it has no clear referent, and in the ballet version this character (the "Superfluous Shade") is not identified with Blok. Toporov[12] regards this phrase as a conflation of texts from two Blok poems, "V neuverennom, zybkom polete" (November 1910) and "Bez slova mysl', volnen'e bez nazvan'ya" (December 1911).

Line 156: Akhmatova noted, "Lysisca–Messalina's pseu⟨⟨donym⟩⟩ in the Rom⟨⟨an⟩⟩ broth⟨⟨els⟩⟩." According to the ancient historians, the empress Messalina was so sexually insatiable that she prostituted herself for amusement, using an assumed name to protect her social position.

Line 159: Akhmatova noted, "The Mamre oak (Bibl⟨⟨ical⟩⟩)." The Book of Genesis, chapter 18, describes Abraham as sitting under the oak (or terebinth) of Mamre when three angels appeared to tell him that Sarah would bear a son. Eastern Orthodox iconography regards the three angels as a foreshadowing of the doctrine of the Trinity, and this angelic visit–the "Old Testament Trinity"–is the subject of one of Andrei Rublyov's greatest icons.

Akhmatova's notebooks contain an omitted stanza that appears to be associated with lines 159–70:

> You didn't twirl at European balls,
> It was you who drew deer upon cave walls,
> You are Gilgamesh, Heser, Hercules.
> Not a poet, but a poet myth,
> Already full-grown striding from the mist
> That shrouds the dawn of nations and creeds.[13]

Line 163: Akhmatova noted, "Hammurabi, Lycurgus, Solon–lawgivers." Hammurabi (ca. 1750 BC), king of Babylon, was the author of the Code of Hammurabi, which like the Mosaic law claimed a divine origin; Lycurgus (eighth to seventh century BC?) is traditionally described as the king of

Sparta who established that city's distinctive way of life; Solon (640–558 BC) established the constitution by which Athens was governed during the period of its greatest glory.

Line 174: Akhmatova noted, "The Ark of the Covenant (Bibl⟨⟨ical⟩⟩)." The Second Book of Samuel, chapter 6, describes how David danced before the Ark of the Covenant in ecstatic inspiration as it was being brought into his new capital of Jerusalem.

Line 177: a draft letter in one of Akhmatova's notebooks[14] comments on this line:

June 24, 1962

Dear Eric Ricardovich,
    Apparently I didn't manage to tell you one more thing about the "Poem": the line "We only dream we hear a cock's crow" ought to be associated with Blok's
> From a blessed land, now unknown and far away,
> Comes the crowing of a cock. ("Steps of theCom⟨⟨mendatore⟩⟩")

It's obvious from the context that in this case the "blessed land" is simply everyday life, where cocks crow, and to which all three of them will never go back. For that reason, in my poem the cock's crow can't even be heard, but only dreamed about.
    ⟨⟨Lines that are⟩⟩ from Macbeth:

> What that would mean is—gravestones are frail
> That would mean granite's softer than wax . . .
> (The apparition of Banquo's ghost at the feast.)

    You, probably, noticed that yourself.

The lines from *Macbeth* that Akhmatova refers to appear to be those spoken by Macbeth as he confronts Banquo's ghost:

> If charnel-houses and our graves must send
> Those that we bury back, our monuments
> Shall be the maws of kites.

Lines 206–17: one of Akhmatova's notebooks[15] contains the following passage:

Someone told me that the appearance of the specter in my "Poem" (the end of the first chapter:

> "Or between the *cupboard* and the stove
> Is there once again someone standing?
> His eyes are *open*, his forehead pale . . .")

calls to mind the scene of Kir⟨⟨illov's⟩⟩ suicide in *The Devils*. I asked N. Il'in to loan me *The Devils*. I opened the book to Kir⟨⟨illov's⟩⟩ conversation with Stavrogin about the suicide itself: "You mean, you love life?" "Yes, I love life, *but there's absolutely no death.*" And I have *the same thing*:

> There is no death, as everyone knows.
> Why repeat that, it's already old.

Who would believe that I wrote that and didn't think of *The Devils*. Sept⟨⟨ember⟩⟩ 22, 1962 (two coincidences in a row). The same thing with "The Queen of Spades" (The shape that flashed past the windowpane), and later *Macbeth*.

The passage of "The Queen of Spades" which Akhmatova had in mind is apparently the one in which Hermann sees (or believes he sees) the ghost of the dead Countess. It starts, "At that moment someone out on the street looked into his window." For the reference to *Macbeth*, see the note above on line 177.

Riccio gives two rejected stanzas which, had they been included, would presumably have been fitted into this chapter:

> Through the charcoal gray of Paris fog
> Once again Modigliani walked
> I'm the one he's following, I'm sure.
> Unfortunately, when he's around
> Even my dreams turn upside down
> And all sorts of disasters occur.

> But to me–his Egyptian–he remains
> What the gray-haired organ grinder plays
> Accompanied by the Paris roar
> Like the roar of a subterranean sea–
> He, too, had more than his fill of grief,
> And hardship and shame he also bore.[16]

Across the Landing

Line 226: "Signor Casanova"–in the Latin alphabet in the original.

Line 229: Akhmatova noted, "Dog–the Stray Dog."

Line 231: Translated literally, "And, alas, Lots of Sodom." As described in the Book of Genesis, chapter 19, Lot was the only righteous man in Sodom and accordingly was given an angelic warning to gather his family and flee before God's wrath was visited upon the sinful city. Thus for even "Lots" to "taste the deadly draft" would imply that everyone, even those who were most resolutely virtuous, had finally yielded to corruption.

Line 237: Akhmatova noted, "Fontanka Grotto–built by Argunov in 1757 in the garden of the Sheremetev Palace on the Fontanka (the so-called Fontanka House), it was destroyed in the early 1910s (cf. Lukomsky, p. ⟨⟨?⟩⟩)."

Lines 241–44. Madame de Lamballe–a close friend and confidante of Marie Antoinette. Arrested after the fall of the monarchy in August 1792, she was killed by an angry mob during the September Massacres, and her severed head was placed on a pike and paraded past the window of the imprisoned royal family. The original Russian of line 241, "Vsekh naryadnee i vsekh vysshe," echoes Akhmatova's description of another celebrated beauty of her youth, Salomeya Andronikova, in "A Shade."

In a diary entry from May 1924, Punin recorded Akhmatova as saying, "When I think of or see the 18th century. . . I always feel that all this carelessness, frivolity, and *joie de vivre* is just for appearances; they wanted to be full of life and happy but they were not so at all. For me these little lambs and shepherds are inseparable from revolution, and the wigs always have and still do remind me of the wigs on those heads on stakes, and that's how we know them." Punin commented, "All this that An. said is very characteristic of her and isn't at all the product of a gloomy world view but of her sense of morality."[17]

Lines 245–48. Some editions give line 245 as "so droll" (*zateinitsa*) rather than "so meek" (*smirennitsa*). Akhmatova's notebooks[18] contain a variant:

> She's meek as a dove, how she enchants
> When, after doing a goat-legged dance,

> She whispers with a shyly raised glance,
> "Que me veut mon Prince Carnaval?"

"Que me veut mon Prince Carnaval?" (Fr.)–"What does my Carnival Prince want from me?"

Following line 248, "Goethe's Brocken": in Goethe's *Faust*, Mount Brocken is the scene of a witches' sabbath, to which Mephistopheles takes Faust. Faust believes that he sees Gretchen there, but Mephistopheles explains that what he is actually seeing is a specter that appears to every man in the form of his first love.

Lines 249–63. Akhmatova's notebooks contain a number of variants on these lines. One entry[19] gives this passage as:

> Like cloven feet stamp her prancing boots,
> Amid blond curls wicked horns peep through,
> Like jingling bells chime [blue] her earring hoops,
> She's drunk with the dance, gone mad, possessed,
> As if from black–figure pottery
> She leapt into life and ran towards the sea
> {So refined and elegant] In full ceremonial undress.
> [And you] Wearing a helmet and cloak, behind her,
> Like a fairy tale, you're disguised, obscure,
> No, that's your daily face, no mystique,
> You, friend of honor and slave of love . . .
> But why does that little speck of blood
> Drip down the petal of your cheek?

Line 257: Akhmatova's notebooks contain the variant: "Running in un-masked, your face unobscured" with the added comment, "Both that he was in a rush and that he was the only one of them all who showed his real face–that's what characterizes him."[20]

Line 258, "Like a fairy–tale youth, your heart is pure." A literal translation of the original would be, "You, Ivanushka of the old fairy tale." The refer-ence could be to either of two well–known Russian fairy–tale heroes: Prince Ivan, who is the youngest and most sympathetic of three royal brothers, and Ivan the Fool, who despite his ignorance of the world has a wisdom of his own. Akhmatova's notebooks contain two rejected variants of this line: "You, the prince from the old fairy tale," and "You, toy soldier from the children's tale" (referring to Hans Christian Andersen's steadfast tin soldier).[21]

Line 261: Akhmatova's notebooks contain three variants: "You, friend of honor and slave of love," "You, honest friend and slave of love," and "How much pain and shame run through your love."[22]

Akhmatova's notebooks[23] contain an omitted stanza apparently related to this section:

> *Masquerade chatter*
> And an everyday envelope enclosed
> An already filled–out form that showed
> The total figures for shedding blood
> Without any cipher or disguise,
> Yet indifferently it gave rise
> To nonexistence's unseen flood.
> March 1961

The Year 1913, Chapter 2

"Or do you see the one who before you knelt . . .": This epigraph is from an earlier poem of Akhmatova's dedicated to Sudeikina, "The Voice of Memory," written in June 1913.

Akhmatova's notebooks[24] contain two variants of the prose. One from early 1962 reads,

> A Sham Rendezvous,
> or
> Confession of a Daughter of the Century
>
> II
>
> Or do you see the one who before you knelt,
> Who sought out white death to escape your spell?

Columbine's [room] bedroom. In the back, above an enormous magnificent "Pavlovsk" bed, her portrait in the role of Confusion. The Columbine in the portrait comes to life and steps out of it. "Meyerhold's blackamoor boys" come running [and] offer a thousand small services (they straighten out the folds of her coat, spritz her with perfume, bring roses*–her flowers). The oldest one [carries a Venetian glass serving tray] brings and sets down on a small table a Venetian glass serving tray and two full [bottles] goblets to greet the New Year, which an old London clock strikes in a strange voice like a waterfall, except for the chimes at the end. A figure [the author] with its back to the viewer, dressed in a long black shawl, pronounces:

> The fur coat's flung open, all satin–lined!
> Don't think, my Dove, it's to be unkind
> That my hand has lifted this goblet high:
> Still the time of reckoning draws close,
> It's myself, not you, I'm punishing now.
> [Do you see, beyond the swirl⟨ing snow⟩]

The blackamoor boys pull open the heavy damask curtain of just such a window (the terrible Petersburg night comes into the room) and in an instant are already playing in the snow outside the window
    And all round us is old Peter City
*and maybe even the offerings of her admirers: verses, music, drawings, they play something celebratory on children's mus⟨ical⟩ instruments . . . and play the same role, as in Molière's "Don Juan." (cf. Vs⟨evolod⟩ Meyerhold's book "On the Theater," p. ?)

Another draft from later that year reads:

Fir⟨⟨st⟩⟩ draft, Sept. 8, 1962
    Chapter II

> You embody the senses' pleasures
> More fully than those alive, radiant shade.
>   –Baratynsky

    The Heroine's bedroom. Wax candles are burning. Over the bed are three portraits of her in her roles. She is the Goat–legged Girl (on the right), Confusion (mid⟨dle⟩), either Donna Anna (or Columbine). One portrait is in shadow. [One] The middle one of the portraits comes to life and steps out of the frame. Outside the attic window on the roof blackamoor boys are having a snowball fight. [The author] A figure in a long lace shawl (her back to the viewer) [speaks] reads from a long scroll:

> The fur coat's flung open, all satin-lined,
> Don't think, my Dove, it's to be unkind ...

"To some it appears to be Columbine, to others Doña Anna (from 'The Steps of the Commendatore')"—reflecting how her suitors behold her: to Pierrot/Knyazev, she is Columbine, to Blok/Don Juan she is Doña Anna.

Line 270, "blackamoor boys (*arapchata*) of Meyerhold": this form of makeup was used by the stagehands (who opened the curtain and moved props in full view of the audience) in Meyerhold's production of Molière's *Le festin de pierre* (*The Stone Guest*) (1910), a treatment of the Don Juan legend—hence the association with the "time of reckoning" which "draws close."

Lines 278–80: this stanza refers to the prima ballerina Anna Pavlova.

Line 281 echoes a scene from *Eugene Onegin*, chapter 1, stanza 21, in which Onegin arrives at the theater after the ballet has already started, yawns at a brilliant performance, and remarks that there's nothing new in it. Evidently the Petersburg snobs of 1913 hadn't changed any from those of Pushkin's day.

Lines 287–92: this stanza refers to Chaliapin. Chukovskaya[25] gives an earlier version:

> And again the voice that won such renown
> Like thunder among the hills resounds,
> Bearing horror, death, forgiveness, love ...
> Like nothing that anyone's ever heard,
> As if proclaiming a holy word,
> Again and again it catches us up.

Line 293: Akhmatova noted, "Peter's Corridor of Colleges—the corridor of Petersburg University." This would not be self-evident to the Russian reader, since in Peter's Russia the loan-word "college" (*kollegia*) referred to a government office. For Akhmatova's comment on these lines, see appendix II, excerpts from notebook 11.

Line 299: Akhmatova's note: "Petrushka's mask—Stravinsky's *Petrouchka*." Stravinsky's opera *Petrouchka* is based on a Russianized version of the *commedia dell'arte*, with the character Petrushka corresponding to Pierrot.

Line 300, "Round the bonfires waiting coachmen dance": Stravinsky's *Petrouchka*, with its evocation of the urban life of St. Petersburg, includes a dance of coachmen around a bonfire.

Line 301: Akhmatova noted, "the Imperial flag, yellow with a bl⟨ack⟩ eagle, wh⟨ich denotes⟩ the monarch's presence"

Lines 304–05: An entry in Akhmatova's notebook[26] reads,

> And the sailor ⟨drunk⟩ was always Tsushima–before the war itself {at age 15?}, when I saw sailors lined up in the ranks, my heart involuntarily ached at the memory of Tsushima–this also was the *first* horror of my generation, which I could not properly express in my poem *At the Edge of the Sea*. (What is the sailor singing? Find out.)

Lines 312–29, "The Demon himself with Tamara's smile . . . There, where the Lethe–Neva flows": these eighteen lines do not appear in early versions of the *Poem*. In 1959, Akhmatova showed these lines to Chukovskaya and explained that they had been written to prevent readers from thinking that the passage immediately preceding them (" . . . is your chevalier / Gabriel or Mephistopheles?") referred to Knyazev rather than to his successful rival.[27]

Lines 325–26, "How the two of you were in a new space, / How outside of time you two arose": Toporov[28] identifies this with two lines from Blok's "Milyi brat! Zavecherelo" (1906): "Slovno my–v prostranstve novom, / Slovno–v novykh vremenakh."

Lines 340–41: Chukovskaya[29] gives an earlier variant of these lines: "And this heavy, stupefying doze / Is so hard for everyone to fight."

Line 353: This line, a relatively late addition to the stanza, has a variant: "In the shade of the Kellomjagi cedar." Kellomjagi (or Kellomjaki) was the Finnish name for Komarovo, suggesting the image of the elderly poet, at her dacha, seeing the spectre of a court that had existed in her youth.[30]

Line 356, "The white–veiled 'shoulders wait to be kissed' ": the words that Akhmatova quotes are from Knyazev's poem "January 1, 1913."

Line 357: Akhmatova noted, "Dove, come!–The Church wedding canticle, sung when the bride steps onto the carpet."

Line 359: Akhmatova noted, "The Maltese Chapel, which was designed by Quarenghi and built (from 1798 to 1800) in an interior courtyard of the Vorontsov Palace, in which the Corps of Pages was located."

Lines 364–67: Chukovskaya's diary for 1955 notes that these lines, which had been present in the Tashkent version of the *Poem*, had subsequently become lost. However, when she reminded Akhmatova of them, Akhmatova replied, "Up till now I'd never remembered them, but now I do, and I remember that you loved them. Let's put them in right now. I was missing the wooden pavements in the *Poem*. What kind of Petersburg is it without wooden pavements!"[31]

Line 374: Akhmatova uses the Russian word *skobar'*, which (as she herself noted) is a derisive term for an inhabitant of Pskov. Sudeikina herself was born in St. Petersburg, but her grandfather was said to be a peasant from Pskov.

Lines 381–86 have a variant:

> The most superstitious of all you enticed,
> With his smile of evening sacrifice,
> Saint Sebastian was less deathly pale,
> Confused and lost, tears dimming his view,
> He sees the roses offered to you,
> Sees his rival flourishing and hale.[32]

Line 390, "I don't mark crosses on doors": compare this with Akhmatova's poem, "What makes this age worse . . . ?" ("Chem khuzhe etot vek . . . ?," 1919), which ends with the lines, "But here the White One [i.e., Death] marks crosses on doors / And calls the ravens, and the ravens fly."

The Year 1913, Chapter 3

Lines 406–08: Chukovskaya gives an earlier version of these three lines:

> Within the living room all grew dark,
> The hot breath stopped blowing from the hearth,
> And cut lilacs drooped beneath its spell.[33]

Line 409, " . . . cursed by the wife the tsar hadn't wanted": a literal translation would be " . . . cursed by Tsaritsa Avdotia." For the legend of the tsaritsa's curse on the city, see above.

During what Akhmatova later described as an unsuccessful "attempt to ground the *Poem*,"[34] line 414 was followed by two subsequently rejected stanzas, which were later published as a separate lyric with the title "Petersburg in 1913":

> Beyond the gate a street organ squawks,
> A gypsy dances, a trained bear walks
> On a spit–stained bridge outside the town.
> [Variant: A workman curses the whole place out.]
> Already the steamer's about to leave
> For the Comforter of All who Grieve,
> Along the Neva its whistle resounds.
> A black wind of rage and freedom blows,
> Surely the Hot Field is very close,
> You could reach out, touch it, if you choose.
> Here my words end their prophetic flight,
> Here the wonders have a sharper bite,
> But let's go–I don't have time to lose.[35]

A church dedicated to the Mother of God, Comfort of All who Grieve, gave its name to the Petersburg district of Skorbyashchaya, which is mentioned in the original Russian; the Hot Field (Goryachee Pole) is described as "an empty lot behind the Neva gate, formerly a garbage dump and a hideout for the criminal element of old Petersburg. After the Revolution it was a site of executions by the Bolsheviks of 'counter-revolutionary elements' in the city."[36]

Lines 427–38: This "lyric digression" evokes the memory of Nikolai Nedobrovo. In her notebook, Akhmatova wrote,

> You! to whom this poem ¾ belongs, since I myself am ¾ made by you, I only let you into a single lyrical digression (Tsarskoe Selo). You and I couldn't get enough of breathing the waterfall–damp air of the parks ("these living waters") and there we saw in 1916 (daffodils along the embankment)
>   . . . the flight of brides in mourning . . . [37]

In a diary entry from 1955, Chukovskaya gives line 432 as "his heart" rather than "your heart" and adds a stanza between lines 432 and 433:

> Beloved from my unforgotten past,
> Who above my stormy youth stood fast,
> A dream that, once dreamed, never returned.
> How once in youthful strength he shone,
> Now his very gravesite is unknown,
> As if he had never lived on earth.[38]

According to Chukovskaya, Akhmatova omitted these lines out of concern that the reference to a forgotten grave might cause them to be misconstrued as referring to the dragoon (Knyazev) rather than to Nedobrovo.

Line 428, "Cameron Gallery": part of the palace complex at Pushkin (Tsarskoe Selo).

Line 431, "the Nine": i.e., the Muses.

Line 435: In her diary for 1955, Chukovskaya mentions an earlier variant of this line, "When the sight of blood hadn't stained our eyes."[39]

The Year 1913, Fourth and Final Chapter

Line 440, "On whose heart lay 'a lock of blond hair'": the words in quotes are cited from Knyazev's poem "Today I rode gaily on the Neva embankment."

Lines 473–74: A literal translation would be, "Not in the accursed Mazurian swamps, / Not on the blue Carpathian heights." Mazuria (in Poland) and the Carpathian Mountains (in the Romanian/Ukrainian border area) were both the sites of deadly and futile battles during World War I. Their names would be as evocative of the fate of a generation of Russian officers as the names of Ypres or the Somme would be for British officers.

A stanza omitted from this section related to the failed attempt to "ground" the poem (see appendix II, excerpts from notebook 4). It depicted the cornet preparing to kill himself and remembering the women he had injured (the gypsy girl and the Smolny debutante). Riccio gives it as follows:

And he hears the words of someone's prayer,
Around him—the beloved shades are there,
They alone remain before his eyes.
And in the night's diamonded gleam,
Like the lure of temptation in a dream,
That enigmatic silhouette shines.[40]

Chukovskaya gives a variant:

Around him—the beloved shades are there,
But all in vain are their words of prayer,
Their call to him fades away and dies.
And in the night's diamonded gleam,
Like the lure of temptation in a dream,
That silhouette, the only one, shines.[41]

Flip Side

Intermezzo: in some manuscripts, this serves as a title, with "Flip Side" as its subtitle; in others, it does not appear at all.

"In my beginning is my end": Akhmatova ascribed this phrase to T. S. Eliot's "East Coker," but, as her manuscripts show, she was also aware of its earlier origin as the motto of Mary, Queen of Scots.

The epigraph following the stage directions is a modified citation from Nikolai Klyuyev's "The Blasphemers of Art." The original reads:

Akhmatova is a jasmine bloom
Surrounded by the gray asphalt's praise,
Can she have lost the path to the caves
Where Dante walked and the air is imbued
And a nymph is spinning crystal flax?

In Klyuyev, the air is "imbued" because it is saturated with poetry (the Russian is *gust*, literally, "thick"); in Akhmatova's modified version, the difficulty of writing is expressed by the air having become "mute" (Russian *pust*, "empty"). In her notebooks, Akhmatova remarked of this epigraph, "The best thing that's been said about my poetry."[42]

A note of Akhmatova's from November 1962 contains a variant of the prose for this section:

Jan⟨⟨uary⟩⟩ 5, 1941

Place: the Fontanka House. In the window, the specter of a snow-covered maple tree. The wind is howling in the pipe, and in this howl one can make out very deeply and cleverly hidden fragments of Requiem. As for what appears in the mirrors, it's better not to think about it. [Complete magnificent silence.] The hellish harlequinade from the year 1913 has just passed, [but over silence silence stands sentry. As for what appears in the mirrors, it's better not to think about it] after rousing the great silent epoch from its wordlessness, leaving behind it the debris common to every holiday or funeral procession—smoke from torches, flowers on the floor, sacred souvenirs lost forever, etc. (However, everything is as it always was.)[43]

A notebook from 1964–1965 contains this prose variant:

January 5, 1941. The Fontanka House. [Night.] A window of the room looks out into a garden which is older than Petersburg, as is evident from the oak tree rings. Under Swedish rule there was a country house here. Peter gave this place to Sheremetev as a reward for victory. When Parasha Zhemchugova was in the pangs of childbirth, stands for the wedding guests [galleries] were built for the upcoming celebration of her wedding. As is well known, Parasha died in childbirth, and a completely different rite [of a different type] was held. Next to the author's rooms is the celebrated "White Hall," the work of Quarenghi, where Pavel I used to hide behind the mirrors and eavesdrop on what the Sheremetevs' ball guests were saying about him. In this hall Parasha sang for the sovereign, and to reward her singing he bestowed upon her a fantastic pearl. The author lived in this house for 35 years and knows everything about it. She thinks, on Jan. 5, 1941, that the most important thing is still ahead.[44]

Akhmatova's notebook contains a stanza dedicated to Parasha which was not included in the final version of the *Poem*:

Midnight, what are you muttering there?
Parasha died, still young and fair,
Rightful lady of palace halls.

> The gallery that should have been filled
> With wedding guests was left half-built—
> There, as Boreas prompts, blowing chill,
> [Here's what] I'm writing all of this down for you.
> From every window incense drifts,
> A lock of the beloved hair is snipped
> And on the oval face darkness falls.[45]

Line 499, "His phone number went under cover": a literal translation would be, "He had his phone number declared classified," an echo of the Stalinist mania for official secrecy.

Lines 533–38,"He's still putting on his old show . . .": not only "the most elegant Satan" but also the reference to Cagliostro point to Kuzmin, who was the author of a novel entitled *The Marvelous Life of Joseph Balsam, Count Cagliostro*. The homosexual Kuzmin may have been hurt that Knyazev not only left him, but left him for a woman. In any event, contemporary accounts describe Kuzmin's reaction to Knyazev's suicide as one of indifference. Such a failure to honor the memory of the dead would have been one of the most certain ways to arouse Akhmatova's contempt and is clearly the motivation for the stanza.

Lines 555–68: As late as 1989 these stanzas were still excluded from *Poem Without a Hero*. Their proper siting in the *Poem* is discussed by Chukovskaya.[46]

Line 545: An entry in Akhmatova's notebooks[47] written after the supposed date of completion of the *Poem* apparently envisions the insertion of a stanza between numbers 8 and 10:

About poetry
July 31, 1963

> No one comes, no knocking at my door,
> Mirror dreams of mirror and nothing more,
> Over silence silence stands sentry.
>   ?
> It all was ready for when my friend came,
> Even the circle of hellish flame—
> But it makes no difference, what happens then—
> Still, I don't know, the meaning's not clear—

> Why does my angel shed such bitter tears,
> The one who holds the scroll and the pen?. . .
> . . . .
> They tortured: "Now tell us what you know!"
> But not a single word or cry or moan
> Gave the enemy anything to use.

Line 558, "Any of those arrested, exiled, caged . . .": the word I have translated as "exiled" is in Russian *stopyatnitsa*, literally, "hundred-and-fiver," referring to a woman who was legally forbidden to live within a hundred kilometers of any major city–the point of the word being that as a result, such women typically settled just outside the forbidden limit. According to Nadezhda Mandelstam, Akhmatova was particularly fond of this word because of its semantic echo of the martyred St. Pyatnitsa.[48]

Line 569, "Shall I plunge into a state hymn and drown?": this would literally be translated as, "Shall I melt away in an official hymn?" The Russian original emphasizes that putting poetry at the service of authority leads to the poet's destruction; my rhyme–forced English suggests the motive for such ill–fated service, the original enthusiasm (plunging) followed by the too-late recognition of one's peril, and fits in with the reference to Mayakovsky in the next two lines.

Line 574 was once followed by this rejected stanza:

> I'll face death and shame and I won't quake,
> It's a cryptogram, a code to break,
> A device like this is not allowed.
> Right up to the edge my pathway goes–
> What a crazy step–and everyone knows
> For what kind of place I've set out.[49]

An entry for 1958 in one of Akhmatova's notebooks[50] appears to be related to this rejected stanza:

> *Flip Side*
> I opened a trunk and dug things out–
> The devil made me do it–but how
> Can it be I'll seize that snowdrop's stalk

> (From *Flip Side*)
> Right up to the edge my pathway leads–
> What a crazy step–everyone can see
> How as if upon piles of silk I walk.
>
> And the bronze tongues of the bells repeated
> The word by which death was defeated
> From every church tower came the song.
>
> But under Columbine's scarf there lay
> The face, greener than the riverside clay,
> Of a drowned woman frozen in the ice.

Line 576: The Russian is not just "a flower" but "a chrysanthemum"–
which, alas, refused to conform to English meter. Chukovskaya suggests
that this image derives from the funeral of Akhmatova's friend, the Push-
kinist D. P. Yakubovich:

> Anna Andreyevna told me that she'd been to Pushkin House for the
> funeral service for Yakubovich.
> "It was good, everyone spoke very warmly about him . . . When the
> coffin was carried downstairs, the clock started chiming on the landing–
> there is an antique clock there with a lovely melodic chime. But he no
> longer heard it. On the steps under the feet of all those carrying the
> coffin, and those following, flowers were strewn at random–chrysan-
> themums. I walked around them, I could not step on them–they are
> alive. He no longer saw them."[51]

Chrysanthemums have been widely used as a funeral flower–see, for
example, D. H. Lawrence's short story "Odor of Chrysanthemums," which
deals with the funeral of a miner killed in a pit accident and the feelings
of his widow as she prepares his body for burial.

Lines 579–80: Luga is a town some sixty miles from Petersburg. The word
that I translated as "satin masks" is *bauta*, which, as Akhmatova noted,
is a domino, or mask with an attached hood and cape. It originated in
Venice.

Line 592, "drawers within drawers": literally, "This chest has a triple
bottom."

Line 600: In a draft for a letter dated January 15, 1963, Akhmatova wrote, "In European painting, the Spaniards are somehow the closest to me, I've always been captivated by El Greco."[52]

Lines 605–10 have a variant:

> So some night, as gleaming Vega ascends
> Over the foggy western land's end,
> Someone will boldly lift up his eyes,
> And to me, a shade vanished into gloom
> He'll offer a branch of lilac in bloom
> In that fair hour when this storm's gone by.[53]

Line 621, "Star Chamber"–a private note of Akhmatova's describes this as "the Eng⟨⟨lish⟩⟩ Cheka ⟨⟨which convened⟩⟩ in a chamber that had a starry sky painted on the ceiling."[54] The version of this note that appears in Soviet editions of *Poem Without a Hero* reads, "A secret court of law; it convened in a chamber that had a starry sky depicted on the ceiling." Presumably the comparison of the notoriously arbitrary proceedings of the Star Chamber to the Cheka was offensive to a Soviet editor, although the offense should have been the other way around: the Star Chamber did not have the power to pass a death sentence, a restriction which never hindered the Cheka or any of its successors.

Line 622: Indulging in irony at the expense of Romantic conventions, Akhmatova put an asterisk after the word "garret" (in Russian, *cherdak*) with a note, "The place where, in the conception of readers, all poetic works are born."

Lines 626–27: Akhmatova noted, "Cf. Shelley's well-known poem, 'To a Skylark.'" Accordingly, I have tried to use a Shelleyan vocabulary in translating these two lines.

Line 628, "George Gordon": Akhmatova merely uses the name George and duly notes, on behalf of those not familiar with one of the most famous scenes in English literature, that the person referred to was known to his readers by his title, Lord Byron.

Line 631, "Clara Gazoul": as Akhmatova noted, this was a pseudonym used by the French Romantic writer Prosper Mérimée.

An entry in Akhmatova's notebooks[55] from September–October 1964 put stanza 11 at the end of this section of the *Poem*:

Flip Side

. . . .

> "And your evil midnight will be repaid
> With the splendor of my royal kiss."

(The banging in the stovepipe falls silent for a minute and the spectator's ear can catch soft muffled sounds. Alternating with the organ's voice are the ravings of several million sleeping women, who even in their sleep cannot forget what their life has turned into):

> Ask any of the women of my age–
> Any of those arrested, exiled, caged–
> And she'll try to make you understand
> How terror left us half-demented,
> How we raised children to be sentenced
> To firing squads or concentration camps.
>   *Finis* {In Latin and underlined in the original}
> [Having tightly sealed our bluish lips,
> The bereaved Hecubas who've lost their wits]
> . . . .
> "We already know what's beyond hell."]
> And Cassandras from Chukhloma as well,
> In a silent chorus we'll proclaim,
> We, united by the brand of shame:
> "We are here, on the far side of hell."
>   Tashkent

Monday.
    Autumn is ending. Now, as you see, I've written a new ending for "Flip Side." Perhaps it will even have its own heading of some sort. I don't know yet.

The following stanzas were written as parts of *Flip Side* but did not fit into its final structure:

> And two orchestras drown each other out,
> From the secret circle each one's sound

Towards the swans' canopy takes its way.
Which is my real voice and which a mock,
Where is help and where a stumbling block,
Which is myself and which only a shade.
How can the second step be forestalled . . . [56]

And above all if a dream reveals
What all too soon must prove to be real:
Death all around—the city aflame,
And Tashkent flower-wreathed like a bride
What free of pain eternally abides
I will hear the wind of Asia proclaim.[56]

Too long I've witnessed the solemn rite
Of civic death—I can't bear the sight.
When I sleep, it comes and fills my dreams.
To find yourself with nothing at all—
No table, no bed—well, worse can befall,
That's the least part of what happened to me.[57]

My guest from beyond the mirror will speak
In a voice of neither joy nor grief,
"Do you forgive me?" is all he'll say.
He'll entwine me, as with pearls on a string,
Then for me, neither will mean a thing,
Not the dark of night nor the light of day.[58]

Epilogue

"May this place be empty": this epigraph, omitted in some manuscripts of the *Poem*, is the curse of Tsaritsa Avdotia (or Yevdokia). An entry in one of Akhmatova's notebooks reads:

> *Lyrical digression*
> Suzdal. The Monastery of the Assumption. The cell of Tsaritsa Yevdokia Fyodorovna Lopukhina. Wandering pilgrims—the shades of the condemned. They tell her fortune. Glebov–Love. Before the house iconostasis she curses Petersburg: "May this place be empty."
> 27 Dec⟨⟨ember⟩⟩ 1959
> Kr⟨⟨asnaya⟩⟩ Kon⟨⟨nitsa⟩⟩[59]

"I love you, Peter's great creation": like the subtitle of part I, "A Petersburg Tale," this line is from Pushkin's *The Bronze Horseman*; the "creation" (*tvoren'e*) is the city of Petersburg.

Line 655, "the star that heralds death and fear": Akhmatova noted, "Mars in the summer of 1941."[60]

Line 657: Tobruk—in Libya; it was garrisoned by Rommel's forces and, as such, was frequently mentioned in Soviet coverage of the North African desert campaign of winter 1941–42.

Lines 659–70, which were inspired by Vladimir Garshin, were significantly revised after his relationship with Akhmatova ended. The original version was:

> You, awe-inspiring, the last there will be,
> Bright listener to dark fantasies,
> Forgiveness, honor, intoxication!
> Like a flame that lights my way you burn,
> Like a banner before me you stand firm,
> And you kiss me sweetly as temptation.
> Lay your arm now upon my shoulder,
> Let the world never grow any older,
> Let the hands of the watch you gave me freeze.
> Ill fate and sorrow will not pass us by
> And the cuckoo will no longer cry
> Amid our leafless fire–blackened trees.

Lines 671–90 are included in the Struve–Filipoff edition of *Poem* but not in Zhirmunsky or any other Soviet edition, for obvious reasons. They also appear in one of Akhmatova's notebooks, where she gives the date of their composition as 1955.[61]

According to Chukovskaya, lines 683–90 were written separately and then formed part of the cycle "From a Burned Notebook" before making their way into the *Poem* in the late 1950s.[62]

Line 678, "the noseless Reaper": literally, "the noseless slut" (in Russian, the word for death is of feminine gender).

Line 686, "Beneath the gun": literally, "under a Nagan." Childers and Crone note that a Nagan pistol was "the then regular service weapon of the KGB."[63]

Line 692: Akhmatova's notebook[64] gives the variant, "You, seditious city, hellish, cherished."

Line 700: Akhmatova noted, "Volkovo Field (the old name of Volkovo Cemetery)." It is a well-known cemetery in Petersburg/Leningrad.

Lines 699–702: In an earlier variant, these lines read,

> Across the bridges my footfalls resound,
> And on the old Volkovo Field,
> Where my tears don't have to be concealed,
> Where new rows of crosses fill the ground.

Akhmatova explained to Chukovskaya that she had revised these lines because "no crosses were put up in Volkovo Cemetery during the blockade."[65]

Line 726, "above Brocken rose": see note on the prose passage following line 248.

Line 728, "the icy Kama River": a river that rises in the Ural Mountains and flows into the Volga. It formed part of the traditional path followed by exiles being marched into Siberia prior to the construction of the Trans–Siberian Railroad.

Line 729, "Quo vadis?": in Latin in Akhmatova's original. According to tradition, at the time of Nero's persecution of Christians, the apostle Peter was persuaded to leave Rome on the grounds that his life was indispensable to his flock. But as he took the road out of the city, he had a vision of Christ appearing to him and asking, "Quo vadis?"–"Where are you going?" Peter then realized that, just as fear for his own life had made him betray Jesus on the night before the Crucifixion, so he had been about to commit a second betrayal. He turned around and went back into the city to accept martyrdom.

The earliest version of the *Poem* does not include lines 709–26. Instead, the line "Into the air above Brocken rose" is followed by a single final stanza:

> And in my wake, lit by mysterious flame,
> A being that took "Seventh" as its name
> Dashed to a festival without peer.

> Disguised as musical notation,
> The Leningrader's renowned creation
> Returned to its ethereal native sphere.

When Akhmatova was evacuated from Leningrad at the end of September 1941 on one of the last flights out of the blockaded city, she carried with her the manuscript of Shostakovich's Seventh ("Leningrad") Symphony.

In a rejected ending, the text following line 742 reads,

> Her lips compressed, with dry downcast eyes
> Russia went at that time to the east.
> But as she retreated, she advanced,
> She met herself, marching sword in hand,
> Like a mirrored image becoming real.
> A storm bursting from the Asian steppes,
> Fearless and faithful, Russia pushed west
> To hail Moscow upon victory's field.[66]

Appendix I: An Early Version of
Poem Without a Hero (Tashkent 1942)

❦ ❦ ❦

Poem Without a Hero
Leningrad (1940)–Tashkent (1942)

Tout le monde a raison.
        –Rochefoucault

PART 1

The Year Nineteen-Thirteen

Di rider finerai
Pria dell'aurora.
    –Don Giovanni

I bear within, like a song or a sorrow,
That final winter before the war.
                –White Flock

Introduction

As from a tower that commands the view,
From nineteen-forty I look down.
As if I bid farewell anew
To what I long since bid farewell,

As if I paused to cross myself
And enter dark vaults underground.
                    1941. August, Leningrad.

Dedication

And since my paper has run out,
I'm using your rough draft for writing.
And there a word not mine shows through,
like a snowflake on my hand alighting,
to melt trustingly, without reproof.
And Antinous' dark downy lashes
rose suddenly—and there's green smoke
and a native breeze began to blow . . .
Is it the sea?
               No, just pine branches
on a grave, and closer, close at hand
in boiling foam comes . . .
                    Marche funèbre. . .
                              Chopin . . .
                         Dec. 26, 1940

                    I

In my hot youth, when George the Third
was king . . .
                         –Byron

I've set the cherished candles alight,
With the guest who didn't arrive
I planned to honor Forty-one's birth.
But . . . God be with us, His power abound!
Within the crystal the flame has drowned
"And the brimming wine like poison burns."
There are splashes of cruel conversations
As long–dead ravings reawaken
Although the hour has not struck yet.
A rush of fear hits me at full force,
Like a ghostly guard I stand by the door

To defend my final haven's rest.
And the bell rings, insistent and shrill,
At its sound I feel a fever chill,
Cold seizes me, I freeze, I burn . . .
Then, as if something came back to mind,
I turn slightly, looking half–behind,
And the words I speak are quiet and firm:
"You've got it wrong–you just went past
The Venice of the Doges . . . but your masks,
Your cloaks, staffs, crowns and all the rest,
You'll have to leave in the entryway.
I've decided to honor you today,
You mischief–making New Year's guests!"
This one's Faust, over there's Don Juan,
Someone goes past with a female faun
To the sound of jingling tambourine bells.
To receive them the walls spread out,
In the distance sirens began to howl,
Like a cupola the ceiling swelled.
Clearly I'm who they want, if not, who's meant?
But not for them is my table set,
And I don't plan to forgive their sins.
The last one is lame, his cough is dry,
I certainly hope that you would shy
From inviting an unclean spirit in.
I'd forgot the lessons you conferred,
False prophets juggling pretty words,
But you hadn't forgotten me.
As in the past the future takes shape
So in the future the past decays,
A hideous fete of rotting leaves.
Something about maskers wakes my fears,
It's just that somehow it always appeared
That some sort of superfluous shade
"Without face or name" had gotten in
Hidden among them . . . But let's begin
The proceedings for this New Year's day.
I'd rather not have the whole world know

About this midnight Hoffmanesque, so
If I could ask a favor . . . Wait,
You there, you're not among those listed
With the Capuchins, clowns, Lysiscas–
Dressed as a milepost in striped array
Painted with crude and gaudy strokes–
You're as old as the Mamre oak,
You converse with the moon through centuries.
You pretend to groan, but no one's fooled,
You use letters of iron to write your rules,
Hammurabi, Lycurgus, Solon too
Would have profited to hear you teach.

    With what strange tastes this being's endowed,
    Not content to wait for gout and renown
    To rush to seat him on display
    In lavish thrones for his jubilee,
    He triumphs out on the flowering heath,
    Through the wilderness he takes his way.
    And there's nothing he needs repent,
    Not a single thing . . . In any event
    Poets and sins don't go together.
    Where the Ark of the Covenant is,
    They must dance or vanish! . . .And about this,
    It's been expressed in verses better.

A cry: "Let's have the hero up front!"
No need to worry: he's sure to come,
He'll replace that tall man, take the floor . . .
Why do you rush off in a throng,
As if each saw the bride for whom he longed,
While I'm left behind to stand forlorn,
Alone in the gloom, facing that black frame
From which there looks out, still the same,
That hour none ever rightly mourned?

    It comes, not all at once, but slowly.
    Like a musical phrase's flowing,
    I hear gusts of words, a broken cry.
    Then–flat steps heading up the stair,

A flash of light and far off somewhere
A clear voice: "I am ready to die."

II

> You embody the senses' pleasures
> More fully than those alive, radiant shade.
> —Baratynsky

The fur coat's flung open, all satin–lined!
Don't think, my Dove, that I'm unkind,
It's myself, not you, I'm punishing now.
Do you see, beyond the swirling snow,
The blackamoor boys who were in the show
Are playing games and horsing around?
Boldly and gaily the sleigh runners chime,
And a goathair lap robe trails behind.
Shades, begone!–He stands alone indeed.
The wall shows his profile, firm and clear.
Say, my lady, is your chevalier
Gabriel or Mephistopheles?
Out of the portrait to me you came,
Upon the wall the empty frame
Will be waiting for you till the dawn.
So go on, dance now–unescorted,
And the role of the fatal chorus
I myself have agreed to take on . . .
You came to Russia out of nowhere,
O my wonder with flaxen hair,
The Columbine of the 1910s!
Why show such a troubled and keen–eyed gaze,
You Petersburg doll, acclaimed on stage–
You're one of my doubles, another me.
That's one more title you must append
To the others. O poets' beloved friend,
The fame you once had is now my own.
To an amazing musical meter
As Leningrad's wind swoops and sweeps here,

I behold dancing courtiers' bones.
Down the wedding candles wax slowly drips,
The white–veiled shoulders wait to be kissed,
The church thunders: "Dove, come to the groom!"
Parma violets in April piled up high,
And the Maltese Chapel rendezvous lies
Deep in your heart like a poisoned wound.
Circus wagons pale beside your home,
Around the altar of Venus go
Cupids with features pitted and gouged.
You made your bedroom a garden retreat,
The people living on your street
Back home in Pskov wouldn't know you now.
Golden candlesticks form a glittering line,
Upon the walls saints in sky blue shine,
These goods aren't quite stolen, but it's close . . .
Like Botticelli's "Spring," flower–bedecked,
You received lovers in your bed,
And anguish filled the sentry Pierrot.

    Where your husband is, I didn't see, couldn't guess,
    I, the hoarfrost against the window pressed
    Or the chiming of the fortress bells.
    Have no fear–I don't mark crosses on doors,
    I'm waiting for you, come boldly forth,
    It's long been known what your stars foretell.

III

    They fall at Bryansk, while Manteshev's
       grow,
    Already he's gone, the young man, our own.
                –Velimir Khlebnikov

To heat the holidays bonfires burned,
And carriages on bridges overturned,
And the black–draped city was borne away,
It drifted on toward an unknown goal,
Following or fighting the Neva's flow–
But always moving away from its graves.

In the Summer Garden a weathervane's tune
Rang delicately, and a silver moon
Hung frozen over the Silver Age.
And through the cold and choking atmosphere
Of prodigal prewar days, one could hear
A low muffled hum, a warning sound.
But then it was still far–off and faint,
And, almost beyond any hearing range,
It sank into the Neva snows and drowned.

After midnight someone paces and stamps
Beneath the windows, a streetcorner lamp
Sheds a merciless and sickly glow–
And then he sees the pretty masker
Coming back from "The Road from Damascus"
Has come home at last, and not alone.
On the landing a lingering scent is sweet,
And a young hussar bearing poetry
And senseless death will ring the bell,
If the courage he calls up doesn't fail,
To you, his Traviata, he will pay
His final respects. Look where he fell:
Not in the mud by some Polish creek. . .
Not upon the blue Carpathian peaks. . .
　　　He is at your door–
　　　There on the floor . . .
　　　Mercy, oh show mercy, Lord!

I, your olden conscience, here affirm:
I tracked down the tale that had been burned,
I went to the deceased's house
And there I laid it down
On a window shelf and then I tiptoed off . . .

Afterword

All's as it should be: the poem rests now,
As usual, with no more to say.
But what if a theme suddenly bursts out,

Knocks with its fists on a windowpane?
And to that summons there replies
A distant sound fraught with alarm—
Gurgling, groaning, and shrieking cries . . .
And a vision of crossed arms.

December 26, 1940
Leningrad. The Fontanka House (night).

PART 2

Flip Side
(Intermezzo)

To V. G. Garshin

. . . I take the waters of Lethe,
Doctor's orders–I'm not allowed to be
    depressed.
                    –Pushkin

My editor was dissatisfied,
Swore he was busy, and sick besides,
His phone number went under cover.
Impossible! Three themes are mixed up here!
The reader gets lost–it's still not clear,
When all is done, who are the lovers.

At first I was ready to yield. But then
Words began to fall in again,
A music box pealed and its echoes rung,
And above the broken flask the glow
Of a mysterious poison rose,
Flamed straight up in a greenish tongue.

And I kept on writing in my dream
A libretto for someone, it seemed,
And the unceasing music poured.
Yes, a dream–but in it some truth stirs!
The "soft embalmer," the long–sought blue bird,
The parapets of Castle Elsinore.

Let me just say that I didn't rejoice
When I heard the distant roaring noise
Set up by that hellish mocking crew.
I kept on hoping, in spite of all,
That the pine branches, like a pall,
Would drift off to the mysterious gloom.

He's still putting on his old show!
That motley clownish Cagliostro
For whom I feel nothing but disgust.
And bats go flying by in a flash,
And across the rooftops hunchbacks dash,
Blood flows, and a gypsy girl licks it up.

No trace of a Roman carnival night–
The Chant of the Angels trembles outside,
Beyond the high windows, barred from entry.
Outside my door no steps draw nearer,
All the mirror's dreams are of a mirror,
Over silence silence stands sentry.

But here's what that theme was like for me–
A flower that fell to the floor unseen
And was crushed when a coffin went past.
Friends, "remember" and "call to mind"
Are as different as Luga's countryside
Is from the city of satin masks.

I opened a trunk and dug things out–
The devil made me do it–well, but how
Does that mean I'm the one most to blame?
I'm simple at heart, I don't try to shock,
You know my books: *Wayside Herb, White Flock* . . .
To defend myself–what can I say?

But know this: if plagiarism's the charge . . .
Well, am I the guiltiest one at large? . . .
But really, this time will be the last . . .
It all turned out badly, yes, I know,
I'll freely let my confusion show,
Not try to hide it behind a mask.

But that hundred–year–old enchantress
Suddenly woke, head full of fancies.
I didn't invite it, I just was there.
Her lace kerchief languidly falls,

From behind the lines her coy looks call
In a Bryullov pose, her shoulders bare.

I drank her in every drop and was cursed
With a raging demonic thirst,
I didn't know what to do, couldn't bear it,
I had to get away from this raver,
I threatened her with the Star Chamber
And forced her back home to her garret,

To the darkness under Manfred's pines
And to where, face turned to see the sky,
Shelley's body lay upon the shore,
And the ethereal sphere was riven
As all earth's skylarks soared to heaven,
And George Gordon held a torch.

But her reply was firm and stately:
"No, I am not that English lady,
And I'm certainly not Clara Gazoul.
I don't claim any forefathers' glories,
Save from the sun and mythical stories
And July itself brought me to you.

"As for your ambiguous fame,
For twenty years left to lie unclaimed,
Yet I shall not have it served like this.
In triumph we two shall celebrate,
And your evil midnight will be repaid
With the splendor of my royal kiss."
> 1941. January (the 3rd–5th)
> Leningrad
> The Fontanka House
> Recopied in Tashkent
> Jan. 19, 1942
> (on a night when there was a minor earthquake)

Epilogue

To my city and my beloved

Under the roof of the Fontanka House
Where the evening langour wanders round
Bearing a lamp and keys on a ring,
I hallooed and distant echoes answered,
And my inappropriate laughter
Troubled the unbroken sleep of things
In the place where each day, at dusk and dawn,
Witness to everything that goes on,
The old maple gazes into my room.
As it sees our parting in advance,
It extends to me a gnarled black hand
As if giving help, remaining true.

But under my feet was burning ground,
And such a star looked balefully down
On the home I hadn't yet fled in fear,
Glaring, watching for the appointed day . . .
It's in Tobruk somewhere—still far away,
It's right around the block—it's almost here.

You, awe–inspiring, the last there will be,
Bright listener to dark fantasies,
Forgiveness, honor, intoxication!
Like a flame that lights my way you burn,
Like a banner before me you stand firm,
And you kiss me sweetly as temptation.
Lay your arm now upon my shoulder,
Let the world never grow any older,
Let the hands of the watch you gave me freeze.
Ill fate and sorrow will not pass us by
And the cuckoo will no longer cry
Amid our leafless fire–blackened trees.

Where I faced doom but didn't perish,
You, city of granite, hellish, cherished,
Have fallen silent, turned deathly white.

My parting from you is only feigned,
Part of each other we still remain,
Upon your buildings my shadow lies,
Upon your waters my image falls,
My steps echo through the Hermitage halls,
Across the bridges my footfalls resound,
And on the old Volkovo Field,
Where my tears don't have to be concealed,
Where new rows of crosses fill the ground.
I fancied that you followed as I fled,
You who stayed behind to meet your death
With gleaming waters and spires of gold.
How you awaited bearers of good news,
They didn't come. . . Now all that's left to you
Is your white nights, still dancing as of old.
And the blest word—home—has become unknown,
All of us who have nowhere of our own
Peer through others' windows from outside.
Some are in New York, some in Tashkent,
And the bitter air of banishment
To the exile is like poisoned wine.
And all of you could marvel, if you wished,
When in the belly of a flying fish
I eluded the malice of foes,
And over Lake Ladoga I soared
Like she who, impelled by demonic force,
Into the air above Brocken rose.
And in my wake, lit by mysterious flame,
A being that took "Seventh" as its name
Dashed to a festival without peer.
Disguised as musical notation,
The Leningrader's renowned creation
Returned to its ethereal native sphere.

1942

Tashkent (finished August 18)

Appendix II

§ § §

Poem Without a Hero:
Excerpts from Akhmatova's Notebooks

The notebooks Akhmatova kept during the last eight years of her life, from 1958 to 1966, contain a number of entries on *Poem Without a Hero*. What follows is a representative sampling of these entries, many of which are repetitive. Not all of Akhmatova's entries are dated; when they are not, I have inferred a date from jottings on pages before or after the entry and have given this date in curly brackets { }. Explanatory material I have added (e.g., English translations of citations that appear in some language other than Russian in Akhmatova's original) is also enclosed in curly brackets. Words or parts of words enclosed by angle brackets (⟨⟨ ⟩⟩) are expansions of material that was abbreviated in Akhmatova's original text. The use of square brackets ([ ]) and parentheses follows Akhmatova's text. All ellipses are in the original.

From notebook 1 {June 1958}[1]

Tonight I saw (or heard) my poem in a dream, as a tragic ballet. (This is the second time, the first time it hap⟨⟨pened⟩⟩ was in 1944.) Let us hope that this is its last return, and that when it appears again, I will already be gone . . . But I wanted to take note of this occurrence, even if just jotting it down, which is what I'm now doing. I remember everything: the music, and the scenery, and the costumes, and the great clock (on the right), wh⟨⟨ich⟩⟩ struck midnight . . . Olga performed *la danse russe rêvée par Debussy* {French, "A Russian Dance as Dreamed by Debussy"}, as ⟨⟨Grand Duke⟩⟩ K⟨⟨irill⟩⟩ V⟨⟨ladimirovich⟩⟩ said about her in 1913, and [danced] did a goat–legged dance, some kind of dance in a fur coat, with a huge muff (like in S⟨⟨udeiki⟩⟩n's portrait) and fur slippers. Then she threw it all off and turned out to be Psyche with wings and in a dense warm yellow glow. The coachmen were dancing, as in Stravinsky's *Petrouchka*, Pavlova was soaring above the Marinsky stage (Nijinsky's last dance), doves were cooing in the middle of Gost⟨⟨iny⟩⟩ Dvor, in the corners before the icons eternal flames burned in golden lamps . . . Blok was awaiting the Commendatore . . . A drum beat . . . (that night 3 pe⟨⟨ople⟩⟩ were very anxious about me).

The dragoon by the streetlamp. Encounters. A blizzard. The Field of Mars. Everything out of my ballet "Sn⟨⟨ow⟩⟩ Mask." A ball of ghosts. A ghostly military parade–military music. The second curtain rises. A march. The dragoon standing motionless in a Nic⟨⟨holas⟩⟩ overcoat. In the depth of the stage a terrifying staircase lit by gas lamps. She (the Goat-Legged Girl) is returning from the masquerade, with her is someone unknown, per-haps the "superfluous shade" (terrifying). Their parting. The kiss. The dragoon's suicide–in music. [his funeral, as in the Dedication]. The fu-neral service, as in Meyerhold's "Masquerade" (candles, veils, incense burning).
. . . By the window ledge–a vision.

From notebook 4 (December 1959)[2]

[I] III
The dragoon by the streetlamp. Encounters: Vera with a malicious note, the General, ⟨⟨they?⟩⟩ leave him, two sluts call to [him] the dragoon–he doesn't go. He sees her image in the window in different forms. Finally as death. (A single instant!) Psyche [in the window]. Behind a tulle curtain. The noise of time! A blizzard.
(Olga is in a theater box watching a fragment of my ballet "The Snow Mask." A lyr⟨⟨ical⟩⟩ digression. Everything is mixed up, as in a dream. The dragoon is writing a poem under the streetlamp. The Field of Mars. A

ghosts' ball. The ghost of the war period. (Military music.) Marches. Procession. Torches. Again the General in a Nich⟨⟨olas⟩⟩ greatcoat. The dragoon, sunk deep in thought, doesn't notice him. In the far recesses of the stage a second curtain rises–a terrifying staircase, gaslit (a blue light). The spectator recognizes the staircase in it–the apparition from the first scene. [The Goat–Legged Girl] O. is returning from the masquerade, the Unknown Man [perhaps the Superfluous Shade] (develop this) is with her. The scene in front of the door. The dragoon stands motionless in a niche.

Their parting, which leaves no doubts whatsoever. The kiss. O. goes into her apartment. The dragoon's suicide . . . A shot. The light goes out. The funeral music. O. comes out and kneels over the body . . .

The door remains wide open, through it one can see everything that happens: both what we know and, beyond that, the unknown

Future

(Psyche)

(Dec⟨⟨ember⟩⟩ 18, 1959. Kr⟨⟨asnaya⟩⟩ Konnitsa)

The door is flung open (becoming wider and taller). Wearing a long black dress, Columbine (with a candle) goes out and kneels by the body. Another figure in the same type of dress and holding the same type of candle goes up a flight of steps, to kneel by the body the same way. Chopin plays.

24 Dec⟨⟨ember⟩⟩1959

I

On a dark stage, only a table is illuminated–two places are set. Candles. "Consecrated candles are burning" {English in the original}. X is sitting, back to the viewer, wearing a long black shawl [as if in mourning], elbows on the table. A clock.–Five minutes to midnight. A conversation with someone who did not come. (He is a portrait or a bust, or a *shade*.) A bell rings. Everything changes. The table into the whole stage–an enormous reception hall. A throng of maskers. Everyone dances: the Demon, Don Juan with the mourning–draped Anna, Faust (an old man) with the de⟨⟨ad⟩⟩ Gretchen, the Milepost (alone), the Goat-Legged Girl leads a Bacchic procession, like on a black–fig⟨⟨ure⟩⟩ vase. X renounces all of them and most of all herself, young, in the celebrated shawl. The "Guest from the Future" walks out of one mirror, *traverse la scène* and walks into another. Everyone is horror–struck. The utterly banal dance of Columbine, Harlequin and Pierrot. Sham prosperity. A court "Russian." ["The Superfluous Shade"] A chiromancer or Rasputin and everyone surrounding him. [In a frock coat, limping.] He shows everyone their future, i.e., a premonition of drowning, to Don Juan–the Commendatore, to Faust, still old–Mephisto⟨⟨pheles⟩⟩, to Cleopatra–the asp, and so on.

And still the specter of Nastasya Filippovna.

Suddenly someone appears, a head taller than everybody else, in a black cloak, wearing a mask. The Superfluous Shade refuses to tell his fortune, he insists, in the depth of the stage arises for an instant the scene of his suicide. He casts off the cloak, takes off the mask–it's the boy–dragoon. He kneels before O., gives her his manuscript. Then he sweeps her into his arms and carries her away. Her portrait. X–in front of the portrait. A new knock. (For an instant it's Mandelstam's Petersburg of 1920.+ Half Venice, half Gonzago decor. So theatrical it's stupefying. ("Chiffon pillows in loges are luxuriantly fluffed.") It's terrifying. Everything's in place–right down to the shop signs–but inside there's already nothing.) Something from here penetrated into the poem.

Something terrible peeped into the window twice. A vision: the dead dragoon "between the cupboard and the stove."

II

(The dragoon's dream: the past and the fut⟨⟨ure⟩⟩)
At Columbine's.

O.'s *intérieur* [the bedroom]. A corner is lit. On the walls are portraits of O., wh⟨⟨ich⟩⟩ at times come to life, exchange glances with each other, not stepping out of their frames. Verka–the little lady's maid. She dresses Columbine. A dining room. In the mirror is reflected the Superfluous Shade . . . People bring notes, flowers. A table. The dragoon arrives. An intimate breakfast. His jealousy. He takes back his letter and roses. Her oaths. Complete reconciliation. *Pas de deux.* The little hall. She cuts off her "lock of pale hair" and gives it to him. ([Perhaps] The meeting in the Malt⟨⟨ese⟩⟩ Chapel.) Requiem [Mozart].

+ No, it's not the 20s, it's 1941–the first bombardment has started–everyone's died long ago.

Two Harlequins–she drives them both off. A reception. Again the bed-room. An altar to Venus. But the dragoon is already forgotten. O., lying down, wearing a lace cap and a nightgown, is receiving her guests. The candles burn in tall gl⟨⟨ass⟩⟩ candlesticks. "And in the round mirror the bed is reflected."

The guests Klyuyev and Yesenin do a wild folk dance, Russian, almost Flagellant. The Demon. Her whole self goes out to him. Black roses. The first scene of the dragoon's jealousy. His despair. The frost peeks in the window. (Byaka–Stravinsky's premonition.) The clocks are chiming: "How glorious . . ."

The scent of *Rose Jaquemineau* {sic}.

A lame and courteous man tries to comfort the dragoon, tempting him with something very dark. (Vyach⟨eslav⟩ Ivanov's "Tower")–[The Super-fluous Shade] The lame and courteous man at home. Antiquity. The Altar of Pergamum comes to life. Oedipus–Antigone. The curse. Pagan Russia (Gorodetsky, Stravinsky's "Rite of Spring," Tolstoy, early Khlebnikov). They're outside. The Tauride Garden in the snow, a blizzard. Specters in the blizzard. (Perhaps even Blok's Twelve, but far–off and unreal.)

> And the mute empty spaces of the squares
> Where people were executed at dawn.

The poem then turns into my memories, wh⟨⟨ich⟩⟩ at least once a year (often in December) demand that I do something with them.

> Things refuse to obey,
> It's the wizard Kashchey
> Sitting there on the painted trunk . . .

. . . "*The Stray Dog*"–the evening for Tamara Karsavina–she's dancing in the mirror. A masquerade–a huge fire buring in the fireplace. The landscape painting on the walls comes to life. Suddenly all the masks become "Su-perfluous Shades." (They exchange glances with each other and laugh.) For some reason the dragoon's eyes are blindfolded, the lights go out. His shoulder straps are torn off. He's supposed to catch someone. The author of the poem (in the limelight, wearing a black domino and a red mask) [approaches him], he mistakenly seizes her, and she gives him a small cross. He recognizes her and . . . wakes up. The *corps de guard*. As punishment for failing to salute the general, the dragoon was sent to the guardhouse, where he dozed off. Outside the window a drum is beating. Drills. They let the dragoon out, he runs again to Columbine. Again Petersburg, but nocturnal, feral. The Neva. Dark windows. All around a terrifying last night. He tries to summon the "dear shades": his mother, his sister—instead of those destroyed by him—the fiancee/Smolny debutante/nun and the dead gypsy girl. Everything's already a deadly circle. He looks for the little cross and notices that he's lost it. He takes out his poems—he renounces them, flings them down in the road, tramples on them. Then he is sorry, picks them up, hides them in his breast together with the lock of pale hair.

[Her glove. Two harlequins . . .]

The magus offers everyone to find out their future by knocking at a terrifying door. The first to knock is Faust[+]—the door opens, Mephistopheles emerges and leads Faust down a staircase—terrifying music. The second to knock is Don Juan, the Commendatore emerges, and they descend together. No one else wants to knock. Only the dragoon is bold enough—the door is flung open, there on a pedestal is Psyche come to life, he takes her for Columbine, dashes toward her, the door slams shut with a bang. Funeral music. The Superfluous Shade knocks at the door three times. Psyche is again marble, the dragoon is lying at her feet.

The line of the "Superfluous Shade"
He appears at the [assembly] ball in the *1st scene*. In a white domino and a red mask, with a lantern and a spade. He has a retinue behind the wings, he summons them with a whistle and dances with them. Everyone runs away. *In the 2nd scene* he peeks into the window of Columbine's room and is reflected in the mirror, doubling, tripling, etc. The mirror is smashed to pieces, foretelling misfortune.

In the (third) 3rd scene he gets out of a carriage wearing a beaver-fur coat and a top hat, invites the dragoon to ride with him . . . The stars—branches of trees in Mikhailovsky Park.

He shakes his head and points to the lock of pale hair. Reaching out a hand in a white glove, the S⟨⟨uperfluous⟩⟩ Shade tries to take the lock. He

---

[+] Punishment, Faust, does come!

seizes the Shade by the hand–the glove is left in his hand, there wasn't a hand in it. In a fury he tears the glove.

> (It's impossible to break the grasp
> Of those greedy, predatory hands
> And take from them what it is they hold.)

Scene II

A light (white in the spotlight) curtain. An unfinished portrait of Columbine–Confusion on the easel. O. steps down out of it in a fur coat, which she tosses to [a little Negro boy] one of the little blackamoors who are scurrying around. X. takes a bottle of wine from a proffered tray, clinks glasses with O. and points out to her something in the distance. The little blackamoors draw the curtain and . . . all around is old Peter City. A New Year's blizzard, almost something out of Hans Christian Andersen. Through it, forms appear (perhaps from "The Snow Mask"). A string of horse–drawn vehicles–carriages, sleighs . . . The Liteiny St. book trade–bent-over bearded owners of secondhand bookstores and eccentric book collectors, nighttime services in churches, "wartime Petersburg" (a drum roll–a soldiers' song–a fragment of a parade–the Guards in arms on the Neva ice. Epiphany). The Vyazemsky Monastery–"the bottom." Columbine, along with five other Columbines, dances a Russian dance at the Tsarskoe Selo palace of K⟨⟨irill⟩⟩ V⟨⟨ladimirovich⟩⟩ (*la dance russe rêvée par Debussy*).

A dance with doubles (all in masks) (Perhaps in the 1st scene)

A shot. The light goes out. The door is flung open (becoming wider and taller). Columbine, wearing a long black dress and holding a candle, goes out and kneels by the body. Another figure in the same type of dress and holding the same type of candle goes up the staircase. Chopin plays.

From notebook 7 (January 1961)[5]

(Jan⟨⟨uary⟩⟩ 2, 1961. Moscow)

Today M. A. Z⟨⟨enkevich⟩⟩ spoke at length and in detail about "Triptych": In his opinion, it is a tragic symphony–it doesn't need music, bec⟨⟨ause⟩⟩ it contains music in itself. The author talks about Fate (Ananke) rising above all–people, time, events. Done very powerfully. An Acmeist work with firmly outlined boundaries. In its fantastic nature, it's similar to "The Lost Streetcar." In the simplicity of its story, which can be retold in a couple of words, to "The Br⟨⟨onze⟩⟩ H⟨⟨orseman⟩⟩."

Dobin called it the apex of the 20th century (summer 1960, Komarovo). X, a requiem for all Europe (1946).

It was this possibility of a voice's sound reaching immeasurably farther than articulate words could that Zhirm⟨⟨unsky⟩⟩ had in mind when he spoke about "Poem Without a Hero." That's why the readers react so differently to the Poem. Some immediately hear that echo, that second step. Others don't hear it and are just looking for sedition, don't find it and are offended.

I understood all this only very recently, and it's possible that this will become my parting with the Poem.

B. Pasternak spoke of the Poem as a dance. (Two figures of the "Russkaya.") "With a kerchief, stepping back"–that's lyric poetry–it conceals itself. Forward, hands outstretched–that's a *poema*. He spoke, as always, unusually–no repeating, no reminding, but always full of quivering life. (Dec⟨⟨ember⟩⟩ 14, 1960. Moscow.)

For ex⟨⟨ample⟩⟩, (Blok about Komissarzhevskaya). V. F. Kom⟨⟨issarzhevskaya's⟩⟩ voice echoed the world orchestra. Because her sum⟨⟨mo⟩⟩ning and tender voice was like the voice of spring, she called us immensely farther than the content of the articulated words.

1. "Triptych" is in no way connected with any of the works of the 1910s, contrary to the wishes of the most asinine readers, wh⟨⟨o⟩⟩ in their "simplicity" suppose that this is the easiest way of giving it the brush-off. "It's old-fashioned–they used to write like that." Who, when?

Maybe it's really bad, but nobody ever wrote like that (including not in the 1910s).

V. M. Zhirmunsky said something very interesting about the Poem. He said that it was the Symbolists' dream come true, i.e., it was what they always preached in theory but never put into practice in their works (magical rhythm, visionary enchantment), that there was nothing of that sort in their long poems. S. M⟨⟨arkish⟩⟩ disagrees . . .

Appendix II

From notebook 9 {spring–summer 1961}[4]

More about the Poem

It's not just by means of the music hidden in it that it's twice gone away from me into ballet. It's straining to go back, somewhere into darkness, into history ("And cursed by the wife the tsar hadn't wanted," 'May this place be empty'), into Petersburg history from Peter to the siege of 1941–1944, or rather into the Petersburg myth. (The Petersburg Hoffmanesque.) (In general this is the apotheosis of the nineteen–tens in all their magnificence and their flaws.)

Another of its features: this enchanted drink, while it's being poured into a vessel, suddenly thickens and turns into my biography, as if seen by someone in a dream or in a row of mirrors ("And I'm happy or not happy walking with y⟨⟨ou⟩⟩.") Sometimes I see it as completely transparent, emanating an incomprehensible light (like the light of a white night, when everything shines from within), unexpected galleries open up and lead nowhere, a second footstep rings out, an echo which regards itself as the most important thing speaks its own word and does not repeat another's. The shadows turn into what is casting them. Everything doubles and triples—right down to the bottom of the chest.

And suddenly this fata morgana breaks off. On the table there are simply lines of verse, quite graceful, skillful, daring ones. No mysterious light, no second footstep, no rebelling echo, no shadows that have acquired a separate existence, and then I begin to understand why it leaves some of its readers cold. This happens mainly when I read it to someone whom it doesn't reach, and, like a boomerang (please forgive the hackneyed comparison), it returns to me, but in what a way (!?), and wounding me itself.

May 17, 1961, Komarovo

The attempt to ground it (on the advise of the late Galkin) wound up as a fiasco. It categorically refused to enter the neighborhoods outside the city's center. Neither the gypsy girl on the spittle–covered road, nor the steamship heading for the Comfort of All the Grieving, nor Khleb–⟨⟨nikov?⟩⟩, nor the Hot Field, [Khleb] it didn't want any of this, it didn't go to the fatal bridge with Mayakovsky, nor to five–kopek public baths smelling of birch twigs, nor to Blok's magical taverns with ships on the walls and all around—mystery and the Petersburg myth—it stubbornly

288

stayed in its fateful corner at the house th⟨⟨at⟩⟩ the br⟨⟨others⟩⟩ Adamini built at the beginning of the 19th C., from which the windows of the Mar⟨⟨ble⟩⟩ Palace were visible and past which to the sound of drums the snub-nosed soldiers of the Pavlovsk regiment returned to their barracks. At the same time, as if showing through a soft wet New Year's snowfall on the Field of Mars, one can see fragments of a hundred May Day parades and

All the Summer Garden's mysteries–

The floodings, the rendezvous, the siege . . .

Someone said "P⟨⟨oem⟩⟩ W⟨⟨ithout a⟩⟩ H⟨⟨ero⟩⟩ is a Requiem for all Europe." Probably he was distracted and was thinking about something else at that moment.

On one occasion I craftily lured it out into the Sheremetev garret ("Flip Side"), having hidden the fact that beneath there lurked Tashkent, and on another occasion Time itself led it almost to the waves of the Pacific Ocean. The poet's grave.

That a *second* music is present is something I finally realized virtually yesterday. Perhaps I'll even hear it sometime. The third (Asiatic) accompanied its harrowing bloodstained youth, and the *first* I'd already dreamed about before its birth and it led me into not the legendary, but the real twentieth century.

(July 27, 1961, Komarovo)

Determining when it began to sound within me is impossible. Either it happened when I was standing with a companion on the Neva (after the dress rehearsal for "Masquerade" on February 25, 1917) and a cavalry charge dashed down the road, or when I was standing, already without my companion, on the Liteiny bridge, when it was unexpectedly lifted open in broad daylight (an event without precedent) to allow the battleships passage through to Smolny to support the Bolsheviks (Oct⟨⟨ober⟩⟩ 25, 1917). How can I know?!

Continuation

(More about the "Poem")

Now I understand: the "Second" or the "Other" ("And along with it goes *Another*"), which has caused such problems almost from the very beginning (at any case in Tashkent) is simply the gaps, the unfilled-in blank spaces, from which, sometimes almost miraculously, I manage to seize something and put it in the text. My activity fundamentally comes down to this, which is what irritates some readers so much. To my chagrin, these fragments are often called "pearls" and people swear that they're better than the text surrounding them. (That's what happened with the lyr⟨⟨ical⟩⟩ digression about the Guest from the Future in Chapter 1.) That's what happened a few days ago with the fragment:

> She's with someone "without face or name"
> . . . .
> And now, time to say good–by, all's done"

and the "Portrait of the Goat–Legged Girl."

It looks as if I left out all the best, turned it over, let's say, to music, and wrote all the worst, but the best continued to crowd in and in places broke through into the printed(?) text, bringing with it the shade, the ghost of the music (but not "musicalness" in the banal sense) in which it had resided. That's the reason for the imperceptible "seams" (which so astonished some people, Ozerov in particular).

The sense of being on the eve, of a holy night–*this* is the axis around which the whole thing revolves like a magic carousel (examples). It's this breath that moves all the details and the surrounding atmosphere itself. (The wind from the morrow.) The reader and listener fall into this revolving atmosphere, that's what creates the magic that makes one's head spin and that some (L. Ya. Ginzburg) have called a forbidden device ("I'll face death and shame and I won't quake, / It's a cryptogram, a code to break, / A device like this is not allowed.")

But it's also, inter alia, what the Symbolists wanted to achieve and what they preached in theory, but what they couldn't achieve when they themselves undertook to write (V. M. Zh⟨⟨irmunsk⟩⟩y, 1960), (develop this).

31 Aug⟨⟨ust⟩⟩ 1961
Leningrad

From notebook 10 (September 1961–January 1962)[5]

After 1946 I didn't write any verses until 1955, but I worked on "Triptych."

More about it.

(*It's broader.*) That's what Vl⟨⟨adimir⟩⟩ Pavl⟨⟨ovich⟩⟩ Mikhailov said. There's a feeling of ⟨⟨unf⟩⟩illed empty spaces where there's something nearby, i.e., there's the illusion they're not filled, because, perhaps, *the most important thing* is right there, and this creates a feeling close to [bordering on] sorcery. These supposedly empty spaces and darknesses are suddenly lit up, now by the sun, now by the moon, now by a Petersburg streetlamp, and they turn out to be now a bit of the city, now the taiga, now Columbine's living room, now the Sheremetev garret, through which whirls the hellish harlequinade of "Flip Side."

In contrast to the editor's commentary, wh⟨⟨ich⟩⟩ will be correct to the point of absurdity, the author's commentary won't contain a single [correct] true word, it will have jokes, both witty and stupid, hints, both comprehensible and incomprehensible, irrelevant references to great figures (Pushkin) and in general everything one finds in life, especially the stanzas which didn't make it into the definitive text, for ex⟨⟨ample⟩⟩, a stanza wandering about in a copy from 1955:

> I left the right–side room, went out the door,
> No hope of a miracle any more,
> In September, in a mirrored night–
> A former love can't sleep, he mutters, pleads
> That more than happiness itself he needs
> To banish the king's daughter from his mind.

(And a note on Lermontov: "The prince rides. . .")

among wh⟨⟨om⟩⟩ the dragoon vainly tries to recognize Columbine. One mistake after another. Finally, the indisputable *She* steps forth: in tiny red boots, a black domino and a splendid red wig (she emerges from a court carriage). Her [thin] [delicate] thin arm in a long white glove enfolds an enormous pile of roses pressed against her breast. A velvet half–mask firmly conceals her face. The dragoon dashes up to her. She is affectionate, looks into his eyes, enfolds him in her arms.* He wants to embrace her–at that minute a terrible whirlwind arises, it awakens the ravens in Mikhailovsky Park,+ they begin to circle around, flying low, cawing

---

* Om⟨⟨itted⟩⟩: throws the roses around his neck like an Indian garland

+ The garland flies around him and turns out to be a simple met⟨⟨al⟩⟩ grave⟨⟨yard⟩⟩ wreath, and he himself turns into just such a cross, into the stone cross by the overgrown wall on the Field of Mars. O.'s voice: "Vs⟨⟨evolod's⟩⟩ grave is somewhere here by the wall." A woman in black.

deafeningly. The wind flings open the "lady in black's" domino. Her mask falls, under it is a skull. The skeleton claps its hands—a crash, the building [falls] is destroyed. A fire . . . The dragoon came to—he had dreamed it all. But worse, the "lady in black" emerges from under the gates and makes a threatening gesture with her finger. (Horrified, he covers his face with his hands).

1st variant—in slow motion:

3rd variant. His own recollections (Waltz: Nothing ⟨⟨illegible⟩⟩)

    Two shades

The cousin—fiancee/Smolny debutante (the Inst⟨⟨itute⟩⟩ ball etc.). Because of Columbine he cools toward her. She enters a convent.

The gypsy girl—tambourine, her fatal dance, death

> Debutante, dear cousin, Juliet! . . .
> You'll wait no more for the cornet,
> In secret you'll take the convent's vow.
> Your tambourine has fallen mute,
> My gypsy girl, and the little wound
> In your left breast has turned black by now.

From the author's commentary

Someone who returned from those parts where people memorize verse brought two stanzas composed by no one knows whom and an implausible novella which I will not undertake to recount.

Text

I

> Like cloven feet stamp her prancing boots,
> Like jingling bells chime her earring hoops,
> Amid blond curls wicked horns peep through,
> She's drunk with the dance, accursed, possessed—
> As if off black–figure pottery
> She leapt into life and ran towards the sea
> In full ceremonial undress.

II

You, in the helmet and cloak, behind her,*
Running in unmasked, your face unobscured,
What is it that chokes your soul with grief?
In your every word pain opens up,
So black a sorrow runs through your love,
And why does that little stream of blood
Drip down the petal of your cheek?

Farther on it seems that there was one more stanza—an utterly enchanting one which, however, was largely washed away when an ocean wave struck the bottle in which the manuscript of the "Poem" was supposedly floating. (A manuscript in a bottle!—cliche. Well, no big deal!—In the worst case it'll do.**)

More for "Prose about the Poem"
    . . . Everything in it doubles and triples. Including, of course—the author herself. One on "Brocken" sees the shade of the living dragoon ("Behind her a man in unif⟨⟨orm⟩⟩"), another sees him in her (Fontanka) apartment and is horrified.
    (The same for everything).
The 19-y⟨⟨ea⟩⟩r-old poet X. said to me in Moscow: "He (the boy, the dragoon) was the best of them all, that's why they killed him." For all its naivete, that response sticks in one's mind, because there are few who have [spoken] expressed themselves so much to the point.

    November 25 {1961}
    . . . So trying it out either as a ballet or a film script, all the time I couldn't understand what exactly I'm doing. The follow⟨⟨ing⟩⟩ quote explained it: "This book may be read as a poem or verse play," Peter Viereck wrote (*The Tree Witch,* 1961) [{quoted in English in original} and then explained the techniques by which a poem is turned into a play. I've been doing that at the same t⟨⟨ime⟩⟩ with *Triptych.* His *The Tree Witch* is a contemporary of my play and, perhaps, that's why the closeness.

---

* (N⟨⟨ote⟩⟩ by the –ian language translator of the manuscript found in a bottle): According to obtained information, dragoons wear not helmets, but shakos. However, there are those who affirm that the author of the *Poem* is a lady. Although I personally do not believe this, such a supposition would make this mistake pardonable.
    ** This no⟨⟨te's⟩⟩ already become God knows what

Another interesting thing: I've noticed that the more I explain it, the more enigmatic and incomprehensible it is. That it's clear to everyone, that I can't explain every last detail and wouldn't want to (wouldn't dare) and all my explanations (for all their insightfulness and ingenuity) are only confusing the matter—that it came from nowhere and went off nowhere, without explaining anything. . . When I read one of my particularly long and exhaustive "explanations" to I⟨⟨vanovsky⟩⟩, he said, "I almost shouted in the middle of it: 'Stop—I can't take any more. Because what you're reading is the "Poem" itself (let's say, "Flip Side"), only in prose—and that's unbearable."

From notebook 11 {January 1962}[6]

For "Prose about the Poem"

I am beginning to think that the "Other," the crumbs of which I am picking up in my "Triptych," is an enormous—gloomy, like a cloud—symphony on the fate of a generation and its best representatives, i.e., about everything that befell us. And something unprecedented* befell, that in the Poem one can hear all time, like the trial in Kafka, and like Time, which I, of course, would not presume to say about my poor "Triptych." But listening to the "Other," i.e., listening to Time

. . . and just this very day I arrived at a definitive formulation of what characterizes my method in the "Poem." Its words never aim straight at the mark: the most complex and deepest things are set forth not in dozens of pages, as is the custom, but in two lines, but everyone understands what the point is and how the author feels. For ex⟨⟨ample⟩⟩:

> Peter's corridor of colleges stretched
> Like an endless line, resonant and straight.

---

 * No generation (in history) has had such a fate, and perhaps there never was such a generation. The twenties, wh⟨⟨ich⟩⟩ it's now the custom to admire so—not at all—they're just the force of inertia. *Blok, Gumilyov, and Khlebnikov* all died at almost the same time. *Remizov, Tsvetayeva and Khodasevich* left the country, along with Chaliapin, M. Chekhov, Stravinsky, Prokofiev and 1/2 the ballet (Pavlova, Nijinsky, Karsavina) The academy lost Rostovtsev, Berdyayev, Vernadsky. B. Pasternak fell silent after his brilliant book of summer 1917 (published in 1921), raised his son, read thick books and wrote his 3 narrative poems. Mand⟨elstam⟩, in Nadya's words, couldn't breathe, and besides he was declared by the Brik salon to be an internal emigre, Akhm⟨atova⟩ was immured somehow or other (from 1925 on) in the first available wall.

> Anything can happen there, it seems,
> But it will stubbornly haunt the dreams
> Of anyone who walks through today.

Isn't this the whole Petersburg academic emigration?

> Or: Everyone's in place, ready for the bell:
> From the Summer Gardens comes the smell
> Of fifth act.

Isn't this the eve of the Revolution?
And more:

> . . . The ghost of Tsushima's hell
> Is there too. A drunken sailor sings . . .

"Tsushima's hell" wasn't there before. I drew it out of the drunk and sing–
ing sailor, where it had always been. (Comparison with a flower.) Thus
unfolding a rose, we find under a torn petal–exactly the same thing.
And in the Epilogue:

> And open before me lay the road (beyond the Urals)
> Along which so many were forced to go
> And my son, too, suffered that cruel command . . .

In those lines every one of us recognizes the times of Yezhov and Beria.
Every one of us had a son (or a husband) forced to go beyond the Urals.
Less important examples:

> That story's being told all over . . .
> You're a mere child, Signor Casanova

etc. etc.
The line "Along which so many were forced to go" already contains the
following one.
This method gives completely unexpected results: I've already written
somewhere else that all the time I felt the reader helping (even almost
prompting). (Especially in Tashkent.) And this "unfolding of the flower"
(in partic⟨⟨ular⟩⟩, a rose) to some extent gives the reader as well a sense–
completely unconscious, of course–of coauthorship. There are poets
who know that readers say about some of their works: "That's about me–

it's as if I wrote it." And then the author can be confident that what he created "made it."

"Poem Without a Hero" was like that, or not quite like that. It's absolutely alien and terrifying to some, and belongs to others as if exclusively.

From notebook 13 {November 1962–January 1963}[7]

About the "Poem"

1. It seems different to everyone:
A poem of conscience (Shklovsk⟨⟨y⟩⟩)
A dance (Berkovsky)
Music (almost everyone)
The Symbolists' dream realiz⟨⟨ed⟩⟩ (Zh⟨⟨irmunsky⟩⟩)
A poem of the eve, the holy night (B. Filippov)
The poem as my biography
A historical picture, the chronicle of an epoch (Chukovsk⟨⟨y⟩⟩)
Why the Revolution occurred (Shtok)
One of the figures of Russian folk dance (hands outspread and forward) (Past⟨⟨ernak⟩⟩).
(Lyrics, stepping away and covered with a kerchief.)
The way magic arises (Nayman)

In the "Poem"

Pushkin–"The Queen of Spades" (at the end of the 1st chapter)
Gogol–Carriages overturned on bridges (not into the river, of course, they just slid back off the steep ramps)
Dostoyevsky–The end of the 1st chapter ("The Devils")
            ("There is no death, as everyone knows")
Paul Valery   Variété V (A Dream . . .)
            (The parapets of Castle Elsinore)
R. Browning   Diis aliter visum {Latin, "The Gods decreed otherwise"}
            (Gout and fame . . .)
Blok–"The Steps of the Commendatore"
("We only dream we hear a cock's crow")
and the black rose in a bottle

Mandelstam
   (I turn slightly, looking half–behind
   and "I am ready to die")
Vs⟨⟨evolod⟩⟩ K⟨⟨nyazev⟩⟩   ("a lock of blond hair")
         ("shoulders wait to be kissed")
Meyerhold   Harlequin as the devil
         cf. "On the Theater," p. . . .
Stravinsky   Petrushka's mask,
         the coachmen's dance, the drums . . .
The Bible–the Mamre oak, the Valley of Jehosaphat, the Ark of the Cove-
nant, the Lots of Sodom
Antiq⟨⟨uity⟩⟩–Hecubas, Cassandras, Sophocles, Antinous' eyelashes
and always music

From notebook 18 (1963)[8]

June 3 (morning). The poem returned again. It demands a second epi-
graph for the first chapter:

> The New Year's splendor lingers on,
> Moist are the stems of New Year's roses.

It demands either a restoration of Baratynsky in the second chapter:

> You embody the senses' pleasures
> More fully than those alive, radiant shade

Or taking the 1921 stanza:

> You prophesy, bitter woman, and then drop your hands,
> On your pale brow, a lock of hair sticks fallen, caught,
> And you're smiling. . .

Move the epigraph of the second chapter to the 4th:

> Or do you see the one who before you knelt,
> Who sought out white death to escape your spell?

But that's not enough for it, it demands new prose.
For the first chapter—something like this:

I

> Fontanka House. December 31, 1940. The old London clock, which (after having struck 13 times out of absent-mindedness) stopped exactly 27 years ago, without any outside intervention started up again, struck a quarter to midnight (in the manner of an orator before the beginning of his speech) and started to tick again so that it could appropriately greet the New Year (which, in its opinion, was presumably 1914). And in these instants the author either heard or foresaw everything that would follow.
> Note. However, because of its English origin and again out of absent-mindedness, during [its] striking [chiming] the clock [mutters] allows itself to mutter: "Consecrated candels are burning, I with him who did not returning Met the year." {In English in the original.}
>   As if someone had returned to someone else sometime.

I've set the cherished candles alight
To give enchantment to this night . . .

Move the present prose II into the "Editor's notes." (Or the other way around.)
In the prose for the Epilogue, here's what needs to be done: after the words, "In the Sheremetev garden, lindens are blooming and a nightingale is singing," need to be added, "A third-floor window, with a crippled maple in front of it, is shattered, and behind it is a gaping black hole."

From notebook 21 (July 1965)[9]

Tell Dobin about the "Poem":

The main thing—the end—where this almost *apologizing tone* comes from. There's nothing traditional in the poem, this just goes perfectly to show it again!
Second: Shostakovich. Correct.
Third: the tens, not the twenties.
Four⟨⟨th⟩⟩: be sure to soften about Olga. Nothing personal.

It mustn't be forgotten that *Acmeism* is a longing for world culture. This line is also in the poem.

Triptych
Poem Without a Hero
(Jubilee Edition)
1940–1965
With a foreword by Anatoly Nayman
Music by Artur Lourie and Al⟨⟨eksei⟩⟩ Kozlovsky
Sets by Boris Anrep, Natan Altman, Dm⟨⟨itri⟩⟩ Bushen
Hist⟨⟨orical⟩⟩ notes on F⟨⟨ontanka⟩⟩ House by Anna Kaminskaya
Leningrad, Tashkent, Moscow

It's now a quarter of a century old.

Notes

Chapter 1. Youth and Early Fame, 1889–1916

1. Lidia Chukovskaya, *The Akhmatova Journals, 1938–1941* (New York: Farrar Straus Giroux, 1993), 73, entry for March 21, 1940.

2. Anna Akhmatova, *My Half-Century: Selected Prose,* ed. and trans. Ronald Meyer (Evanston: Northwestern University Press, 1997), 6; Chukovskaya, *Akhmatova Journals,* 157, entry for September 17, 1940.

3. Chukovskaya, *Akhmatova Journals,* 120, entry for June 25, 1940; Akhmatova, *My Half-Century,* 7.

4. This account of Gumilyov's courtship relies heavily on Vera Luknitskaya's biography *Nikolai Gumilyov. Zhizn' poeta po materialam domashnego arkhiva sem'i Luknitskikh* (Leningrad: Lenizdat, 1990) and to a lesser extent on Amanda Haight's *Anna Akhmatova: A Poetic Pilgrimage* (New York: Oxford University Press, 1976). Luknitskaya's book drew on the unpublished work of Pavel Luknitsky, who in the 1920s undertook to write a biography of Gumilyov with Akhmatova's assistance, as described in chapter 2 below. Haight was personally acquainted with Akhmatova in the last years of her life.

5. V. Chernykh, *Letopis' zhizn i tvorchestva Anna Akhmatovoi,* 3 vols. (Moscow: Editorial URSS, 1996–2001), 1:22.

6. Akhmatova, *My Half-Century,* 25.

7. Ibid., 275, 278–79.

8. Luknitskaya, *Nikolai Gumilyov,* 48.

9. Chernykh, *Letopis',* 1:32.

10. Anna Akhmatova, *Zapisnye knizhki Anny Akhmatovoi (1958–1966)* (Moscow: Rossiysky gosudarstvenny arkhiv literatury i iskusstva; Turin: Giulio Einaudi, 1996), 275.

11. Akhmatova, *My Half-Century,* 26.

12. Luknitskaya, *Nikolai Gumilyov,* 109.

13. Akhmatova, *Zapisnye knizhki,* 220.

14. Akhmatova, *My Half-Century,* 44.

15. Ibid., 26, 46.

16. Pavel Luknitsky, *Akumiana. Vstrechi s Annoi Akhmatovoi,* 2 vols. (Paris: YMCA Press, 1991–97), 1:191–92.

17. Akhmatova, *My Half-Century,* 47; a similar account is given in Chukovskaya, *Akhmatova Journals,* 109, entry for June 8, 1940.

18. Akhmatova, *My Half-Century,* 79.

19. Ibid., 9.

20. Ibid., 26.

21. Akhmatova, *Zapisnye knizhki,* 342.

22. Luknitskaya, *Nikolai Gumilyov,* 125.

23. *Ibid.,* 159–60.

24. In Russian, "Palchiki-to, palchiki-to, Bozhe ty moi!" Georgy Adamovich, "Moi vstrechi s Annoi Akhmatovoi," *Ob Anne Akhmatovoi: stikhi, esse, vospominaniya, pis'ma,* comp. Mikhail Kralin (Leningrad: Lenizdat, 1990), 93.

25. Haight, *Anna Akhmatova,* 30.

26. The wartime demand for coverage of current events held up the publication of Nedobrovo's article, which first appeared in the journal *Russkaya mysl'* in 1915. This quotation is from Alan Myers's translation in *Russian Literature Triquarterly* 9 (Spring 1974), 232. For Akhmatova's view of this article, see Chukovskaya, *Akhmatova Journals* 98–99, entry for May 24, 1940.

27. Akhmatova's remark is recalled by Vyacheslav Nechayev in "Akhmatova i Ranevskaya," *Vestnik Russkogo Khristianskogo Dvizheniya* 156 (1989): 153.

28. Akhmatova, *Zapisnye knizhki,* 190.

29. Akhmatova, *My Half-Century,* 48.

30. Akhmatova, *Zapisnye knizhki,* 652.

31. Ibid., 342.

32. Boris Eikhenbaum, *Anna Akhmatova: opyt analiza,* reprinted in *Anna Akhmatova: pro et contra,* comp. Sv. Kovalenko (St. Petersburg: Izdatel'stvo RKhGI, 2001), 535.

33. Akhmatova, *My Half-Century,* 9.

Chapter 2. Revolution and Civil War, 1917–1922

1. Akhmatova, *My Half-Century,* 9. She gives the date as January 20, but Chernykh, *Letopis',* 1:95–96, gives evidence that on the twentieth she was still at Slepnyovo and did not arrive in Petrograd until a few days later.

2. Luknitskaya, *Nikolai Gumilyov,* 196.

3. Boris Anrep, "The Black Ring," *Anna Akhmatova and Her Circle,* comp. Konstantin Polivanov (Fayetteville: University of Arkansas Press, 1994), 85. This night was also the inspiration for a rejected stanza of *Poem Without a Hero* given in Carlo Riccio, *Materiali per un'edizione critica di "Poema bez geroja" di Anna Achmatova,* Testi e documente 4 (Macerata: Giardini, 1996), 68:

I was happy, or wasn't, on the night
We came from "Masquerade," you and I,
And after that, where shall we two go?
All round is the fearsome cityscape,
The same as in "The Queen of Spades,"
Each step will take you farther from home.

4. This letter and the next one are cited in Timenchik, "Posle vsego," *Literaturnoe obozrenie*, 5 (1989): 23.

5. Akhmatova, *My Half-Century*, 52.

6. Chernykh, *Letopis,'* 1:101.

7. D. S. Mirsky, *Contemporary Russian Literature, 1881–1925* (New York: Kraus Reprint, 1972), 257.

8. Akhmatova, *Zapisnye knizhki*, 584–585.

9. Luknitsky, *Akumiana*, 1:44.

10. Quoted in *Anna Akhmatova and Her Circle*, 59.

11. Chukovskaya, *Akhmatova Journals*, 148, entry for August 19, 1940.

12. Akhmatova, *My Half-Century*, 32.

13. N. Mandelstam, *Hope Abandoned* (London: Collins and Harvill, 1974), 78.

14. Mikhail Heller and Aleksandr Nekrich, *Utopia in Power: The History of the Soviet Union from 1917 to the Present*, trans. Phillis B. Carlos (London: Hutchinson, 1986), 100.

15. Robert Service, *Lenin: A Biography* (Cambridge: Harvard University Press, 2000), 364.

16. Nicholas V. Riasanovsky, *A History of Russia*, 3d ed. (New York: Oxford University Press, 1977), 541.

17. Robert Service, *A History of Twentieth-Century Russia* (Cambridge: Harvard University Press, 1998), 109.

18. J. N. Westwood, *Endurance and Endeavour: Russian History 1812–1980*, 2d ed. (Oxford: Oxford University Press, 1981), 277.

19. Heller and Nekrich, *Utopia in Power*, 117–21.

20. Luknitskaya, *Nikolai Gumilyov*, 254.

21. Lidia Chukovskaya, *Zapiski ob Anne Akhmatovoi*, 2 vols. (Paris: YMCA Press, 1980–84), 2:432, entry for Sept. 19, 1962.

22. N. I. Popova and O. E. Rubinchik, *Anna Akhmatova i Fontanny Dom* (St. Petersburg: Nevsky Dialekt, 2000), 43.

23. Anna Akhmatova, *Sobranie sochinenii v shesti tomakh*, 6 vols., comp. N. V. Koroleva (Moscow: Ellis Lak, 1998–), 1:617.

24. Chernykh, *Letopis,'* 2:16.

25. Haight, *Anna Akhmatova*, 55.

26. *Ibid.*, 127.

27. Akhmatova, *Zapisnye knizhki*, p. 183.

Chapter 3. Outcast in the New Order, 1922–1935

1. Kornei Chukovsky, "Akhmatova and Mayakovsky," *Major Soviet Writers: Essays in Criticism,* ed. Edward J. Brown (New York: Oxford University Press, 1973), 52–53.

2. G. Lelevich, "Anna Akhmatova (belye zametki)," reprinted in *Anna Akhmatova: pro et contra,* 480.

3. V. Pertsov, "Po literaturnym vodorazdelam," reprinted in *Anna Akhmatova: pro et contra,* 696. (The reprint contains a typographical error in the quoted passage: it should read "yazyka," not "yazvy.")

4. Akhmatova, *My Half-Century,* 56.

5. N. Mandelstam, *Hope Abandoned,* 308.

6. Nikolai Punin, *Diaries of Nikolai Punin,* ed. Sidney Monas and Jennifer Greene Krupala, trans. Jennifer Greene Krupala (Austin: University of Texas Press, 1999), 82.

7. Luknitsky, *Akumiana,* 1:40.

8. Punin, *Diaries of Nikolai Punin,* 106.

9. Ibid., 146.

10. N. Mandelstam, *Hope Against Hope,* trans. Max Hayward (New York: Atheneum, 1970), 135.

11. Adam B. Ulam, *Stalin: The Man and His Era* (New York: Viking, 1973), 332.

12. Chris Ward, *Stalin's Russia* (London: Edward Arnold, 1993), 60–61.

13. Luknitsky, *Akumiana,* 1:312.

14. Quoted in Chernykh, *Letopis',* 2:129.

15. Vera Luknitskaya, *Pered toboi zemlya* (Leningrad: Lenizdat, 1988), 120.

16. N. Mandelstam, *Hope Against Hope,* 246.

17. Akhmatova, *My Half-Century,* 99.

18. Ibid., 101.

19. This translation by Max Hayward is given in Nadezhda Mandelstam, *Hope Against Hope,* 13. I have not seen any English translation that fully captures the savagery of the original Russian, which would be worthy of Swift; but this at least gives a shadow of it.

20. This account draws upon the reminiscences of Nadezhda Mandelstam and Akhmatova as supplemented and in some instances corrected by Vitaly Shentalinsky in *The KGB's Literary Archive* (London: Harvill, 1995). After the collapse of the Soviet Union, Shentalinsky was allowed to see a number of secret police files relating to literature, including those on Mandelstam's arrest and interrogation. The date of May 16–17 is established by the case file; Nadezhda Mandelstam remembered it as May 13–14.

21. Ibid., 183.

22. Akhmatova, *My Half-Century,* 103.

23. N. Mandelstam, *Hope Against Hope,* 148.

24. Ibid., 159.

25. Ward, *Stalin's Russia,* 113.

26. N. Mandelstam, *Hope Against Hope*, 98.

27. Chukovskaya, *Akhmatova Journals*, 38, entry for 27 Sept. 1939.

28. Luknitskaya, *Pered toboi zemlya*, 291.

29. N. Mandelstam, *Hope Abandoned*, 415.

30. N. Mandelstam, *Hope Against Hope*, 15.

31. Emma Gershtein, *Memuary* (Moscow: Zakharov, 2002), 292.

32. Popova and Rubinchik, *Anna Akhmatova i Fontanny Dom*, 69.

33. Gershtein, *Memuary*, 293.

34. Ibid., 294.

35. Zinaida Pasternak says that her husband posted his letter separately from Akhmatova's; *Vospominaniya o Borise Pasternake*, comp. Ye. B. Pasternak and M. I. Feinberg (Moscow: Slovo, 1993), 194. However, Pasternak's son, Yevgeny, who relied on Gershtein for his information, says that Akhmatova took the two letters together; see V. M. Borisov and Ye. B. Pasternak, "Materialy k tvorcheskoi istorii romana B. Pasternaka *Doktor Zhivago*," *Novy mir* 6 (1988): 212. Since the impact of the appeal would be greater if both letters were read at once, it seems likely Akhmatova would want them delivered simultaneously.

36. Chernykh, *Letopis*,' 3:16.

Chapter 4. Terror and the Muse, 1936–1941

1. Punin, *Diaries of Nikolai Punin*, 182.

2. Akhmatova, *Zapisnye knizhki*, 311.

3. N. V. Nedobrovo, "Anna Akhmatova," *Russian Literature Triquarterly* 9 (Spring 1974): 231.

4. N. Mandelstam, *Hope Against Hope*, 210–11.

5. Robert Thurston, *Life and Terror in Stalin's Russia, 1934–1941* (New Haven: Yale University Press, 1996), 63.

6. Eugenia Ginzburg, *Journey into the Whirlwind*, trans. Paul Stevenson and Max Hayward (New York: Harcourt Brace Jovanovich, 1975), 181–82.

7. For the purge's effect on the Central Committee, see Service, *History of Twentieth-Century Russia*, 224–25; for the army, J. N. Westwood, *Endurance and Endeavour*, 316.

8. Shentalinsky, *The KGB's Literary Archive*, 156.

9. Ibid., 204–05.

10. Akhmatova, *My Half-Century*, 108.

11. Conquest, *The Great Terror: A Reassessment*, 269.

12. Lyov told Akhmatova about the beatings he witnessed in June 1938, and she in turn quoted his words to her friend Lyubov Shaporina, who recorded them in a diary entry dated July 17, 1939; see "Anna Akhmatova v dnevnikakh L. V. Shaporinoy (1930-e–1950-e gody)," *Akhmatovsky sbornik* (Paris: Institut d'Études slaves, 1989), 206. Gumilyov described how he himself was beaten in an interview published under the title, " . . . Inache poeta net," *Zvezda* 6 (1989): 129.

13. Gershtein, *Memuary*, 350.

14. Akhmatova, *Requiem*, ed. R. D. Timenchik and K. M. Polivanov (Moscow: MPI, 1989), 21; cf. Akhmatova, *My Half-Century*, 31.

15. Chernykh, *Letopis*,' 3:39.

16. Gershtein, *Memuary*, 388–89.

17. Chernykh, *Letopis*,' 3:49–50.

18. Chukovskaya, *Akhmatova Journals*, 175–76, entry for November 13, 1940.

19. Ibid., 10, 149, entries for November 10, 1938 and August 19, 1940. Lermontov's poem tells of the ill-fated love of a human prince for a mermaid, the daughter of the Sea King–an evocative image, given Akhmatova's youthful love of the sea and her reputation as a strong and fearless swimmer. The poem's final couplet reads, "As onward the prince rides, his thoughts turn behind, / Long, long the king's daughter will stay in his mind!" The breakup would find an echo two decades later in a stanza omitted from *Poem Without a Hero* (quoted in appendix II, excerpts from notebook 10).

20. Recollections of Irina Punina, quoted in Popova and Rubinchik, *Anna Akhmatova i Fontanny Dom*, 147.

21. Gershtein, *Memuary*, 364.

22. For both this quote and the following one, see Chukovskaya, "Instead of a Foreword," *Akhmatova Journals*, 7.

23. Chukovskaya, *Zapiski*, 2:453, entry for October 30, 1962.

24. Chukovskaya, *Akhmatova Journals*, 56, entry for January 23, 1940.

25. Akhmatova, *Stikhotvoreniya i poemy*, Biblioteka poeta, bolshaya seriya, 2d ed., ed. with notes by V. M. Zhirmunsky (Sovetsky pisatel': Leningradskoe otdelenie, 1979), 511.

26. The English translation of the entire letter from which this is quoted is given in Haight, *Anna Akhmatova*, 112–13.

27. Akhmatova, *My Half-Century*, 127.

28. How and when Sergei Efron died was not known until after the fall of the Soviet Union, when the opening of secret police archives showed that he was one of 136 inmates of Butyrki Prison in Moscow who were executed on October 16, 1941, when the prisons were being hastily emptied as the German army approached Moscow; see Shentalinsky, *The KGB's Literary Archive*, 220–21.

29. "A. A. Akhmatova v pis'makh k N. I. Khardzhievu," *Voprosy literatury* 6 (1989): 227.

30. Akhmatova, *My Half-Century*, 121.

Chapter 5. War and Late Stalinism, 1941–1953

1. Ulam, *Stalin*, 539.

2. Akhmatova, *Requiem*, ed. Timenchik and Polivanov, 167.

3. E. Babayev, "Na ulitse Zhukovskoi . . ." *Vospominaniya ob Anne Akhmatovoi*, ed. Ya. V. Vilenkin and V. A. Chernykh (Moscow: Sovetsky pisatel,' 1991), 408.

4. Haight, *Anna Akhmatova*, 127.

5. Punin, *Diaries of Nikolai Punin*, 194, entry for Sept. 23, 1942.

6. This is quoted from the English translation of the entire letter given in Haight, *Anna Akhmatova*, 128.

7. J. Czapski, "Oblaka i golubi: vstrechi s Akhmatovoy v Tashkente (1942 g.)," *Vestnik russkogo khristianskogo dvizheniya* 156 (1989): 160.

8. Zoya Tomashevskaya, *Peterburg Akhmatovoi: semeinye khroniki. Zoya Borisovna Tomashevskaya rasskazyvaet* (St. Petersburg: Nevsky Dialekt, 2001), 21.

9. Akhmatova, *Sobranie sochinenii v shesti tomakh*, 2(1): 350.

10. Budyko, "Istoriya odnogo posvyashcheniya," *Russkaya literatura* 1 (1984): 237. This letter is undated but apparently was written in summer 1943.

11. Punin, *Diaries of Nikolai Punin*, 202, entry for 24 Feb. 1945.

12. See Margarita Aliger's reminiscences in *Vospominaniya ob Anne Akhmatovoi*, 353.

13. The available information regarding Akhmatova's breakup with Garshin and his later life is summarized in Budyko's "Istoriya odnogo posvyashcheniya," 235–38.

14. Punin, *Diaries of Nikolai Punin*, 208–09 (entry for Feb. 23, 1945); ellipses in original.

15. Gershtein, *Memuary*, 268.

16. Punin, *Mir svetel lyubov'yu. Dnevniki. Pis'ma*, ed. L. A. Zykov (Moscow: Izd-vo "Artist. Rezhisser. Teatr," 2000), 399; this diary entry, for Nov. 16, 1945, is not included in the English translation of Punin's diaries.

17. Sir Isaiah Berlin, *Personal Impressions* (New York: Viking, 1980), 190.

18. Ibid., 199.

19. N. Mandelstam, *Hope Abandoned*, 372.

20. For Akhmatova's response to the call for encores, see Natalia Roskina in *Anna Akhmatova and Her Circle*, 165, and Nadezhda Mandelstam, *Hope Against Hope*, 375, which also mentions the Stalin anecdote. Akhmatova's remark on the photograph is quoted by György Dalos, *The Guest from the Future: Anna Akhmatova and Isaiah Berlin*, trans. Antony Wood (London: John Murray, 1998), 68.

21. N. Mandelstam, *Hope Abandoned*, 375.

22. Akhmatova, *Zapisnye knizhki*, 665.

23. Oleg Kalugin, "Delo KGB na Annu Akhmatovu," *Gosbezopasnost' i literatura na opyte Rossii i Germanii (SSSR i GDP)* (Moscow: Rudomino, 1994), 77.

24. Punin, *Diaries of Nikolai Punin*, 212.

25. Gumilyov, "Inache poeta net...," 130.

26. Gershtein, *Memuary*, 477.

27. Punin, *Diaries of Nikolai Punin*, 223.

28. Reminiscences of Irina Punina, in Popova and Rubinchik, *Anna Akhmatova i Fontanny Dom*, 151–52.

Chapter 6. Late Fame and Final Years, 1953–1966

1. Chukovskaya, *Zapiski*, 2:229–30, entry for March 26, 1958; emphasis and ellipsis in original.

2. Ibid., 2:335, entry for June 19–20, 1960.

3. Ibid., 2:259, entry for October 29, 1958.

4. Ibid., 2:274, entry for November 26, 1958.

5. See Petrovykh's reminiscences in *Vospominaniya ob Anne Akhmatovoi*, 414.

6. Chukovskaya, *Zapiski*, 2:329, entry for June 2, 1960.

7. Akhmatova, *My Half-Century*, 39.

8. Natalia Ilyina, "Anna Akhmatova v poslednie gody ee zhizni," *Oktyabr'* 2 (1977): 130.

9. Raisa Orlova and Lev Kopelev, "Anna vseya Rusi," *Lituraturnoe obozrenie* 5 (1989): 102.

10. Chukovskaya, *Zapiski*, 2:450, entry for October 30, 1962.

11. Aleksandr Solzhenitsyn, *The Oak and the Calf: Sketches of Literary Life in the Soviet Union*, trans. Harry Willetts (New York: Harper and Row, 1979), 239.

12. Orlova and Kopelev, "Anna vseya Rusi," 103.

13. Akhmatova, *Zapisnye knizhki*, 269.

14. Anatoly Nayman, *Remembering Anna Akhmatova*, trans. Wendy Rosslyn (London: Peter Halban, 1991), 5.

15. Ibid., 135.

16. Dalos, *The Guest from the Future*, 175.

17. Akhmatova, *Zapisnye knizhki*, 667.

18. Akhmatova, *My Half-Century*, 66.

19. Orlova and Kopelev, "Anna vseya Rusi," 107

Bearing the Burden of Witness: *Requiem*

1. According to Chukovskaya, "Already madness' outstretched wing" was not written until May 4, 1940 (Chukovskaya, *Akhmatova Journals*, 79, entry for May 6, 1940), while Akhmatova recited "No, it's not I . . ." to Chukovskaya for the first time on November 7, 1940 (*Akhmatova Journals*, 173, entry for 7 Nov. 1940).

2. N. Mandelstam, *Hope Against Hope*, 285–86.

3. Chukovskaya, *Akhmatova Journals*, 58n, entry for January 31, 1940.

4. Akhmatova was certainly aware of this passage in *Poltava*. Chukovskaya, in her diary entry for May 29, 1939 (*Akhmatova Journals*, 19), notes that she told Akhmatova about a friend's account of her prison experiences. This account included a quote of two lines spoken by Kochubey, who laments that when he was tortured, his honor was lost. Akhmatova was struck by Pushkin's recognition of the sense of personal degradation which, illogically enough, attaches itself to the victim rather than the criminal and exclaimed, "How did he know? How did he know everything?"

5. Gershtein, *Memuary*, 358.

6. Typhus was a veritable barometer of social disorder and deprivation: it was epidemic during the Revolution, and Akhmatova contracted it during World War II, when she was living in refugee-choked Tashkent. It was also a common prison disease; Mandelstam died in a transit camp during a typhus epidemic.

Efim Etkind, pointing to this fact and to the similarity of the images in "To Death" and Mandelstam's poem "For the thunderous valor of coming ages . . ." suggests that "To Death" was inspired by Mandelstam's fate (E. Etkind, "Bessmertie pam-yati. Poema Anny Akhmatovoi *Rekviem*," *Studia Slavica Finlandensia* 8 [1991]: 116). However, it was not until many years after the fact that those close to Mandelstam learned that the immediate medical cause of his death was typhus, and it is no more surprising that two poems referring to Siberian exile should both mention the Yenisei River and the stars in the polar night than that two poems about Alaska should both mention Denali and the northern lights. Mandelstam's fate adds an extra layer of meaning to this poem, but the case for its being a major source of inspiration, in the way that it inspired lyrics like "Voronezh" or "A Little Geography," is weak.

Forward into the Past: *The Way of All the Earth*

1. Akhmatova, *Stikhotvoreniya i poemy*, ed. V. M. Zhirmunsky, Biblioteka poeta, bolshaya seriya, 2d edition (Sovetsky pisatel': Leningradskoe otdelenie, 1979), 506–07.
2. Akhmatova, *My Half-Century*, 6.
3. The poem consists of lines of five to seven syllables; each line has two accented syllablesand two unaccented syllables between them. This meter is a variant of the two-foot anapestic, which Unbegaun notes was regularly used by Alexei Koltsov (1809–42), the most famous poetic imitator of Russian folk songs; see Boris Unbegaun, *Russian Versification* (Oxford: Clarendon Press, 1956), 50. I have retained this distinctively songlike meter in translation; but while in Russian *The Way of All the Earth* is rhymed as abab, in translation I have followed the looser rhyme scheme characteristic of English folk songs and used an abcb stanza.
4. Verheul, *The Theme of Time in the Poetry of Anna Akhmatova* (The Hague: Mouton, 1971), 142n.
5. Akhmatova, *Zapisnye knizhki*, 174, 175, 210.
6. Valentin Tomberg, "Introduction to the Kitezh Legend," in *Kitezh: The Russian Grail Legends*, trans. by Tony Langham (London: Aquarian, 1991), 93.

Rediscovering a Lost Generation: *Poem Without a Hero*

1. Akhmatova, *Zapisnye knizhki*, 222.
2. Ibid., 248.
3. Ibid., 207–08.
4. N. Mandelstam, *Hope Abandoned*, 426.
5. Akhmatova, *Zapisnye knizhki*, 650.
6. Ibid., 155.
7. Popova and Rubinchik, *Anna Akhmatova i Fontanny Dom*, 30–34.
8. Akhmatova, *Zapisnye knizhki*, 551.
9. R. D. Timenchik, "Rizhsky episod v *Poeme bez geroya*," *Daugava* 2 (80)

(February 1984): 120. The shot was not immediately fatal; Knyazev died a week later, on April 5.

10. Ya. V. Vilenkin, *V sto pervom zerkale* (Moscow: Sovetsky pisatel',' 1987), 252.

11. Chukovskaya, *Zapiski*, 2:181–82, diary entry for Jan. 3, 1957.

12. In a marginal note on the libretto for *Poem*, Akhmatova wrote, "Misha Lindeberg–24 Dec. 1911." The same date is written above a fragment: "Vsevolod Knyazev was not the first killed and was never my lover, but his suicide was so much like another catastrophe. . . that they have become fused together forever for me." See Timenchik, *Daugava* 2 (1984): 121.

13. Akhmatova, *Zapisnye knizhki*, 141.

14. Vilenkin, *V sto pervom zerkale*, 271, states that on a typewritten copy of the *Poem Without a Hero* he saw a note by Akhmatova: "Apropos of Confusion. All that I knew about her until yesterday (July 6, 1958) was the title and the portrait of O.A. in that role painted by S. Sudeikin . . . I even, God forgive me, confused it with another play by the same author, *Psyche*, which I hadn't read either. Hence the line: 'Can it be you, Confusion-Psyche.'" This is confirmed by an entry in one of Akhmatova's notebooks, "Confusion–the heroine of a play by Yu. Belyayev–the whole point is just in the costume, S. Sudeikin's wo⟨⟨rk⟩⟩." (Akhmatova, *Zapisnye knizhki*, 178)

15. "A bacchanale" and "extremely provocative": see Wendy Rosslyn, "Akhmatova's *Poema bez Geroia*: Ballet and Poem," in *The Speech of Unknown Eyes: Akhmatova's Readers on her Poetry*, ed. Rosslyn (Nottingham: Astra, 1990), 65. The newspaper review, dated March 30, 1913, is quoted in B. Kats and R. D. Timenchik, *Anna Akhmatova i muzyka* (Leningrad: Sovetsky kompozitor, 1989), 194 n. 2.

16. Akhmatova, *My Half-Century*, 128.

17. Akhmatova, *Sochineniya* (Moscow, 1986), 2:226. I have translated this passage myself, rather than using the translation given in *My Half-Century*, 133, to ensure that the citations in the quote can be readily matched to the relevant passages in my translation of *Poem Without a Hero*.

18. J. Malmsted, "Mixail Kuzmin: A Chronicle," in Mikhail Kuzmin, *Sobranie stikhov*, 3 vols., ed. V. Markov and J. Malmstad (Munich: William Fink, 1977), 3:108.

19. Chukovskaya, *Akhmatova Journals*, 138, entry for August 8, 1940.

20. Akhmatova, *Zapisnye knizhki* 259, 276.

21. Nikolai Gogol, "Nevsky Prospekt," *The Collected Tales and Plays of Nikolai Gogol*, ed. Leonard J. Kent, Constant Garnett translation revised by the editor (New York: Octagon Books, 1978), 452.

22. Akhmatova, *Zapisnye knizhki*, 137.

23. Fyodor Dostoevsky, *The Adolescent*, trans. Andrew MacAndrew (New York: W. W. Norton, 1981), 136.

24. Chukovskaya, *Zapiski*, 2:310 note 303.

25. N. Mandelstam, *Hope Abandoned*, 434.

26. This point is made by David Wells in *Anna Akhmatova: Her Poetry* (Oxford: Berg, 1996), 117.

27. Akhmatova, *Stikhotvoreniya i poemy* (ed. Zhirmunsky), 378.

28. Chukovskaya, "Polumertvaya i nemaya," *Kontinent* 7 (1976): 433–34; Akhmatova, *Zapisnye knizhki*, 491, 496.

29. Susan Amert, *In a Shattered Mirror: The Later Poetry of Anna Akhmatova* (Stanford: Stanford University Press, 1992), 112.

30. Akhmatova, *My Half-Century*, 127.

31. Chukovskaya, *Zapiski*, 2:399, entry for January 1, 1962.

32. Timenchik et al., "Akhmatova i Kuzmin," 230; Malmsted, *Mixail Kuzmin: A Chronicle*, 179.

33. Akhmatova is quoted as having said, "Let us remember the first Russian *poema, Eugene Onegin.* We should not be troubled by the fact that the author called it a novel. Pushkin found a special 14-line stanza and a particular intonation for it. It would have seemed that so happily found a stanza and intonation would root itself in Russian poetry. But *Eugene Onegin* came out and a crossing beam swung down behind it. Anyone who tried to put Pushkin's 'discovery' to use failed . . . Only Nekrasov understood that new paths had to be sought out. That's when *Frost the Red-Nosed* appeared. Blok also understood this . . . in his *poema The Twelve.*" (Etkind, "Bessmertie pamyati," 101–02, citing *Literaturnaya gazeta*, 23 Nov. 1965)

34. Nayman, *Remembering Anna Akhmatova*, 118.

Commentary on *Poem Without a Hero*

1. Akhmatova's own explanatory notes on the *Poem* are given in Akhmatova, *Zapisnye knizhki*, 178, 200–01, and *Stikhotvoreniya i poemy* (ed. Zhirmunsky), 357–58.

2. Rory Childers and Anna Lisa Crone, "The Mandelstam Presence in the Dedications of *Poema bez Geroja*," *Russian Literature* 15, no. 1 (1984): 54–55.

3. Chukovskaya, *Zapiski*, 2:179.

4. Chukovskaya, *Akhmatova Journals*, 137, entry for August 8, 1940.

5. Quoted in Zhirmunsky, *Tvorchestvo Anny Akhmatovoi* (Leningrad: Nauka, 1973), 159–60.

7. Akhmatova, *Zapisnye knizhki*, 386–87.

8. Akhmatova, *My Half-Century*, 342.

9. R. D. Timenchik, V. N. Toporov, and T. V. Tsiv'yan, "Akhmatova i Kuzmin," *Russian Literature* 6 (1978): 248–49.

10. Riccio, *Materiali per un'edizione critica*, 69.

11. Akhmatova, *Zapisnye knizhki*, 181.

12. V. Toporov, *Akhmatova i Blok*, Modern Russian Literature and Culture 5 (Berkeley: Berkeley Slavic Studies, 1981), 16.

13. Akhmatova, *Zapisnye knizhki*, 398.

14. *Ibid.*, 112.

15. *Ibid.*, 155.

16. Riccio, *Materiali per un'edizione critica*, 249.

17. Punin, *Diaries of Nikolai Punin*, 125.

18. Akhmatova, *Zapisnye knizhki*, 183–84.

19. *Ibid.*, 176.

20. *Ibid.*, 188.

21. *Ibid.*, 182.

22. *Ibid.*, 176, 182, 184.

23. *Ibid.*, 20.

24. *Ibid.*, 213–214, 255.

25. Chukovskaya, *Zapiski*, 2:180, entry for January 3, 1957.

26. Akhmatova, *Zapisnye knizhki*, 189.

27. Chukovskaya, *Zapiski*, 2:297–98, entry for December 23, 1959.

28. V. Toporov, *Akhmatova i Blok*, 24.

29. Chukovskaya, *Zapiski*, 2:74, entry for May 12, 1955.

30. Riccio, *Materiali per un'edizione critica*, 121–123.

31. Chukovskaya, *Zapiski*, 2:92, entry for June 11, 1955.

32. Akhmatova, *Stikhotvoreniya i poemy* (ed. Zhirmunsky), 429; cf. *Zapisnye knizhki*, 88.

33. Chukovskaya, *Zapiski*, 2:273, entry for November 26, 1958.

34. Akhmatova, *Zapisnye knizhki*, 138; cf. appendix II, excerpts from notebook 9.

35. *Ibid.*, 56, 570, 591; cf. Akhmatova, *Stikhotvoreniya i poemy* (ed. Zhirmunsky), 429.

36. Judith Hemschemeyer, *Complete Poems of Anna Akhmatova*, updated and expanded edition (Boston: Zephyr, 1997), 850.

37. Akhmatova, *Zapisnye knizhki*, 190.

38. Chukovskaya, *Zapiski*, 2:75 note 76, entry for May 12, 1955.

39. *Ibid.*, 2:72, entry for May 6, 1955.

40. Riccio, *Materiali per un'edizione critica*, 248.

41. Chukovskaya, *Zapiski*, 2:315, entry for May 11, 1960.

42. Akhmatova, *Zapisnye knizhki*, 176.

43. *Ibid.*, 260–61.

44. *Ibid.*, 551–52.

45. *Ibid.*, 470.

46. Chukovskaya, "Polumertvaya i nemaya," *Kontinent* 7 (1976): 430–36.

47. Akhmatova, *Zapisnye knizhki*, 389–90.

48. N. Mandelstam, *Hope Against Hope*, 344.

49. Akhmatova, *Stikhotvoreniya i poemy* (ed. Zhirmunsky), 430.

50. Akhmatova, *Zapisnye knizhki*, 7–8.

51. Chukovskaya, *Akhmatova Journals*, 100–01, entry for June 3, 1940.

52. Akhmatova, *Zapisnye knizhki*, 286.

53. Akhmatova, *Stikhotvoreniya i poemy* (ed. Zhirmunsky), 439.

54. Akhmatova, *Zapisnye knizhki*, 200; compare with Akhmatova, *Stikhotvoreniia i poemy* (ed. Zhirmunsky), 378.

55. Akhmatova, *Zapisnye knizhki*, 491.

56. Akhmatova, *Stikhotvoreniya i poemy* (ed. Zhirmunsky), 380.

57. Akhmatova, *Zapisnye knizhki*, 569; cf. 479.
58. *Ibid.*, 389–90. The lines are headed "In *Flip Side*" and dated "1963. Aug. 3. Komarovo. In a dream."
59. *Ibid.*, 89.
60. Akhmatova, *Stikhotvoreniya i poemy* (ed. Zhirmunsky), 375.
61. Akhmatova, *Zapisnye knizhki*, 135.
62. Chukovskaya, *Zapiski*, 2:457 note 434, entry for November 4, 1962.
63. Childers and Crone, "The Mandelstam Presence," 72.
64. Akhmatova, *Zapisnye knizhki*, 135.
65. Chukovskaya, *Zapiski*, 2:180, entry for January 3, 1957.
66. Akhmatova, *Stikhotvoreniya i poemy* (ed. Zhirmunsky), 430.

Appendix II

1. Akhmatova, *Zapisnye knizhki*, 19, 21.
2. *Ibid.*, 84–87, 90, 93–94.
3. *Ibid.*, 108–09.
4. *Ibid.*, 137–38, 144, 147–48, 154.
5. *Ibid.*, 173, 179–82, 185, 189–90.
6. *Ibid.*, 208–10.
7. *Ibid.*, 261, 276.
8. *Ibid.*, 520.
9. *Ibid.*, 650, 651.

Bibliography

§ § §

Akhmatova, Anna. *The Complete Poems of Anna Akhmatova.* Updated and expanded edition. Translated by Judish Hemschemeyer. Edited and introduced by Roberta Reeder. Boston: Zephyr, 1997.

——. *My Half-Century: Selected Prose.* Edited by Ronald Meyer. Evanston: Northwestern University Press, 1997.

——. *Poems of Akhmatova.* Selected, translated, and introduced by Stanley Kunitz with Max Hayward. Boston: Little, Brown, 1973.

——. *Requiem.* Edited by R. D. Timenchik and K. M. Polivanov. Moscow: MPI, 1989.

——. *Requiem and Poem Without a Hero.* Translated by D. M. Thomas. London: Paul Elek, 1976.

——. *Selected Poems.* Edited and translated by Walter Arndt. With *Requiem,* translated by Robin Kemball, and *A Poem Without a Hero,* translated and annotated by Carl R. Proffer. Ann Arbor, Mich.: Ardis, 1976.

——. *Sobranie sochinenii v shesti tomakh.* Edited with articles and commentaries by N. V. Koroleva. Moscow: Ellis Lak, 1998–.

——. *Sochineniya.* 3 vols. Vols. 1 and 2 edited by G. P. Struve and B. A. Filipoff. Munich: Inter–Language Literary Associates, 1967–68. Vol. 3 edited by G. P. Struve, N. A. Struve, and B. A. Filipoff. Paris: YMCA Press, 1983.

——. *Sochineniya.* 2 vols. Vol. 1 edited by V. A. Chernykh, intro. by Mikhail Dudin. Vol. 2 edited by E. G. Gershtein, L. A. Mandry Kina, V. A. Chernykh, and N. N. Glen. Moscow: Khudozhestvennaya literatura, 1986.

——. *Stikhotvoreniya i poemy.* Edited by V. M. Zhirmunsky. Biblioteka poeta, bolshaya seriya, 2d edition. Sovetsky pisatel': Leningradskoe otdelenie, 1979.

——. *Tale Without a Hero and Twenty-Two Poems.* Translated and edited by Jeanne van der Eng–Liedmeier and Kees Verheul. Dutch Studies in Russian Literature, 3. The Hague: Mouton, 1973.

——. *Way of All the Earth.* Translated by D. M. Thomas. London: Secker and Warburg, 1979.

—. *Zapisnye knizhki Anny Akhmatovoi (1958–1966)*. Moscow: Rossiysky gosudar-stvenny arkhiv literatury i iskusstva; Turin: Giulio Einaudi, 1996.

Amert, Susan. *In a Shattered Mirror: The Later Poetry of Anna Akhmatova*. Stanford: Stanford University Press, 1992.

Ardov, Mikhail Viktorovich. "Legendarnaya Ordynka." *Novyi mir* 4 (1994): 3–43 and 5 (1994): 113–55.

Azadovsky, K. M. "Menya nazval 'kitezhankoi.'" *Literaturnoe obozrenie* 5 (1989): 66–70.

Babayev, E., ed. "A. A. Akhmatova v pis'makh k N. I.Khardzhievu (1930–1960–e gg.)." *Voprosy literatury* 6 (1989): 214–47.

Ballardini, Elio, et al., editors. *La pietroburgo di Anna Achmatova = Peterburg Anny Akhmatovoi*. Bologna: Grafis, 1996. (In Italian and Russian)

Berlin, Sir Isaiah. *Personal Impressions*. New York: Viking, 1980.

Borisov, V. M., and E. B. Pasternak. "Materialy k tvorcheskoy istorii romana B. Pasternaka *Doktor Zhivago*." *Novyi mir* 6 (1988): 205–48.

Brodsky, Joseph. "The Keening Muse" in *Less Than One: Selected Essays*, 34–52. New York: Farrar Straus Giroux, 1986.

Brown, Clarence. *Mandelstam*. Cambridge: Cambridge University Press, 1973.

Brown, Edward J. *The Proletarian Episode in Russian Literature, 1928–1932*. New York: Columbia University Press, 1953.

Budyko, Iu. I. "Istoriya odnogo posvyashcheniya." *Russkaya literatura* 1 (1984): 235–38.

—. "Ya poslal tebe chernuyu rozu v bokale." *Russkaya literature* 4 (1984): 217–21.

Bulgakova, Yelena. *Dnevnik Yeleny Bulgakovoi*. Edited with a commentary by Viktor Losev and Lidia Yanovskaya. Moscow: Knizhnaya palata, 1990.

Chernykh, V. *Letopis' zhizn i tvorchestva Anna Akhmatovoi*. 3 vols. Vol. 1, 1889–1917. Moscow: Editorial URSS, 1996. Vol. 2, 1918–34. Moscow: Editorial URSS, 1998. Vol. 3, 1935–45. Moscow: Editorial URSS, 2001.

Childers, Rory, and Anna Lisa Crone. "The Mandel'stam Presence in the Dedications of *Poèma bez geroja*." *Russian Literature* 15, no. 1 (1984): 51–84.

Chukovskaya, Lidia. "Polumertvaya i nemaya." *Kontinent* 7 (1976): 430–36.

—. *Zapiski ob Anne Akhmatovoi*. 2 vols. Vol. 1, 2d ed. Paris: YMCA–Press, 1984. Vol. 2, Paris: YMCA–Press, 1980. Volume 1 has been translated by Milena Michalski and Sylva Rubashova as *The Akhmatova Journals, 1938–1941*. New York: Farrar Straus Giroux, 1993.

Chukovsky, Kornei. "Akhmatova and Mayakovsky." In *Major Soviet Writers: Essays in Criticism*, edited by Edward J. Brown, 33–53. New York: Oxford University Press, 1973.

—. "Anna Akhmatova." In Kornei Chukovsky, *Sobranie sochinenii v shesti tomakh*, 5:725–55. Moscow: Khudozhestvennaya literatura, 1967.

—. "Chitaya Akhmatovu." *Moskva* 5 (1964): 200–03.

Conquest, Robert. *The Great Terror: A Reassessment*. New York: Oxford University Press, 1990.

Czapski, Jozef. "Oblaka i golubi: vstrechi s Akhmatovoi v Tashkente (1942 g.)." *Vestnik russkogo khristianskogo dvizheniya* 156 (1989): 157–63.

Dalos, György. *The Guest from the Future: Anna Akhmatova and Isaiah Berlin*. With the collaboration of Andrea Dunai. Translated from the German by Antony Wood. London: John Murray, 1998.

Dedulinek, Serge, and Gabriel Superfin, editors. *Akhmatovsky sbornik*. Bibliothèque Russe de l'Institut d'Études slaves, vol. 85. Paris: Institut d'Études slaves, 1989.

Dobin, E. "*Poema bez geroya* Anny Akhmatovoi." *Voprosy literatury* 9 (1966): 63–79.

———. *Poeziya Anny Akhmatovoi*. Leningrad: Sovetsky pisatel, 1968.

Dolgopolov, L. "Po zakonam pritiazheniya: O lit. traditsiyakh v *Poeme bez geroya* A. Akhmatovoi." *Russkaya literatura* 4 (1979): 38–57.

Driver, Sam. *Anna Akhmatova*. New York: Twayne, 1972.

Eng-Liedmeier, Jeanne van der. "Reception as a Theme in Akhmatova's Later Poetry." *Russian Literature* 15 (1984): 360–94.

Erdmann-Pand'iæ, Elisabeth von. *AEPoema bez gerojaAF von Anna A. Achmatova: Variantenedition und Interpretation von Symbolstrukturen*. Baustine zur Geschichte der Literatur bei den Slaven. Volume 25. Cologne: Böhlau Verlag, 1987.

Etkind, Efim. "Bessmertie pamyati. Poema Anny Akhmatovoi *Rekviem*." *Studia Slavica Finlandensia* 8 (1991): 98–133.

Gershtein, E. G. *Memuary*. Moscow: Zakharov, 2002.

Ginzburg, Lidia. *O lirike*. 2d ed. Leningrad: Sovetsky pisatel', 1974.

Gumilyov, Lev. " . . . Inache poeta net," *Zvezda* 6 (1989): 127–33.

———. "Zakony vremen. Beseda korrespondenta *LO* Evg. Kanchukova s L'vom Gumilevym." *Literaturnoe obozrenie* 3 (1990): 3–9.

Haight, Amanda. *Anna Akhmatova: A Poetic Pilgrimage*. New York: Oxford University Press, 1976.

———. "Anna Akhmatova's *Poema bez geroja*." *Slavonic and Eastern European Review* 45 (1967): 474–96.

Heller, Mikhail, and Aleksandr Nekrich. *Utopia in Power: The History of the Soviet Union from 1917 to the Present*. Translated from the Russian by Phillis B. Carlos. London: Hutchinson, 1986.

Ilyina, Natalia. "Anna Akhmatova v poslednie gody ee zhizni." *Oktyabr'* 2 (1977): 107–34.

Jovanovich, Milivoe. "K razboru 'chuzhikh golosov' v *Rekvieme* Akhmatovoi." *Russian Literature* 15 (1984): 169–81.

Kalugin, Oleg. "Delo KGB na Annu Akhmatovu." In *Gosbezopasnost' i literatura na opyte Rossii i Germanii (SSSR i GDP)*, 72–@80. Moscow: Rudomino, 1994.

Kats, B., and R. Timenchik. *Anna Akhmatova i muzyka*. Leningrad: Sovetsky kompozitor, 1989.

Ketchian, Sonia. *The Poetry of Anna Akhmatova: A Conquest of Time and Space*. Slavistische Beiträge. Volume 196. Munich: Otto Sagner, 1986.

Kovalenko, Sv., compiler. *Anna Akhmatova: pro et contra*. St. Petersburg: Izdatel'stvo RKhGI, 2001.

Kralin, Mikhail, compiler. *Ob Anne Akhmatovoi: stikhi, esse, vospominaniya, pis'ma*. Leningrad: Lenizdat, 1990.

Leiter, Sharon. *Akhmatova's Petersburg*. Philadelphia: University of Pennsylvania Press, 1983.

Levin, Yu. I., D. M. Segal, R. D. Timenchik, V. N. Toporov, and T. V. Tsiv'yan. "Russkaya semanticheskaya poetika kak potential'naya kul'turnaya paradigma." *Russian Literature* 7/8 (1974): 47–82.

Losev, L., ed. "Akhmatova i Ranevskaya." *Vestnik russkogo khristianskogo dvizheniya* 156 (1989): 150–56.

Luknitskaya, Vera. *Nikolai Gumilyov. Zhizn' poeta po materialam domashnego arkhiva sem'i Luknitskikh*. Leningrad: Lenizdat, 1990.

—. *Pered toboi zemlya*. Leningrad: Lenizdat, 1988.

Luknitsky, P. N. *Akumiana. Vstrechi s Annoi Akhmatovoi*. 2 vols. Vol. 1, 1924–25. Paris: YMCA Press, 1991. Vol. 2, 1926–27. Paris: YMCA Press, 1997.

Malmstad, J. "Mixail Kuzmin: A Chronicle of His Life and Times." In Mikhail Kuzmin, *Sobranie stikhov*, 3 vols, edited by. V. Markov and J. Malmstad, 3:7–319. Munich: William Fink, 1977.

Mandelstam, Nadezhda. *Vospominaniya*. New York: Izd-vo im. Chekhova, 1970. Translated by Max Hayward as *Hope Against Hope*. New York: Atheneum, 1970.

—. *Vtoraya kniga*. Paris: YMCA-Press, 1978. Translated by Max Hayward as *Hope Abandoned*. London: Collins and Harvill, 1974.

Mirsky, D. S. *Contemporary Russian Literature, 1881–1925*. New York: Kraus Reprint, 1972.

Moch–Bickert, Elaine. *Kolombina desyatykh godov...* Translated by Vera Rumyantseva, edited by Yu. A. Molok. Paris: Grzhebina–AO "Arsis," 1993. (Russian translation of *Olga Glebova-Soudeikina*. Paris: Service de reproduction des thèses université de Lille, 1972.)

Mochulsky, Konstantin. *Aleksandr Blok*. Translated by Doris V. Johnson. Detroit: Wayne State University Press, 1983.

Nayman, Anatoly. *Rasskazy ob Anne Akhmatovoi*. Moscow: Khudozhestvennaya literatura, 1989. Translated by Wendy Rosslyn as *Remembering Anna Akhmatova*. Introduction by Joseph Brodsky. London: Peter Halban, 1991.

Nederlander, Munin. *Kitezh: The Russian Grail Legends*. Translated from the Dutch by Tony Langham. London: Aquarian, 1991.

Nedobrovo, N. V. "Anna Akhmatova." *Russkaya musl'* 7 (1915): sec. 2, 50–68. Reprinted in Akhmatova, *Sochineniya* (ed. Struve and Filipoff), 3:473–95. Translated by Alan Myers in *Russian Literature Triquarterly* 9 (Spring 1974): 221–36.

Nove, Alec. *Stalinism and After*. London: George Allen and Unwin Ltd., 1975.

Orlova, Raisa, and Lev Kopelev. "Anna vseya Rusi." *Lituraturnoe obozrenie* 5 (1989): 100–09.

Pasternak, Ye. B., and M. I. Feinberg, compilers. *Vospominaniya o Borise Pasternake*. Moskva: Slovo, 1993.

Polivanov, Konstantin, compiler. *Anna Akhmatova and Her Circle*. Translated from the Russian by Patricia Beriozkina. Fayetteville: University of Arkansas Press, 1994. (Translation of *Anna Akhmatova i ee okruzhenie*, Progress Publishers, 1991)

Popova, N. I., and O. E. Rubinchik. *Anna Akhmatova i Fontanny Dom.* St. Peterburg: Nevsky Dialekt, 2000.

Proffer, Ellendea. *Bulgakov: Life and Work.* Ann Arbor: Ardis, 1984.

Punin, Nikolai. *Mir svetel lyubov'yu. Dnevniki. Pis'ma.* Edited with a foreword and notes by L. A. Zykov. Moscow: Izd-vo "Artist. Rezhisser. Teatr," 2000. Much of this material is included in *The Diaries of Nikolai Punin, 1904–1953,* edited by Sidney Monas and Jennifer Greene Krupala and trans. by Jennifer Greene Krupala. Austin: University of Texas Press, 1999.

Reeder, Roberta. *Anna Akhmatova: Poet and Prophet.* New York: St. Martin's, 1994.

Riccio, Carlo. *Materiali per un'edizione critica di "Poema bez geroja" di Anna Achmatova.* Testi e documente 4. Macerata: Giardini, 1996.

Rosslyn, Wendy. "Not a Whiff of a Roman Carnival: Akhmatova's *Poema bez geroia.*" In *Russian and Yugoslav Culture in the Age of Modernism,* edited by Cynthia Marsh and Wendy Rosslyn, 69–87. Nottingham: Astra, 1991.

—, ed. *The Speech of Unknown Eyes: Akhmatova's Readers on her Poetry.* Nottingham: Astra, 1990.

Rude, Jeanne. *Anna Akhmatova.* Poètes d'aujourd'hui, 179. Paris: Seghers, 1968.

Service, Robert. *A History of Twentieth-Century Russia.* Cambridge: Harvard University Press, 1998.

—. *Lenin: A Biography.* Cambridge: Harvard University Press, 2000.

Shentalinsky, Vitaly. *The KGB's Literary Archive.* Translated and abridged by John Crowfoot. London: Harvill, 1995.

Solzhenitsyn, Aleksandr. *The Oak and the Calf: Sketches of Literary Life in the Soviet Union.* Translated from the Russian by Harry Willetts. New York: Harper and Row, 1817.

Struve, Gleb. *Russian Literature Under Lenin and Stalin.* Norman: University of Oklahoma Press, 1971.

Thurston, Robert. *Life and Terror in Stalin's Russia, 1934–1941.* New Haven: Yale University Press, 1996.

Timenchik, R. D. "Akhmatova's Macbeth." Translated by Howard Goldman. *Slavic and Eastern European Journal* 24, no. 4 (1980): 362–68.

—. "Avtometaopisanie u Akhmatovoi." *Russian Literature* 10/11 (1975): 213–26.

—. "Posle vsego." *Literaturnoe obozrenie* 5 (1989): 22–26.

—. "Rizhsky episod v *Poeme bez geroya* Anny Akhmatovoi." *Daugava* 2 (80) (Feb. 1984): 113–21.

Timenchik, R. D., V. N. Toporov, and T. V. Tsiv'yan. "Akhmatova i Kuzmin." *Russian Literature* 6 (1978): 213–305.

Tomashevskaya, Zoya. *Peterburg Akhmatovoi: semeinye khroniki. Zoya Borisovna Tomashevskaya rasskazyvaet.* St. Petersburg: Nevsky Dialekt, 2001.

Toporov, V. N. *Akhmatova i Blok.* Modern Russian Literature and Culture, 5. Berkeley: Berkeley Slavic Studies, 1981.

Tsiv'yan, T. V. "Akhmatova i muzyka." *Russian Literature* 10/11 (1975): 173–212.

—. "Materialy k poetike Anny Akhmatovoi." *Trudy po znakovym sistemam* 3 (1967): Issue 198:180–208.

—. "Zametki k deshifrovke *Poemy bez geroya.*" *Trudy po znakovym sistemam* 5 (1971): Issue 284:255–80.

Ulam, Adam B. *Stalin: The Man and His Era.* New York: Viking, 1973.

Unbegaun, Boris. *Russian Versification.* Oxford: Clarendon Press, 1956.

Verheul, Kees. *The Theme of Time in the Poetry of Anna Akhmatova.* The Hague: Mouton, 1971.

Vilenkin, Ya. V. *V sto pervom zerkale.* Moscow: Sovetsky pisatel,' 1987.

—, and V. A. Chernykh, eds. *Vospominaniya ob Anne Akhmatovoi.* Moscow: Sovetsky pisatel,' 1991.

Ward, Chris. *Stalin's Russia.* London: Edward Arnold, 1993.

Wells, David. *Anna Akhmatova: Her Poetry.* Oxford: Berg, 1996.

Westwood, J. N. *Endurance and Endeavour: Russian History 1812–1980.* 2d ed. Oxford: Oxford University Press, 1981.

Zhirmunsky, V. M. "Anna Akhmatova i Aleksandr Blok." *Russkaya literatura* 3 (1970): 57–@82.

—. *Tvorchestvo Anny Akhmatovoi.* Leningrad: Nauka, 1973.

Index